Europeanization and Multilevel Governance

GOVERNANCE IN EUROPE

Europeanization and Multilevel Governance

Cohesion Policy in the European Union and Britain

Ian Bache

ROWMAN & LITTLEFIELD PUBLISHERS, INC.
Lanham • Boulder • New York • Toronto • Plymouth, UK

ROWMAN & LITTLEFIELD PUBLISHERS, INC.

Published in the United States of America
by Rowman & Littlefield Publishers, Inc.
A wholly owned subsidiary of The Rowman & Littlefield Publishing Group, Inc.
4501 Forbes Boulevard, Suite 200, Lanham, Maryland 20706
www.rowmanlittlefield.com

Estover Road, Plymouth PL6 7PY, United Kingdom

British Library Cataloguing in Publication Information Available

Library of Congress Cataloging-in-Publication Data

Bache, Ian.
  Europeanization and multilevel governance : cohesion policy in the European Union
and Britain / Ian Bache.
    p. cm. — (Governance in Europe)
  Includes bibliographical references and index.
  ISBN-13: 978-0-7425-4132-0 (cloth : alk. paper)
  ISBN-10: 0-7425-4132-0 (cloth : alk. paper)
  ISBN-13: 978-0-7425-4133-7 (pbk. : alk. paper)
  ISBN-10: 0-7425-4133-9 (pbk. : alk. paper)
  1. Central-local government relations—European Union countries.
2. Decentralization in government—European Union countries. 3. Regionalism—
European Union countries. 4. Regionalism (International organization) 5. European
Union—Great Britain. 6. Central-local government relations—Great Britain.
7. Decentralization in government—Great Britain. 8. Regionalism—Great Britain.
I. Title.
JN34.5.B33 2008
320.8094—dc22

                                                              2007021583

Printed in the United States of America

∞™ The paper used in this publication meets the minimum requirements of American
National Standard for Information Sciences—Permanence of Paper for Printed Library
Materials, ANSI/NISO Z39.48-1992.

This book is dedicated to the memory of Hedley Salt

Contents

Acknowledgments

Europeanization and Multilevel Governance draws on a number of studies I have conducted both solely and jointly over the past few years. I am most grateful to my collaborators for allowing me to draw on some of our joint material here. Specific acknowledgments are given at the appropriate points of the text. More generally, I have learned an enormous amount from my collaborations on these and other relevant studies with the following individuals: Maura Adshead, Gillian Bristow, Philip Catney, Rachael Chapman, Thomas Conzelmann, Matthew Flinders, Stephen George, Rachael Jones, Andrew Jordan, Adam Marshall, James Mitchell, Jan Olsson, and Andrew Taylor. To all of these individuals and to colleagues and students at the department of politics at the University of Sheffield, who are too numerous to mention, I express my sincere thanks.

For comments on draft material, I would like to thank Philip Catney, Andrew Geddes, Stephen George, Andrew Jordan, Vasilis Leontitsis, and Vivien Schmidt. In addition, the comments of the anonymous reviewer for Rowman & Littlefield were very helpful. The editorial director at Rowman & Littlefield, Susan McEachern, and the series editor, Gary Marks, have been very helpful and encouraging throughout and I am grateful to the staff at R&L— Melissa Ollila, Anna Schmöhe, and Meg Tilton—for the very professional way in which they guided the book through its final stages.

Finally, and for many reasons, I would like to thank my family—Pamela, Anna, and Thomas.

Ian Bache
Matlock, June 2007

Abbreviations and Acronyms

CAP	Common Agricultural Policy
CBI	Confederation of British Industry
CDP	Community Development Project
CED	Community Economic Development
CEE	Central and Eastern Europe
CEECs	Central and Eastern European Countries
CI	Community Initiative
CSFs	Community Support Frameworks
CSR	Comprehensive Spending Review
DETR	Department for the Environment, Transport and the Regions
DG	Directorate General
DoE	Department of the Environment
DoT	Department of Transport
DTI	Department of Trade and Industry
EAGGF	European Agricultural Guarantee and Guidance Fund
EC	European Community
EEC	European Economic Community
EIB	European Investment Bank
EMU	Economic and Monetary Union
ERDF	European Regional Development Fund
ESF	European Social Fund
EU	European Union
EUA	European Unit of Account
FCO	Foreign and Commonwealth Office
GDP	Gross Domestic Product
GNP	Gross National Product

GO	Government Office
GOEM	Government Office East Midlands
GOYH	Government Office for Yorkshire and Humber/Humberside
IMPs	Integrated Mediterranean Programmes
ISPA	Instrument for Structural Policies Pre-Accession
LAU	Local Administrative Unit
LEA	Local Education Authority
LEC	Local Enterprise Company
MEP	Member of the European Parliament
MLG	Multilevel Governance
MP	Member of Parliament
NAW	National Assembly for Wales
NDC	Northern Development Company
NEDC	National Economic Development Council
NGO	Nongovernmental Organization
NUM	National Union of Mineworkers (Britain)
NUTS	Nomenclature of Territorial Units for Statistics
ODPM	Office of the Deputy Prime Minister
PES	Public Expenditure System
Phare	Poland–Hungary: Actions for Economic Reconstruction
PMC	Programme Monitoring Committee
PR	Proportional Representation
RDA	Regional Development Agency
Rechar	Community Initiative Programme for the Conversion of Coal-mining Areas
SAPARD	Special Accession Programme for Agriculture and Rural Development
SDP	Social Democratic Party
SEA	Single European Act
SMEs	Small and Medium-sized Enterprises
SNAs	Subnational Actors
SPD	Single Programming Document
SRB	Single Regeneration Budget
TEC	Training and Enterprise Council
TUC	Trades Union Congress
UDC	Urban Development Corporation
UK	United Kingdom
WEPE	Welsh European Programme Executive

1

Introduction

Europeanization and multilevel governance are concepts that share a concern with explaining governance change in Europe, but the relationship between them is relatively unexplored. Europeanization has become a major theme of European studies in recent years and, while its meaning remains contested, there is a generally accepted differentiation between European integration as the process of creating a polity at the EU level and Europeanization as the effects of the EU on its member and accession states. Multilevel governance has emerged as an important concept highlighting both shifts in horizontal relations between state and society and changes in the vertical relations between actors located at different territorial levels. This book considers the extent to which Europeanization advances multilevel governance within member states and, if so, of what type(s), and through what processes.

The empirical focus is on EU cohesion policy[1] and the main case study is Britain, a member state whose political system has been increasingly characterized by multilevel governance in the period of EU membership. The British case is analyzed in relation to developments across the EU. The main purpose of the book is to establish whether EU cohesion policy (independent variable) has promoted multilevel governance in Britain and other member states (dependent variable) and, therefore, to assess whether any identified governance change can be characterized as a process of Europeanization. Beyond this are a number of related purposes:

1. To distinguish between the effects of EU cohesion policy on what Marks and Hooghe (2004) describe as type I multilevel governance (general purpose bodies) and type II multilevel governance (functionally specific

bodies) in domestic politics and to account for any variation across types;
2. To identify and explain the main causes of and constraints on change (to include a discussion of relevant intervening variables);
3. To reflect on the implications of any changes in governance for the role, power, and authority of the state;
4. To reflect on the utility of the framework of Europeanization developed for the book and on the utility of the multilevel governance concept and suggest how it might be strengthened analytically by drawing on the findings of the book.

SIMPLE AND COMPOUND POLITIES

In developing the comparative analysis, a distinction is drawn between EU effects in "compound" and "simple" polities (see table 1.1). In the former, "power, influence and voice are diffused through multiple levels and modes of governance" (e.g., Germany, Italy, Spain), while in the latter, "power, influence and voice are more concentrated in a single level and mode of governance" (e.g., Britain, France, Greece) (Schmidt 2003, 2). This distinction highlights both state structures and policy processes, and places these alongside analysis of the nature of politics. Here, changes in the former relate to changes in the vertical dimension of multilevel governance as new state structures emerge or are strengthened at levels above and below the nation state, while changes to the latter relate to the sideways movement of power to nonstate actors that relate to the horizontal dimension of multilevel governance.

Schmidt's (2006) approach builds on Lijphart's (1984, 1989) influential dichotomy between majoritarian and consensus democracies and is best understood in relation to this. However, the refinements it adds are important for

Table 1.1.   Key characteristics of compound and simple polities

	Structures	*Power*	*Authorities*
Simple polities (Fr, UK)	Unitary	Concentrated	Single
Compound polities (Sp, It)	Regionalized	Partially diffuse	Somewhat multiple
Compound polities (Ger, U.S.)	Federal	Diffuse	Multiple
Highly compound (EU)	Quasi-federal	Highly diffuse	Highly multiple

Source: Adapted from Schmidt 2006, 51.

Fr   Gr   UK   It   Ger   Sw   NL

Statist   Corporatist

Figure 1.1.   Member states along a continuum from statist to corporatist processes
Source: Schmidt 2006, 108.

the study of multilevel governance. First, it adds a third category of nation state structures to the two identified by Lijphart (federal and unitary), that is, *regionalized.* A number of EU states now fit into this category (Spain and Italy being the most obvious), while others may follow. Indeed, postdevolution Britain might be categorized as moving in the direction of a regionalized state, albeit unevenly (chapter 6). Second, it replaces Lijphart's executive-parties categorization of politics with two more nuanced categories of *representative politics* and *policy-making processes.* Third, Lijphart's twofold categorization of policy-making processes as pluralist and corporatist is made threefold to include *statist* processes (see figure 1.1).

In relation to politics, which for Lijphart is the overarching dichotomy between consensual and majoritarian systems, Schmidt includes it within the larger dichotomy between compound and simple polities. The politics dimension is separated from the systems dimension, because "Lijphart's distinction implies that majoritarian democracies will always have confrontation and consensus ones the opposite. But in real life this is not the case" (Schmidt 2006, 229). This point is amply demonstrated in relation to developments in British politics (chapter 6).

In short, the term *compound polity* refers to a state with a combination of a proportional representation system, corporatist policy-making processes, and regionalized or federalized structures. The term *simple polity* refers to a

                                                                                          EU

UK   Fr   Ire   Sw   NL   It   Ger   Sp   B

Simple polity   Compound polity

Figure 1.2.   EU and member states on a continuum between simple and compound polity
Source: Schmidt 2006, 229.
Note: While some member states do not figure on this diagram, Schmidt (2006) confirmed in correspondence with the author for this research that France, Greece, Ireland, Portugal, and the UK are classified as "simple" polities and Austria, Belgium, Germany, Spain, and Italy as "compound" polities. Denmark, Finland, Netherlands, and Sweden do not fall neatly into one category or the other; they are on the compound side of the continuum, but closer to the middle, having unitary structures but corporatist policy-making processes and proportional representation systems.

state with a combination of a majoritarian system of representation, statist policy-making processes, and a unitary state structure (Schmidt 2006, 227). Using these categories, the EU is defined as a *highly compound* regional polity, which places it at the extreme end of the continuum that includes its member states (figure 1.2), and one that tends to pull all member states—irrespective of their place on the continuum—in this direction.

However, and consistent with the "goodness of fit" argument, the pressure on states farthest away from the EU on this continuum is likely to be comparatively greater. This leads us neatly to the main case study.

BRITAIN

The case study of Britain draws on a number of research projects conducted by the author over a fifteen-year period (1991–2006) and over two hundred interviews conducted with policy makers and others. Over this period, Britain has undergone profound governance changes that have led to an increasing number of commentators characterizing it as a system of multilevel governance (chapter 6). Some of these developments have been formal and high profile (e.g., devolution to Scotland, Wales, Northern Ireland, and the English regions), while others have been more informal and generally lower profile (e.g., the proliferation of agencies, quangos, and partnerships; see chapter 7). While this general claim is often made, to date there has been no attempt to refine this claim by either distinguishing between different types of multilevel governance or relating developments of these typologies to the process of European integration; that is, to consider the extent to which types of multilevel governance are produced or promoted by features of European integration (here, cohesion policy), and, therefore, to assess whether any governance change identified can be characterized as a process of Europeanization.

The nature and duration of the research undertaken allows for a careful process tracing approach (see Checkel 2005) and the close focus on a single member state has a number of advantages. First, it allows detailed consideration of the domestic sources of multilevel governance as well as those of the EU; this avoids the criticism that those looking for Europeanization tend to find it (see chapter 2). Second, it provides detailed analysis over a significant time period: an important finding of Europeanization research is that deep-seated change involving learning takes place gradually (Bulmer and Burch 1998; Radaelli 2003, 52). Third, it provides the opportunity to explore the Europeanization effects of EU cohesion policy beyond the traditional focus on regions (see chapter 6) to identify other governance effects (i.e., both type I and type II).

THE STRUCTURE OF THE BOOK

The remainder of the book is structured as follows. Chapter 2 explains the concept of Europeanization and sets out the analytical framework guiding subsequent chapters. It traces the development of the concept and highlights its main uses and definitions before explaining and outlining the approach taken and the definition adopted here. In doing so, it provides a substantial revision of the three-step approach to understanding Europeanization (Risse, Cowles, and Caporaso 2001; see chapter 2) to include a new definition, to identify additional intervening variables, and to add categorizations of domestic change. This approach is then further developed to model simultaneously for complex and noncomplex causality. In addition, a test variable is identified to indicate *deep* Europeanization—that is, the transference of EU policies, practices, and preferences into domestic policies and practices as a result of changes in actors' preferences through their engagement with the EU. The chapter ends by highlighting issues for consideration in the empirical chapters of the book.

Chapter 3 explains why multilevel governance has become a central analytical concept in understanding the transformation of governance in the EU and its member states and clarifies how the concept is utilized in this study. It outlines the key contributions to the literature and, in particular, distinguishes between and explains the nature of types I and II multilevel governance (Hooghe and Marks 2003). The chapter identifies weaknesses in the concept and proposes the policy networks approach as a conceptual complement to address some of these weaknesses and to provide a bridge between the concept and that of Europeanization.

Chapter 4 sets out the emergence and development of EU cohesion policy. It portrays a highly contested policy area, which has been the site of significant struggles between supranational and intergovernmental forces. More specifically, it has been at the center of innovations in governance requirements that have often challenged existing practices within member states and promoted the idea of multilevel governance. Of particular importance in this respect are the administrative requirements of regionalization, partnership, and programming, which are explained here. These requirements have remained constant since the introduction of cohesion policy in 1989.

Chapter 5 explores and explains the effects of EU cohesion policy on multilevel governance patterns across EU member states, distinguishing between simple and compound polities and assessing the "goodness of fit" argument. There is a separate discussion of the specific experience of the simple polity states of central and eastern Europe (CEE) that acceded in 2004, which relates mainly to the preaccession effects of EU cohesion policy. The cases of the EU15 covered in the simple polity category are Ireland, Greece, and Portugal, and the compound polities covered are Germany, Spain, Sweden, and Finland. These cases are analyzed before the discussion turns to the CEE countries, namely Poland, the Czech Republic, and Hungary. In each of these three categories (simple, compound, and simple CEE), there is also a brief discussion of "other" cases.

The three subsequent chapters focus on the case of Britain. Before discussing the relationship between EU cohesion policy and British governance, chapter 6 outlines the main changes in British government and politics that have led to its characterization as a system of multilevel governance. It identifies the traditional features of British governance and specifically the notion of the Westminster model, the traditional organizing perspective, before tracing key developments in the postwar period under successive governments. There is a particular focus on change under New Labour since 1997, distinguishing between vertical change (devolution) that relates closely to type I multilevel governance and horizontal change (agencies, networks, and partnerships) that resemble type II multilevel governance. The final section of the chapter considers findings on the broad relationship between Europeanization and British politics and government effects and suggests that the effects of the EU generally and cohesion policy specifically are most likely to be found in relation to type II multilevel governance. Understanding the British conception of sovereignty is identified as central to understanding the prospects for multilevel governance through Europeanization.

Chapters 7 and 8 turn specifically to considering the relationship between EU cohesion policy and British governance. On this relationship, there is no easy way of dividing the historical narrative. The landmark year in cohesion policy for the EU was 1989, and this provides the starting point for the study; before that time there were a number of financial instruments that related to the goals of cohesion, such as the European Regional Development Fund (ERDF), but no administrative requirements that had implications for domestic governance. Since 1989, the EU requirements relevant to this study have remained in place. As such, the division of the narrative between pre- and post-1997, when there was a change of government in Britain for the first time in eighteen years, allows us to examine a domestic variable that deserves close attention, according to previous research on Europeanization and Britain (Bache and Jordan 2006a). Thus, chapter 7 considers the period 1989–1997 and chapter 8 considers the period 1997–2006. Both chapters consider both cohesion policy effects on type I and type II multilevel governance. In doing so, each chapter focuses on a number of cases relating to both the vertical dimension of multilevel governance (e.g., the development of the English regional tier) and the horizontal dimension (e.g., partnership governance).

Chapter 9 considers the extent to which EU cohesion policy has promoted multilevel governance in European states and whether this should be understood as a process of Europeanization. In doing so, it analyzes developments in Britain in comparative perspective and reflects on their significance. The chapter reflects on the utility of the main analytical tools of Europeanization, multilevel governance and policy networks, and the connections between them. It concludes by looking at the main explanations for change and offers the notion of the *learning state* to emphasize the interaction between ideas and interests in the process of change at the heart of contemporary multilevel governance.

NOTE

1. Cohesion policy is the EU's main redistributive policy (chapter 4), aiming to reduce social and economic inequalities across Europe. The main financial instruments of cohesion policy, the structural funds, are aimed largely at promoting the development of disadvantaged regions and localities in the single European market. Cohesion policy covers a substantial part of the EU's territory, accounts for approximately one-third of the EU's total budget, and remains an important source of funding for both regions and localities in both established and new member states.

2

Europeanization: A Framework for Analysis

Europeanization has become a leading concept in the field of European studies. Yet its purpose and utility is hotly contested, leading to a number of conceptual approaches and typologies.[1] For some, understanding Europeanization as the domestic effects of engagement with the EU is an overly narrow usage of the term (Wallace 2000). Yet this has become the dominant application for empirical studies of Europeanization. And, while acknowledging the argument that the EU itself may be best understood as both a feature and cause of Europeanization, the term is used here to mean the effects of the EU on domestic politics.[2] Specifically, Europeanization is understood as "the reorientation or reshaping of politics[3] in the domestic arena in ways that reflect policies, practices or preferences[4] advanced through the EU system of governance" (Bache and Jordan 2006c, 30). The purpose of adopting this narrower understanding is simple: it places a boundary around what is already a complex task of empirical research—that of tracing EU–member state relations.

Europeanization research on EU–member state relations has made comparisons both across different dimensions of politics and across different states (Featherstone and Radaelli 2003); focused more on different dimensions within one state (e.g., Dyson and Goetz 2003 on Germany; Bache and Jordan 2006a on Britain); examined one policy sector across a number of countries (e.g., Jordan and Liefferink 2004 on the environment); and, most recently, considered the accession process of central and eastern European (CEE) states (Hughes, Sasse, and Gordon 2004; Schimmelfennig and Sedelmeier 2005). Over time, definitions and models of Europeanization have become more sophisticated and the development of the field largely reflects broader trends in theorizing on the EU: namely, a growing interest in the debate between rationalists and reflectivists, particularly through the contrasting varieties of new institutionalism (below).

The remainder of this chapter has three parts. The first part sets out the background to the concept of Europeanization, the second part provides the analytical framework for the book, and the concluding section summarizes the main questions that guide the empirical investigation.

EUROPEANIZATION

Europeanization is not a new term, but only relatively recently have academics given it precise meaning in order to utilize it for empirical research. The first important attempt to do this was Robert Ladrech's (1994) article on the EU and France, in which he defined Europeanization as "an incremental process reorienting the direction and shape of politics to the degree that EC political and economic dynamics become part of the organizational logic of national politics and policy-making" (Ladrech 1994, 69). Ladrech was keen to point out that while EU membership had distinct effects in France, the mediating influence of domestic factors meant that fears of homogenization across states through European integration were unfounded. Moreover, he argued for a bottom-up approach to research to identify the nation-specific adaptation to cross-national inputs (Ladrech 1994, 84). Similar conclusions were drawn by Bulmer and Burch's (1998, 603) work on Britain, which found that "while change has been substantial, it has been more or less wholly in keeping with British traditions." Numerous subsequent studies have revealed a similar pattern of adaptation to the EU with "national colours" (e.g., Cowles, Caporaso, and Risse 2001; Olsen 2002).

Yet if the starting point of early research was to understand Europeanization as a top-down process in which the EU impacted on states, research revealed a more complex interactive dynamic: member states did not simply passively "download" policies from the EU, but also actively "uploaded" their preferences to the EU level: they understood that the greater their influence on the EU position, the less the subsequent problems of adapting. On this point, Tanya Börzel (2002) distinguished between those governments that successfully uploaded, calling them "pacesetters," and those that did not upload but preferred to delay or obstruct, calling them "foot-draggers." The third category, "fence-sitters," referred to those governments that neither uploaded nor blocked, but worked strategically with either type, policy pacesetters or foot-draggers, in exchange for their support on other issues. Governments' strategies were determined by both their preferences and their capacity to act.

Modeling Europeanization

While Europeanization has been increasingly viewed as a two-way or circular process (see Saurugger 2005), the most influential model for conducting empirical research on domestic effects remains essentially top-down. This is the three-step approach developed by Risse, Cowles, and Caporaso (2001, 6–12). Here, the first step is to identify the relevant EU-level processes (whether formal rules or informal processes) that imply some measure of domestic change. The second step is to identify the compatibility or "goodness of fit" between the EU-level requirements and domestic arrangements: poor fit implies strong adaptational pressure on the member state, good fit implies weak pressure. Step three of the approach suggests that the extent to which adaptational pressure leads to domestic change depends on five intervening factors: multiple veto points in the domestic structure; facilitating institutions; political and organizational cultures; the differential empowerment of domestic actors; and learning. In this schema, the EU is most likely to produce domestic structural change when it a) generates significant adaptational pressures; and b) facilitating factors are present that enable domestic actors to "induce or push through institutional change" (Risse, Cowles, and Caporaso 2001, 12).

In a subsequent contribution, Olsen (2002, 933) sought to specify more precisely the pressures likely from different types of EU requirements, highlighting among other factors the importance of the precision of their legal foundation. In the same vein, Bulmer and Radaelli (2005) related Europeanization pressures to different governance mechanisms of the EU. Simplified here, *governance by negotiation* provided member states with the opportunity to upload, and *governance by hierarchy* and *facilitated coordination* were the two downloading mechanisms. Governance by hierarchy, characterized by strong supranational power and the use of command and control instruments, generates the greatest pressure for change (other things being equal). Facilitated coordination refers to policy areas in which national governments are most powerful, where EU law is not prominent, unanimous voting is often in place, or the EU is primarily a forum for the exchange of ideas. Here, Europeanization takes place through learning rather than pressure.

Börzel and Risse (2003, 69–70) provided a threefold categorization of the outcome of domestic change in response to Europeanization pressures that ranges from transformation to absorption. This categorization is adapted to relate more specifically to the definition used here in table 2.1.

In short, then, Europeanization research has settled on understanding the relationship between the EU and its member (and accession) states. A consensus

Table 2.1.   Categorizing domestic responses to the EU

Category	Features	Degree of Domestic Change
Transformation	States fundamentally change existing policies, practices, and/or preferences or replace them with new ones.	High
Accommodation	States adapt existing policies, practices, and/or preferences without changing their essential features.	Modest
Absorption	States incorporate EU policies, practices, and/or preferences without substantially modifying existing policies, practices, and/or preferences.	Low

Source: Adapted from Börzel and Risse 2003, 69–70.

has grown around the need to understand this as a two-way relationship, but one that has been modeled primarily in terms of the downward flow of effects. There is consensus also on needing to understand both the force of what is "coming down" in terms of EU requirements (e.g., legal status) and how this "fits" with and is mediated by domestic factors. The effect is then categorized according to the nature and degree of change that takes place.

New Institutionalist Refinements

Much of the Europeanization literature is institutionalist by nature (e.g., Knill 2001; Knill and Lehmkuhl 1999; Börzel 1999; Radaelli 2003) and, indeed, Bulmer (2007, 51) has argued that "an awareness of the new institutionalisms is indispensable for understanding how Europeanization is theorized." This is partly because institutionalism lends itself well to mesolevel concerns of domestic policy and governance change, but also because new institutionalism is a broad church that seeks to explain an array of political phenomena. Over time though, Europeanization research has utilized new institutionalist approaches that are more nuanced and differentiated. In particular, a useful contrast is made between the respective arguments of rational choice, sociological and historical variants of new institutionalism, and particularly on the claims of the logic of consequentiality versus the logic of appropriateness (Börzel and Risse 2003; Hix and Goetz 2000; Vink 2003). While the former emphasizes rational goal-driven action and the latter emphasizes a more complex process of social learning in which actors' goals and preferences are transformed, as March and Olsen (1998, 10) have argued, "any particular action probably involves elements of each."

Table 2.2. **Rationalist and sociological assumptions**

Assumptions	Rationalist Accounts	Sociological Accounts
Power	Zero-sum	Positive-sum
Interests	Fixed	Malleable
Mechanism of Europeanization	Redistribution of power resources	Socialization/learning

An appreciation of the new institutionalisms is helpful in understanding the relationship between Europeanization and multilevel governance through EU cohesion policy. Here, Thielemann's (1999) work is particularly instructive because it sets out two positions on the implications for European governance of the partnership principle of EU cohesion policy (see chapter 4) and links the rationalist-sociological debate with the discussion of policy networks (chapter 3). In this debate, there are two main views: one emphasizes partnership as a mechanism for creating new opportunities for strategic interaction, the other suggests that it provides the potential for a deeper transformation of actor behavior and preferences. The first position, linked to the Rhodes model of policy networks (chapter 3) "is informed very much by a consequentialist/rational choice underpinning as it regards networks as an opportunity for strategic interaction" (Thielemann 1999, 185). In this view, power is zero-sum and Europeanization results from a redistribution of power resources between actors in the domestic arena resulting from EU membership. The alternative position on network governance, most closely associated with Beate Kohler-Koch (1996) and her collaborators, is that the EU is producing a transformation in European governance. In this view, the regular interaction promoted by the partnership principle can generate trust through socialization that promotes problem solving rather than bargaining as the decision-making style (Thielemann 1999, 187–88).

Here is a clear contrast between rationalist and sociological strands in parallel debates on new institutionalism and policy networks, which generate contrasting hypotheses in relation to the nature and extent of the transformation of governance that has taken place through EU cohesion policy. A rationalist account would assume power to be zero-sum, expect national actors to continue pursuing established goals (albeit in a changing environment), and ascribe shifts toward multilevel governance to a redistribution of power resources brought by EU policies. By contrast, a sociological perspective would assume power to be positive-sum, expect actors to change their preferences through socialization in a changing environment, and ascribe shifts toward multilevel governance to a learning process (see table 2.2).

In both accounts, learning is seen to be a feature of change, but has a different meaning in each. The central distinction is between "thin" (single loop) and "thick" (double loop)[5] forms of learning (Radaelli 2003, 52). "Thin learning" refers to the readjustment of actor strategies to allow them to achieve unchanged goals in a new context or "how to get around an obstacle by using a menu of well-known responses in various ingenious ways" (Radaelli 2003, 38). "Thick learning" involves a modification of actors' values and thus a reshaping of their preferences and goals. The notion of learning provides a further bridge between Europeanization, policy networks, and multilevel governance (chapter 3) through the argument that thick learning depends on "the way in which the system of institutional interactions is shaped, on the adequacy of information and communication flows, and on the presence of forums for dialogue among the actors" (Paraskevopoulos 2001, 254); and, more specifically, on the argument that policy networks can play a crucial role in generating social capital—trust and shared norms—among actors. Here, the norm of generalized reciprocity is particularly important, based on "a continuing relationship of exchange involving mutual expectations that a benefit granted now should be repaid in future" (Paraskevopoulos 2001, 260). In this view, social capital is generated through the interaction of actors in dense policy networks, such as those constructed through structural fund processes (chapter 4), and contributes to the socialization of those actors. In this context, social capital facilitates collective action and learning and adaptation to change through Europeanization becomes easier as a result. In his research on Greece, Paraskevopoulos (2001, 276) found evidence that "vindicates the role of social capital and institutional networks as important components of the institutional infrastructure that facilitate the process of social learning" (see also chapter 5).

So far, this rationalist-reflectivist dichotomy is relatively straightforward, but does not account for historical institutionalism, a key component in Europeanization research (Bulmer and Burch 1998; Bulmer and Radaelli 2004). As an approach, it incorporates both rationalist and sociological elements, but emphasizes the importance of practices embedded over time in explaining how institutions respond to external pressures for change. As Pierson (2000, 264) put it, "rather than assume relative efficiency as an explanation, we have to go back and look." Central to this argument is that institutions over time become path dependent[6] and are characterized by "stickiness." Consequently, historical institutionalism is often most useful in explaining responses approximating inertia or incremental change, although the approach anticipates occasional sudden change through "seismic events that trigger a 'critical juncture' or 'punctuate' the pre-existing equilibrium" (Bulmer 2007, 50). Thus, the main contribution of historical institutionalism here is not as a counterpoint to rationalist and sociological positions, but as a complement highlighting the potential significance of the temporal dimension in understanding institutional responses to the EU.

A FRAMEWORK FOR ANALYSIS

To recap, while Europeanization remains a relatively new field of research, it has begun to settle around a common empirical focus—on domestic change brought about by EU membership (or the prospect of membership)—and has a broad conceptual agreement on the value of the new institutionalisms. However, on this last point there is a caveat to be entered, which relates to the degree that institutional dynamics have been prioritized to the exclusion of political dynamics. Peter Mair (2004, 344) argued that "there seems little room for political or partisan contestation in Europeanization—whether we speak of the actors involved, who usually tend to favour depoliticization in any case, or of the analysts and scholars, who tend to see politics as being irrelevant to the issues at stake." This view demands that research focus more on issues of domestic political legitimacy and political contestation. In a study of Britain, where the majoritarian system brings sudden and substantive shifts in the political outlook of government (chapter 6), this point is well taken.

A further caveat is that while we are concerned with identifying Europeanization, the research design must allow for alternative sources of domestic change and, in particular, accommodate Radaelli's (2000, 220) argument that analysis of the effects of the EU on domestic systems "should be conducted in parallel to the investigation of endogenous processes." Inevitably, disentangling key variables in explaining domestic change is difficult. To manage this task, the focus here on a single state is important in facilitating in-depth investigation of the effects of domestic processes as well as EU and other international processes over a significant period of time. However, understanding developments in a comparative context provides additional means for teasing out the distinctive EU effects from other effects (Saurugger 2005, 292). This is the central purpose of the discussion in chapter 5.

Having set out a definition and some basic typologies of Europeanization, this study takes as its conceptual starting point the "three-step" framework developed by Risse, Cowles, and Caporaso (2001, 6), where step 1 involves identifying the relevant EU-level processes, step 2 assesses the "goodness of fit" with domestic politics, and step 3 identifies the relevant mediating factors (figure 2.1). Understanding the relationship between these three aspects is the key to explaining Europeanization.

However, there is need for some amendment to this framework. First, the definition of Europeanization applied by Risse, Cowles, and Caporaso (2001, 1), "the emergence and the development at the European level of distinct structures of governance," closely resembles the concept of European integration and does not acknowledge domestic change as a key component of Europeanization. As such, the definition set out earlier in the chapter is preferred

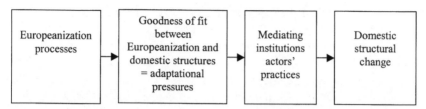

Figure 2.1.   Europeanization and domestic structural change
Source: Risse, Cowles, and Caporaso 2001, 6.

and thus the first part of the revised schema (figure 2.2) refers to "EU policies, practices, and preferences." It is also noted that in reflecting on the pressures "coming down" from the EU in this schema, it is helpful to keep in mind their legal status and precision.

Second, while the notion of "goodness of fit" remains a useful device for this study, its use has to be qualified in response to a number of criticisms. Most important among these is the argument that EU frameworks and policies have no "absolute" existence, but are subject to interpretation (Dyson and Goetz 2003, 16; see also Buller 2006; Geddes 2006). Moreover, while it is widely acknowledged that misfit may be a precondition for domestic change, alone it is not sufficient: a number of domestic political, institutional, and cultural variables are important in mediating change. However, misfit is seen to be particularly useful where there is a clear EU requirement or model (Knill and Lehmkuhl 2002). In this case, EU cohesion policy appears to fit the bill, with regulations setting out clear principles of governance within the domestic arena (chapter 4).

Third, the identification of potentially important mediating factors requires some explanation and a little development. To recap, five key mediating factors are identified by Risse, Cowles, and Caporaso (2001, 9–12): *multiple veto points* in the domestic structure, *facilitating institutions, political and organizational cultures*, the *differential empowerment of domestic actors*, and *learning*. The first three factors focus on institutional mediating factors, the last two on factors that relate to agency. In response to the observation that the political dynamics of Europeanization are often neglected, a sixth factor is added to this list: *political or partisan contestation*.

Multiple veto points in the domestic structure provide the argument that the more dispersed power is within the domestic arena, the more likely it is that adaptational pressures from EU sources will be slowed or even blocked. The existence of *facilitating formal institutions* can empower domestic actors to bring about change. These two institutional factors can work against each other, although both are consistent with rationalist assumptions about consequentiality. *Political and organizational cultures* are further "institutional"

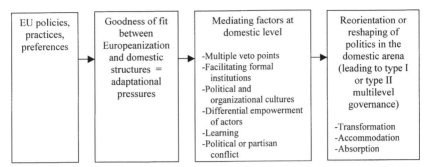

Figure 2.2. Europeanization and domestic change
Source: Adapted from Risse, Cowles, and Caporaso 2001, 6.

factors, but these speak to the sociological logic of appropriateness. Specifically, for this research, this factor raises the contrast between consensus-oriented (or cooperative) decision-making cultures and majoritarian (or "winner-take-all") cultures. As the EU system is generally characterized by the former, EU governance norms should provide more misfit and therefore greater adaptational pressures in majoritarian states. *Differential empowerment of actors* relates to the rationalist argument that Europeanization depends on a redistribution of power resources within the domestic arena. *Learning* refers to the potential for Europeanization to lead to the redefinition of actors' interests and preferences—that is, thick learning. *Political or partisan contestation* is the argument that EU effects are mediated by political or partisan conflicts within the domestic arena, more specifically, in the majoritarian British system, that the outcome of national elections can transform the prospects for Europeanization depending on the value structure of the party in government.

The final box in the Risse, Cowles, and Caporaso schema, which refers to "domestic structural change," is also amended here to fit more precisely with the focus of this research and to bring it into line with the definition adopted (see figure 2.2). Added to this are the refinements provided by Börzel and Risse (2003) for categorizing the degree of domestic change.

While this adapted model provides a valuable starting point for the study here, it has two important limitations. The first is that it models Europeanization as a linear rather than a dynamic or circular process. This shortcoming is addressed by Saurugger's (2005, 301) complex causality model (see figure 2.3).

These two models appear to provide a straightforward choice in terms of alternative research design: either top-down or interactive. However, the view taken here is that both approaches may have something to offer in relation to the case study, or at least, at this stage of the investigation, neither approach

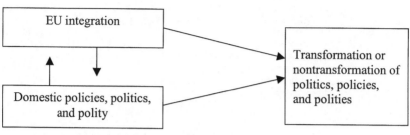

Figure 2.3.   Complex causality
Source: Saurugger 2005, 301.

should be ruled out. As such, an adjustment to the Saurugger schema is made to incorporate both the potential for complex causality and noncomplex causality (figure 2.4).

The second limitation of the Risse, Cowles, and Caporaso approach is that it does not model for the effects of domestic processes that proceed in relative isolation from the EU. Nor, indeed, does it model for the effects of processes that are neither domestic nor EU in origin. This is true also of the Saurugger schema. Moreover, while the latter models for the interactive dynamic of Europeanization, research should be open to the possibility that there may be EU factors that develop in relative isolation from national inputs, at least in the short to medium term. As such, the interactive dimension may not be a central part of the explanation for EU effects in all cases. The argument here is that complex and noncomplex processes may offer alternative explanations for Europeanization, but they may also occur simultaneously and each offer part of the explanation. The point is not to model exclusively for one of the possibilities but for both and to test them empirically (see figure 2.4).

The final part of this framework is the identification of a test variable for measuring the degree of Europeanization (Saurugger 2005, 292). As is typical of Europeanization research, this study is looking for evidence of change, specifically the "reorientation or reshaping of politics in the domestic arena." In this definition, reorientation equates to the more strategic response characteristic of thin learning, while reshaping relates more to thick learning. Understanding the type of learning that has taken place is the key to understanding whether Europeanization has been transformative or not. Saurugger's (2005, 297) argument is that "if in-depth change has occurred in behaviour, we must be able to observe it outside the EU as well"; this is used as the test variable in her study of interest groups. In this study, the test variable for indicating deep Europeanization is evidence of EU policies, practices, and preferences being voluntarily used to shape domestic policies and

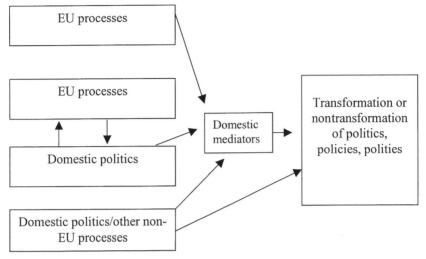

Figure 2.4.   Simultaneous complex and noncomplex causality

practices as a result of actor preferences changing through engagement with the EU. Moreover, given the focus of this study, we would expect these domestic arrangements to display characteristics of multilevel governance.

CONCLUSION AND KEY QUESTIONS

In simple terms, this study of Europeanization takes the governing principles of EU cohesion policy as the independent variable, domestic change (the emergence of multilevel governance) as the dependent variable, and identifies a range of intervening variables at the domestic level. However, the discussion above has signaled some of the challenges involved in the empirical study of Europeanization and produced a broad model of simultaneous complex and noncomplex causality to guide the research, which will also draw on the more specific insights of Risse, Cowles, and Caporaso (2001), among others. In doing so, the following questions guide investigation of the empirical material:

1. What are the relevant aspects of EU cohesion policy for analyzing its effects on multilevel governance and through what mechanisms and with what degree of force do these impact states?
2. What is the degree of "fit" between these relevant aspects of EU cohesion policy and domestic arrangements in Britain? How does this compare

with other member (and accession) states and are there different adaptational pressures in compound versus simple polities (chapter 1)?
3. To what extent has EU cohesion policy promoted multilevel governance
   in Britain and how should this be characterized (type I or type II; weak
   or strong; see chapter 3)? How does this compare with other member
   states?
4. What explains the degree of Europeanization that is evident?

NOTES

1. Bache and George (2006, 60) identified six uses of Europeanization that were
EU-specific: a top-down process of change deriving from the EU, the creation of new
EU powers, the creation of a European lodestar of domestic politics, an increasingly
two-way interaction between states and the EU, changes in external boundaries, and
a smokescreen for domestic maneuvers. In addition, they identified a further two non-
EU-specific uses of the term: horizontal transfer or "crossloading" between states and
exporting forms of political organization (Bache and George 2006, 61). See also
Bache and Jordan (2006b, 20–23).

2. Bulmer and Lequesne (2005, 11) suggested that the impact of the EU on member states "might better be termed 'EU-ization,' were it not for this being a dreadful
word."

3. In this definition, politics is used broadly to capture their concerns with polity,
politics, and policy dimensions. Thus, "politics" incorporates notions of governance
change, which is the concern here.

4. A preference here is taken to mean an "expressed desire," whether driven by instrumental or value-laden motives.

5. For a discussion of "single loop" and "double loop" learning, see Risse, Cowles,
and Caporaso (2001, 12). Here, the categories of thin/thick and single/double-loop
learning are used interchangeably.

6. As Hall and Taylor (1996, 941) put it, "forces will be mediated by the contex-
tual features of a given situation often inherited from the past." In some circumstances, path dependence can lead to "lock-in" (Pierson 1996) where the inherent bias
of the institution effectively rules out alternative courses of action.

3

Multilevel Governance and Policy Networks

The term *governance* has taken central place in the political science literature. It features prominently in debate on domestic politics (e.g., Marinetto 2003; Rhodes 1997; Stoker 1998), international politics (e.g., Rosenau 2004; Welsh and Kennedy-Pipe 2004), and where the boundaries between domestic and international politics have blurred in the context of European integration. It is here that that concept of multilevel governance has become most important.

There are many definitions of governance (for an overview see Bevir and Rhodes 2003, 45–52; Kjaer 2004; Pierre 2000; Richards and Smith 2002, 17–18). In its broadest sense, governance may be understood as "the continuous political process of setting explicit goals for society and intervening in it in order to achieve these goals" (Jachtenfuchs and Kohler-Koch 2004, 99). More narrowly, the term is used to capture the increasing fragmentation of public decision making and an increasing degree of interdependence between state and nonstate actors in this sphere, specifically, "governing with and through networks at the boundary of the state and civil society" (Bevir and Rhodes 2003, 9). On this issue, there is consensus that state-society relations are changing and that the boundary between the two is being redrawn, but "there is little agreement on how, why, or whether it is desirable" (Bevir and Rhodes 2003, 198). In the context of European integration, multilevel governance draws attention not only to shifts in the horizontal relationship between state and society, but also in vertical relations and boundaries between actors at national, supranational, and subnational levels.

In this tradition, there is an established conceptual toolkit for analyzing governance change through the work of Rod Rhodes and his associates on policy networks (e.g., Marsh and Rhodes 1992; Marsh and Smith 2000; Rhodes 1988, 1997). Moreover, and significantly for this study, there is a close conceptual fit between the policy networks approach and multilevel governance (Adshead 2002; Bache 1998; Rhodes, Bache, and George 1996a; Warleigh 2006). To date, however, the analytical potential arising from this fit remains underdeveloped. This chapter seeks to develop this potential and suggests that the policy networks approach provides a helpful conceptual bridge between Europeanization (chapter 2) and multilevel governance. The discussion at the end of this chapter considers in more detail how policy networks can be linked to the conceptual frames of Europeanization and multilevel governance to inform analysis of domestic governance change through EU membership. At this point though, we turn specifically to understanding multilevel governance.

BACKGROUND AND DEVELOPMENT

Origins

The intellectual context in which multilevel governance emerged is described in a number of places (e.g., Hooghe and Marks 2001; Pollack 2005; Rosamond 2000) but some restatement is useful here. Until the mid-1980s, the study of the EU was dominated by approaches developed from the study of international relations (IR) that were concerned with understanding the process of integration. From the IR tradition of pluralism, neofunctionalists (Haas 1958; Lindberg 1963) argued that the national governments who had initiated the integration process were losing control in an increasingly complex web of interdependence, a web that involved supranational, subnational, and nonstate actors. The counterview came from intergovernmentalism (Hoffmann 1964, 1966), informed by realist approaches in IR. More critical perspectives (e.g., structuralism, constructivism) came relatively late to prominence in debate on the EU (for an overview, see Bache and George 2006, 1–78).

The neofunctionalist argument fitted neatly with events until the mid-1960s, when the reassertion of national authority strengthened the counterclaims of intergovernmentalists that governments retained control over the important issues—not least through the persistence of the national veto in most areas. The period from the mid-1960s to the mid-1980s is generally seen as one in which intergovernmentalist explanations prevailed; although while the period was not marked by rapid advances in integration through significant new treaties or other headline developments, a considerable amount of lower-level integration continued to take place.

The turning point in relation to theorizing on the EU came with a renewed push for integration in the form of the single market program, culminating in the Single European Act (SEA) signed in 1986. This initiative led to an expansion in EU competences and revised decision-making procedures, most notably to eliminate the national veto in a number of areas to facilitate faster integration. The effects of the single market program on the process of integration and, in turn, on the nature of the EU as a political system prompted a new wave of theory challenging the dominant intergovernmental-supranational debate. Increasingly, parallels were drawn between the EU and domestic political systems, and tools and approaches from the study of domestic and comparative politics were utilized (Hix 1994).

Multilevel governance emerged in this period and drew upon both the old and new debates. Gary Marks (1992) first used the phrase "multilevel governance" to capture developments in EC structural policy after it was reformed in 1988. Subsequently, Marks and others developed the "multilevel governance" approach to apply more broadly to EU decision making (Marks, Hooghe, and Blank 1996; Hooghe and Marks 2001). The approach drew insights from both the study of domestic/comparative politics and the study of international politics. In particular, it had connections to the work by Fritz Scharpf (1988) and others on German federalism, resembled aspects of neofunctionalism, and was replete with network metaphors. While cohesion policy is covered in more detail later in the book (see chapters 4 to 8), a summary of the significance of the 1988 reform of the structural funds is important here for understanding the development of the multilevel governance approach.

EU Cohesion Policy and Multilevel Governance

EU cohesion policy has both social and economic aspects and focuses particularly on developing disadvantaged regions in the context of market integration. The main financial instruments of cohesion policy are the structural funds, which are governed by "structural policy," which differs in some respects from the policies for other instruments of cohesion policy (see chapter 4). As such, while the concern in this book is with a range of cohesion policy instruments, the term *structural policy* will be used where it is more accurate.

In the context of the acceleration of market integration in the 1980s and an increase in the number of relatively disadvantaged regions through the accession of Greece, Portugal, and Spain, structural policy underwent a major reform in 1988. In addition to agreeing to double the funding allocated, national governments also agreed to a new set of governing principles for structural policy, not least to ensure that funds were spent effectively. These were the principles of partnership, additionality, programming, and concentration, the first two of which became central to the case study from which multilevel governance was developed.

The partnership principle required that the structural funds be administered through partnerships established in each assisted region. These partnerships were to consist of national, subnational (regional and/or local), and supranational (EU Commission) actors. This decision gave subnational actors a formal role in the EU policy-making process for the first time. In subsequent years the Commission pushed for and secured agreement to a greater role in the partnerships for nonstate actors (trade unions, environmental organizations, voluntary and community groups, and so on).

The additionality principle required that EU funds be spent in addition to any planned expenditure in the member states. The requirement had been in place since the introduction of EU regional policy in 1975 but was strengthened in 1988, having been regularly ignored to that point—in particular by the British government, which treated EU funds as a reimbursement to the Treasury for its payments to the EU budget. Following the 1988 reform, the Commission took the British government to task over additionality and—with the support of British local authorities—forced a change in the government's approach. This case of joint supranational-subnational action was taken as further evidence of an emerging multilevel polity. Gary Marks (1993, 403) suggested that "Several aspects of the conflict—the way in which local actors were mobilized, their alliance with the Commission, and the effectiveness of their efforts in shifting the government's position—confirm the claim that structural policy has provided subnational governments and the Commission with new political resources and opportunities in an emerging multilevel policy arena."

In its early manifestation, *multilevel governance* referred to "continuous negotiation among nested governments at several territorial tiers" (Marks 1993, 392) and described how "supranational, national, regional and local governments are enmeshed in territorially overarching policy networks" (Marks 1993, 402–3). "Multilevel" referred to the increased vertical interactions and interdependence between governments operating at different territorial levels, while "governance" signaled the growing horizontal interactions and interdependence between governments and nongovernmental actors. Although not a theory of integration, the approach had strong neofunctionalist antecedents in its argument that supranational actors and interest groups were significant players in EU politics, although multilevel governance placed more emphasis on the importance of subnational actors. Both approaches shared the view that states had lost some control in this changing context, although the position of multilevel governance theorists is nuanced and requires further explanation.

Multilevel Governance and State Power

As noted above, multilevel governance was developed as a counterview to the state-centrism that dominated the study of the EU from the 1960s to the 1980s, and which found a contemporary voice in the post-SEA period through the work on liberal intergovernmentalism of Andrew Moravcsik (1991, 1993, 1994, 1998). Moravcsik (1994, 9) argued that the control of state executives at the agenda-setting stage of EU policy making conferred on them "gate-keeping" power: "the power to veto proposed policies, permits executives to block negotiation or agreement at the international level, thereby imposing a *de facto* domestic veto." Yet multilevel governance did not reject the central role played by state executives in EU decision making; rather, it acknowledged them as "the most important pieces of the European puzzle" (Hooghe and Marks 2001, 3). However, it suggested that "when one asserts that the state no longer monopolizes European level policy-making or the aggregation of domestic interests, a very different polity comes into focus" (2001, 3). On this issue, the multilevel governance model makes three claims:

1. Decision-making competences are shared by actors at different levels rather than monopolized by state executives.
2. Collective decision making among states involves a significant loss of control for individual state executives (notably, through qualified majority voting in the Council).
3. Political arenas are interconnected rather than nested. Subnational actors operate in both national and supranational arenas, creating transnational associations in the process (Hooghe and Marks 2001, 3–4).

In explaining why state sovereignty is transferred or lost, the multilevel governance approach sees an important distinction between institutions and actors—a point of contrast with state-centric models. For Hooghe and Marks (2001, 70), political institutions "specify the structure and allocation of authority in a given territory," while political actors, individuals, and groups of individuals "operate in the context of those institutions, but they may also try to change them" (2001, 70). To understand how institutions change, therefore, it is important to focus on the preferences of actors within institutions who are the actual participants in decision making. This focus is important in challenging the assumption that institutional interests and the interests of actors within those institutions are necessarily the same. Therefore, in addressing questions of why and how states lose or transfer control to the EU, the focus should be on the actors within state institutions. As Marks, Hooghe, and Blank (1996, 348) put it,

It makes little sense to conceive of whole states or national governments as the key actors in European decision-making. One cannot assume that those serving in national governments give priority to sustaining the state as an institution. This is an empirical matter. Institutions influence the goals of those who hold positions of power within them, but it is unlikely that political actors will define their own preferences solely in terms of what will benefit their institution. The degree to which an actor's preferences will reflect institutional goals depends, in general, on the extent to which an institution structures the totality of the individual's life, on how positively or negatively the institution is viewed, on the strength of the contending institutional, personal and ideological loyalties, and on the length of time in which the individual expects to stay within that institution.

The first part of this argument has resonance with the "core executive" arguments of Rhodes and others on the need for analysis that disaggregates the state (below). In the context of EU decision making, the important state actors are the elected politicians in the central executive. Once this focus is established, it is easier to understand how and why "states" agree to shift decision making to the EU level. Understanding the normative goals and private preferences of state actors that may lead them to weaken the institutions in which they are located is seen as "the key to explaining multilevel governance" (Hooghe and Marks 2001, 79).

Applications and Criticisms

The arguments of multilevel governance have been examined most regularly on the "home ground" of EU structural policy. Hooghe's (1996a) edited volume on the implementation of structural policy across the EU found considerable variations in the evidence for multilevel governance across states, with the preexisting balance of territorial relations a key part of the explanation. These findings were confirmed in a Commission-funded study (Kelleher, Batterbury, and Stern 1999). Studies of Britain demonstrated variations both across issues within structural policy and across different regions within the country (Bache, George, and Rhodes 1996; Bache 1999). On the additionality issue, the change in the government's approach to implementation failed to lead to the anticipated extra spending in Britain's regions. Policy control that the state "gatekeeper" lost through pressure from joint supranational-subnational action (above) was clawed back at a later stage of the policy process (Bache 1999). Here it was argued that defining the role of gatekeeper in the traditional sense, of controlling the flow of connections between nested arenas of international and domestic politics, missed an essential point: that it is the influence over outcomes from the policy process that matters most—

not control over the interconnections between actors. More specifically, in modeling a two-stage process of policy making, Moravcsik's (1993) liberal intergovernmentalism overlooked the important third stage of the process—policy implementation—where the decisions taken at the EU level are put into effect. This stage involves further political activity, the outcomes from which provide a more complete picture of state power.

A number of other criticisms of multilevel governance emerged, in particular that it focused more on relations between state actors at different levels than on relations across sectors (i.e., multilevel *government* not *governance*), that it was more descriptive than explanatory, and that it overstated the autonomy of subnational actors (for an overview of criticisms and a response, see Jordan 2001 and George 2004). In a subsequent development of the approach, Hooghe and Marks (2003) and Marks and Hooghe (2004) developed a twofold typology of multilevel governance, which clarified aspects of the approach that had been criticized. In particular, they clarified that the empirical concerns of multilevel governance were with both intergovernmental relations (type I) and the less orderly governing arrangements (type II) that did not always nest within these relations.

Two Types of Multilevel Governance

Type I multilevel governance has echoes of federalism. It describes system-wide governing arrangements in which the dispersion of authority is restricted to a limited number of clearly defined, nonoverlapping jurisdictions at a limited number of territorial levels, each of which has responsibility for a "bundle" of functions. By contrast, type II multilevel governance describes governing arrangements in which the jurisdiction of authority is task-specific, where jurisdictions operate at numerous territorial levels and may be overlapping. In type I, authority is relatively stable, but in type II it is more flexible, to deal with the changing demands of governance (see table 3.1).

Table 3.1. Types of multilevel governance

Type I	Type II
General-purpose jurisdictions	Task-specific jurisdictions
Nonintersecting memberships	Intersecting memberships
Jurisdictions at a limited number of levels	No limit to the number of jurisdictional levels
System-wide architecture	Flexible design

Source: Marks and Hooghe 2004, 17.

These types of multilevel governance are not mutually exclusive, but can and do coexist. Britain is a case in point (chapters 6 to 8), where general-purpose jurisdictions exist alongside special-purpose jurisdictions: formal institutions of government operate alongside, and indeed create, special-purpose bodies designed to carry out particular tasks. Their coexistence may lead to tensions, but such tensions (and their resolution) are a characteristic feature of multilevel governance.

UTILIZING MULTILEVEL GOVERNANCE

In the conclusion to their collection on multilevel governance, Bache and Flinders (2004c, 197) identified four areas of agreement in the disparate contributions:

1. That decision making at various territorial levels is characterized by the increased participation of nonstate actors;
2. That the identification of discrete or nested territorial levels of decision making is becoming more difficult in the context of complex overlapping networks;
3. That in this changing context the role of the state is being transformed as state actors develop new strategies of coordination, steering, and networking to protect, and in some cases to enhance, state autonomy;
4. That in this changing context the nature of democratic accountability has been challenged.

Beyond these common strands lay areas of dispute in relation to the value of multilevel governance and how it should employed in academic research. The next section explains how multilevel governance is employed in this study and highlights its potential value.

The Contribution of Multilevel Governance

It is a strength of multilevel governance that it draws on ideas and concepts from across political science and contributes to a growing awareness that many contemporary issues and challenges require analysis that transcends traditional disciplinary boundaries. Most specifically, multilevel governance crosses the traditionally separate academic terrains of domestic and international politics to emphasize the blurring of the distinction between the two through the process of European integration. Here, the link with the concept of Europeanization (chapter 2) is obvious. Moreover, as will be developed further in chapter 6, multilevel governance increasingly captures the nature of domestic politics and governance in Britain, with some suggesting that "multi-level governance has become a new mantra" in British politics (Marsh, Richards, and Smith 2003, 314). While an increasing number of scholars are making similar claims (see chapter 6), to date there has been no attempt to refine this general claim by both distinguishing between type I and type II multilevel governance within Britain and then seeking to examine these developments in relation to the process of European integration, that is, to consider the extent to which the two types of multilevel governance (dependent variable) are produced or promoted by European integration (independent variable) and, therefore, whether any governance change identified can be characterized as a process of Europeanization. The examination of domestic change of this type through engagement with EU cohesion policy (as a particular feature of European integration) is the central purpose of this book.

Type I multilevel governance, with its federalist overtones, speaks increasingly to the formal devolution of powers in Britain (chapter 6), particularly in creating new general-purpose jurisdictions. Type II multilevel governance is altogether more messy and ad hoc, capturing the complex array of quangos, agencies, and partnerships and so on that exist not only at territorial levels marked out by devolution, but also in the spaces in between and below (intraregional, subregional, sublocal, and so on). One might imagine a complex diagram in which the orderly institutional backbone of the British system of governance is overlaid, sometimes neatly, often less so, with a less formal mosaic of governing arrangements for different issues and policy areas. Chapter 8 (see figure 8.1) gives a flavor of this image with an illustration of how type II multilevel governance in the field of structural policy in just one subregion of England maps on to type I formal institutions.

By starting with this understanding of how informal and disorderly governance relates to and overlays orderly and formal governance, we can sharpen the questions about the mechanisms, strategies, and tactics that are used to govern in the context of multilevel governance, not just by those in national government seeking to maximize influence in the context of devolution and fragmentation, but also by the regional and subnational actors seeking to maximize influence in this changing environment. This issue inevitably connects us to the central question in the debate: what is happening to the role, power, and authority of the state in this context?

The relationship between multilevel governance and state power remains controversial. It would be a misreading of multilevel governance to see it as a claim that the nation state is in terminal decline. Marks and Hooghe (2004, 19) restated their position that some control has "slipped away" from governments in the context of multilevel governance but acknowledged that they continue to be "central actors." A similar position is taken elsewhere in the governance literature, whether relating to global developments (Rosenau 2004) or domestic politics (Rhodes 1997). The challenge is to understand more about the extent to which power has slipped away from states, in what circumstances, and with what effect.

However, it is also important to recognize that there may be circumstances where multilevel governance does not necessarily undermine state power. As Jessop (2004, 65) argued, "a shift to governance can enhance the capacity to project state power and achieve state objectives by mobilizing knowledge and power resources from influential non-governmental partners or stakeholders." Empirically, there is evidence that the state has orchestrated a shift to governance in some fields to enhance its power. In the case of British urban policy, the Conservative governments of the 1990s introduced local partnership arrangements to weaken the position of Labour local authorities and empower more sympathetic private sector actors to achieve centrally determined objectives more effectively (Bache 2001). In the case of education policy, the Labour government after 1997 introduced new actors into local decision making and policy delivery as a way of bypassing local education authorities that failed to meet central objectives successfully, thus again promoting governance to maximize central control (Bache 2003). As such, part of the research objective has to be aimed at understanding how and why the development of (multilevel) governance might be advantageous to central government and indeed form part of state strategy.

Jessop (2004, 65) argued that countering the shift toward multilevel governance is the increased role of government in "metagovernance":

> political authorities (on and across all levels) are becoming more involved in all aspects of metagovernance: they get involved in redesigning markets, in constitutional change and the juridical re-regulation of organizational forms and objectives, in organizing the conditions for self-organization, and, most importantly, in the overall process of collibration [*sic*].

It is through the role of governments in setting these ground rules that (multilevel) governance is said to take place "in the shadow of hierarchy" (Scharpf 1994, 40, in Jessop 2004, 65). This argument does have echoes in the multilevel governance literature, where Marks and Hooghe (2004, 24) suggest that "Type II multilevel governance tends to be embedded in legal frameworks determined by Type I jurisdictions."

Yet while, as Jessop suggests, governments are becoming "more involved" in metagovernance, the extent to which they are successful in their efforts must be a question for empirical investigation. For example, in the EU, the "ground rules" for governance (whether they are hard law or soft law) emerge from a complex set of interactions that gave rise to the intergovernmental-supranational and other debates referred to above. In other words, national governments are not the only actors seeking to set the ground rules for governance. As such, there may be an argument for applying the insights of multilevel governance and the related tools of policy networks and power dependence to investigate the role of governments (and other actors) in metagovernance. Before turning to these tools, a key outstanding issue in debates on multilevel governance is addressed.

Governance or Participation?

A key criticism of multilevel governance has been its failure to distinguish governance from other counterdescriptions of (multilevel) participation (Bache 1999), mobilization (Jeffery 2000), or dialogue (Wilson 2003). These three alternative descriptions essentially amount to the same claim, that there is often an increase in the number of actors involved in policy making but the effects of this extra activity on policy outcomes is unclear. For the sake of brevity and consistency, the term *participation* is used here to represent these three similar ideas.

What has been missing in the debate so far is identification of the empirical indicators that tell us whether we are witnessing governance or participation; to paraphrase Radaelli (2003, 38), we need to locate the "fence" that separates the two. The literature does not make a clear distinction between the two terms, but there is an obvious one to be drawn from the debate: *participation* refers to engagement in the decision-making process, while *governance* infers that engagement involves some influence over the outcomes of this process. Thus, to distinguish between the two we need to identify empirically whether participants influence policy outcomes. Finding a more precise answer to this empirical question would also contribute to more informed normative debates around the virtues (or otherwise) of multilevel governance. The policy networks approach can inform this endeavor.

POLICY NETWORKS

As observed above, it is perhaps surprising that, given the explicit connections made by Marks, Hooghe, and others between multilevel governance and "transnational" and "territorially overarching" networks, more has not been made of the potential for developing a more coherent relationship between multilevel governance and the policy networks approach. Not only are there similarities in terms of language and metaphor, but also both approaches share a concern with detailed empirical investigation of multiple interactions within policy processes, particularly sector-specific, from policy initiation through to and including policy implementation. In particular, and this is the approach here, more might be made of the policy networks approach for exploring changing dynamics and power relations as a means of assessing shifts to multilevel governance.

The emphasis on policy implementation is particularly pertinent in relation to Europeanization, understood as the reorientation or reshaping of politics in the domestic arena in ways that reflect policies, practices, or preferences advanced through the EU system of governance (see chapter 2). The nature of EU policy making offers considerable scope for the domestic actors responsible for implementation to shape outcomes at this stage of the process. This point has been long recognized by some EU scholars (e.g., Wallace 1977, 57). Despite this, much theorizing continues to focus on EU negotiations and decisions to the exclusion of the effects of this on outcomes on the ground. However, this is not so with the two approaches discussed here. Marks, Hooghe, and Blank (1996, 365) suggested that multilevel governance is "prominent in the implementation stage," while, from a policy networks perspective, Rhodes has emphasized that "Policy does not 'fail' but is actually made in the course of negotiations between the (ostensible) implementers" (Rhodes 1986, 14).

Peterson (2004, 119) identified three basic assumptions of the policy networks approach: that modern governance is frequently nonhierarchical, that the policy process must be disaggregated to be understood because of the variations between groups and governments in different policy sectors, and that while governments "remain ultimately responsible for governance," this is not the whole story. Peterson (2004), Jachtenfuchs (2001), and others have argued strongly that the EU is particularly apposite for policy network analysis, highlighting the fluid institutional structure, fragmented (often sector-specific) policy making, the high number of participants engaging through multiple access points, and the absence of a strong center of power. Jachtenfuchs and Kohler-Koch (2004, 100) have suggested that "networking is the most characteristic feature of EU governance." To the extent that the policy networks approach has been used in conjunction with or in relation to multilevel governance (notably, contributions to the Hooghe 1996a collection by Anderson; Bache, George, and Rhodes; and Balme and Jouve), the point of departure has usually been the "Rhodes model." This is also true of most other applications of the policy networks approach to the study of the EU more generally (e.g., Bomberg and Peterson 1998; Peterson and Sharp 1998; Smith 1990; Daugbjerg 1999).

In the Rhodes model, a policy network is a set of resource-dependent organizations. These networks vary along five key dimensions: the constellation of interests, membership, vertical interdependence, horizontal interdependence, and the distribution of resources (Rhodes 1988, 77–78). The model provides a continuum of network types, from highly integrated policy communities (high interdependence, stable relationships, restricted membership, insulation from other networks) to loosely integrated issue networks (limited interdependence, open membership, less stable relationships, less insulated from other networks). In relation to network typologies, a key claim of the Rhodes model is that highly interdependent, stable, and relatively closed policy communities are more able to shape policy outcomes and resist external pressures than are less interdependent, less stable, and relatively open issue networks.

Resource Dependence

Rhodes described resource dependence as the "explanatory motor" for the network-based differentiated polity perspective that he adopted for the study of Britain (chapter 7). In particular, it explains why different levels of government interact (Rhodes 1997, 9). While the typologies of policy networks and their key characteristics are widely discussed and understood, the concept of resource dependence—which is central to the Rhodes model—is relatively underutilized, but is arguably the aspect of the policy networks approach that is of greatest analytical utility in assessing the development of multilevel governance. It states that organizations are bound together within networks by interdependence: each organization is dependent on others for certain resources. These "resource dependencies" are the key variable in shaping policy outcomes. As Peterson and Bomberg (1993, 28) put it, "They set the 'chessboard' where private and public interests manoeuvre for advantage" (we might add the voluntary sector here). However, interdependence is generally asymmetrical and in some cases it is possible to talk of "unilateral leadership" within networks (Rhodes 1986, 5). In this study, we can gain a more nuanced understanding of how European integration can redistribute resources of various types between domestic actors to promote (or constrain) the development of multilevel governance.

The key resources identified by Rhodes (1997, 37) are financial, informational, political, organizational, and constitutional-legal. Interestingly, one of the leading (liberal) intergovernmentalist protagonists in the state-centric versus multilevel governance debate identified a similar set of categories in seeking to explain how and when international cooperation "redistributes domestic power resources between state and society" (Moravcsik 1994, 1). Here,

Moravcsik advanced three arguments: that international negotiations and institutions reallocate political resources by changing the domestic, institutional,
and ideological context in which domestic policy is made; that this realloca-
tion of control over domestic political resources generally favors those who
participate directly in international negotiations (generally, national executives); and that this shift in domestic power resources toward executives feeds
back into international bargaining, often facilitating international cooperation
(Moravcsik 1994, 1–2). The power resources that were redistributed in this
process fell into four categories: initiative, institutions, information, and ideas.
The first two of these were procedural, the latter two cognitive. *Initiative* referred to the ability to introduce (or block the introduction of) issues onto the
domestic agenda; *institutions* to the procedures by which domestic decisions
are legally adopted; *information* to political and technical knowledge; and
ideas to the supply of legitimate justifications for specific policies. Moravcsik
(1994, 5) argued that "the art of democratic governance consists in exploiting
these four procedural and persuasive resources to realize political goals."

Stephen George (2001) suggested that each of the five resources identified
by Rhodes could be fitted into Moravcsik's categories, with the exception of
financial resources, which he argued was a "strange omission" given the importance of the EU budgetary line in at least some policy sectors. Clearly,
consideration of the (re)distribution of financial resources is important in relation to cohesion policy. Thus if not for the direct link with the policy networks approach, the inclusion of financial resources in the power dependence
framework alone makes it preferable for this study.

The Core Executive Approach

The second aspect of the policy networks approach that has potential for con-
tributing to understanding the development of multilevel governance is the
core executive approach. As noted above, it has resonance with the argument
of multilevel governance scholars that to conceive whole states or national
governments as the key actors in decision making conceals the potential for
the interests of individual actors to differ from those of the institutions in
which they serve. The core executive approach emphasizes the complexity of
central policy making, in which there are differences of view and conflicts of
interest both within and between the important formal institutions of government as well as between these institutions and the policy network participants
that surround them. The relative influence of individual government departments depends, like that of other network participants, on the extent to which
they control and can effectively deploy relevant power resources in a given
situation. In this context, the formal institutional arrangements are important

in structuring the distribution of resources, but this alone does not determine policy positions. The effectiveness of central government (and other participants) is in part dependent on "the tactics, choices and strategies they adopt in using their resources" (Smith 1999, 5).

The complexity of central policy making and coordination is acknowledged in a growing number of studies of domestic politics and policy making. In their comparative study of six European core executives, Wright and Hayward (2000, 33) highlighted the limits to core executive coordination, suggesting that it is "largely negative, based on persistent compartmentalisation, mutual avoidance and friction reduction between powerful bureaux or ministries." Moreover, there is growing empirical evidence that this complexity relates equally to core executive policy making on foreign affairs generally and on the EU specifically (Allen and Oliver 2006; Bulmer and Burch 2005). To some degree, this argument would be accepted by liberal intergovernmentalists, who recognize that a pluralistic domestic process shapes foreign policy positions (see Moravcsik 1993). In the context of arguments on Europeanization, however, this previously "domestic" process can no longer be understood as purely domestic. For example, the network participants who influence "British" policy on EU matters are ones whose position has often been shaped by prior engagement with the EU and, in some cases, whose very participation in the relevant network is owed to EU policies: cohesion policy is a case in point (chapters 7 and 8).

More generally, the core executive approach's emphasis on difference and interdependence at the core of government, on both formal institutions and informal processes, and thus on the need for a disaggregated analysis of the state, provides added sensitivity to understanding the influence of central government in mediating Europeanization processes.

Criticisms

An important criticism of the policy networks approach that may partly explain its underutilization in connection with multilevel governance is the inadequate treatment it has given to the role of ideas in the policy process—at least in the earlier versions of the Rhodes model (Marsh, Richards, and Smith 2003, 310). This shortcoming is particularly unfortunate for advocates of applying the approach to the EU in light of the recent constructivist turn in European studies (for a discussion, see Pollack 2005, 365–68), which provides a strong ideas-based counterargument to the interest-based claim that participants in policy making coalesce (within and between networks) because they are bound together by resource dependence. If this counterpossibility is not identified prominently in the research framework, studies adopting the policy networks approach are likely to underplay the significance of ideas in policy making. However, in more recent work, Rhodes has placed a greater emphasis on the role of ideas, arguing that "'objective' positions in a structure do not determine the beliefs and actions of individuals" and that "even when an institution maintains similar routines while personnel changes, it does so mainly because the successive personnel pass on similar beliefs and preferences" (Bevir and Rhodes 2003, 41).[1] These arguments dovetail neatly both with the actor-centered approach of multilevel governance (above) and also with the sociological institutionalist dimensions of Europeanization (chapter 2) and, as such, enhance the potential of the policy networks approach to provide a conceptual bridge between the two.

A Conceptual Bridge

Applying a purely rationalist policy networks approach as a conceptual bridge, the argument postulated would be that Europeanization that promotes a shift toward multilevel governance within states would require a redistribution of domestic power resources in favor of subnational and nonstate actors. While the policy networks approach is not a predictive theory, by being used to connect multilevel governance to Europeanization it contributes this strong hypothesis. Moreover, its framework of power dependence facilitates a nuanced typology for guiding empirical research toward identifying and isolating the decisive resource exchanges. The counterhypothesis that arises from criticisms of the rationalist approach to policy networks is that where there is evidence of Europeanization promoting multilevel governance *without* related evidence of a redistribution of power resources, this development must be explained in terms of dominant actors changing their values and preferences, that is, through a process of thick learning. Of course, any investigation of the potential for Europeanization effects here has to proceed alongside exploration of other (non-EU) sources of change.

POWER AND SOVEREIGNTY IN MULTILEVEL GOVERNANCE

The final issue that must be dealt with in connecting multilevel governance and policy networks is how they deal with the related issues of power and sovereignty. Much of the debate around both has conceptualized power as zero-sum: what one actor gains, another must lose. Thus, in relation to multilevel governance, it is often assumed that to the extent that subnational, supranational, and nonstate actors have gained power through the process of European integration, this must be at the expense of national state actors. Yet there is nothing inevitable in this reading of power in relation to multilevel governance and policy networks. Indeed, a closer look at the literature reveals variance in how power is conceived in different contributions.

While traditionally rationalist, the Rhodes model has been developed to provide a more nuanced understanding of power in different types of network. Bevir and Rhodes (2003, 57) argued that in a policy community "although one group may dominate, power must be a positive-sum game if community is to persist," whereas in looser issue networks, power is a zero-sum game. Multilevel governance theorists also distinguish between two conceptions of power. The zero-sum notion conceives power narrowly as "control over persons," while a broader understanding of power as "the ability to achieve desired outcomes" is preferred (Hooghe and Marks 2001, 5). It is the latter conception that offers an explanation for why states sometimes transfer authority to supranational bodies.

The debate on sovereignty closely follows the debate on power. Multilevel governance theorists take a broader view of sovereignty than the Weberian focus on formal, legislative authority, which is the emphasis of state-centric accounts of the EU (Hooghe and Marks 2001, 6). They highlight a broader range of resources, including information, expertise, and legitimacy, and identify political control as the defining element of sovereignty: control which is considered sovereign "when it exists independently of an external power or body" (Aalberts 2004, 31). Here again, both the focus and language of multilevel governance closely resemble key features of the Rhodes model and particularly the resource dependence framework. However, this emphasis in multilevel governance on understanding sovereignty as effective control may obscure the explanation for enduring sovereign statehood in the context of European integration, namely that "in their interaction with multilevel governance structures, states are reconstituting in the meantime their mutual quality as sovereign states" (Aalberts 2004, 41). Again, this infers a deeper process of reshaping through learning rather than simply strategic reorientation in a changing opportunity structure. This distinction is considered in relation to British notions of sovereignty in the context of multilevel governance (chapter 6 and chapter 9).

CONCLUSION

This chapter has explained the development and nature of multilevel governance and its relevance for this study. It has argued that multilevel governance directs attention to increasingly complex vertical and horizontal relations between actors and sharpens questions about the mechanisms, strategies, and tactics through which governing takes place in this context. This connects us inevitably to the question of what is happening to the role, power, and authority of the state within and beyond national boundaries.

It has identified the connections between multilevel governance and the policy networks approach and set out how the latter provides a conceptual bridge connecting Europeanization and emerging multilevel governance in domestic politics. The tools of the networks approach can guide empirical research in locating the fence that separates multilevel governance from multilevel participation. Moreover, in its rationalist form, the policy networks approach provides the hypothesis that a shift toward multilevel governance in Britain requires a redistribution of power resources among relevant domestic actors, specifically, in favor of subnational and nonstate actors. The counterhypothesis that arises from criticisms of the rationalist approach to policy networks is that where there is evidence of Europeanization promoting multilevel governance, but no related evidence of a redistribution of domestic power, this development must be explained in terms of dominant actors changing their preferences; that is, through a thick learning process.

Finally, the chapter considers the concepts of power and sovereignty in the debates on multilevel governance and policy networks. It suggests that much of the debate surrounding multilevel governance has assumed zero-sum conceptualizations of power—particularly state-centric criticisms. However, a closer look at the literature on multilevel governance and the more recent contributions to the policy networks approach suggest a broader understanding of the notions of power and sovereignty that are integral to understanding why states voluntarily concede power (narrowly defined) to other actors.

The relevance of these issues is explored in subsequent chapters and in relation to the British case in particular. The contribution of multilevel governance to this study is then evaluated in the concluding chapter.

NOTE

1. In this later work, Rhodes added a footnote suggesting that his original policy networks model did not neglect the realm of ideas entirely. While acknowledging that it "was clearly rooted in a positive epistemology," it also "genuflected in the direction of a more intepretive approach through its reference to Sir Geoffrey Vickers and the idea of appreciate systems" (Bevir and Rhodes 2003, 78).

4

EU Cohesion Policy

In essence, cohesion policy refers to the governing principles of the EU structural funds and the Cohesion Fund, which are explained below. The policy is aimed at addressing economic and social inequalities. In the terms of Lowi's (1964) classic threefold categorization of public policies as either redistributive, distributive, or regulatory, cohesion policy should be understood as the main redistributive policy of the EU.[1] As Lowi acknowledged, these typologies are not straightforward: regulatory and distributive policies may be redistributive in the longer term and thus, the typologies are most useful in categorizing the short term. This is useful to highlight here because a theme of the discussion in subsequent chapters is that it is both the regulatory and financial aspects of cohesion policy that have had redistributive effects. Moreover, the redistribution of nonfinancial resources through regulation is a central concern here.

Not least because of its innovative experiments in governance, cohesion policy has received considerable attention from political scientists. The purpose here is not to rehearse the whole of this debate,[2] but to set the scene for the analysis of Europeanization and multilevel governance through cohesion policy that follows in subsequent chapters. This requires some attention to the development of the policy—not least to identify any uploading from member states—and to the nature and force of its requirements on member states. The narrative takes the story of cohesion policy requirements up to the end of 2006, although the significance of the most recent reform requirements (for the period 2007–2113) is also reflected on briefly.

The chapter has four substantive parts. The first part provides a brief background to, or "prehistory," of cohesion policy; the second part discusses the nature of the cohesion policy created in 1988; part three teases out and explains

39

the aspects of cohesion policy most relevant to multilevel governance; and part four explores the motivations for and values informing cohesion policy.

THE PREHISTORY

While economic and social disparities across and within member states were significant from the outset, it was not until the 1970s that the then-EEC made any serious attempt to address them. Agreement to create the European Regional Development Fund (ERDF) at the Paris Summit of 1972 reflected the increased salience of the issue of regional disparities in the context of the impending enlargement to include Britain, Denmark, and Ireland. The British government in particular pushed for the fund, being in need of something tangible to persuade a reluctant public and Parliament of the benefits of EEC membership. The other influential factors in the creation for the ERDF were a push toward Economic and Monetary Union (EMU) provided by the Werner Report of 1970 and Commission plans to control member states' aid to industries (see Bache 1998, 36–37).

From the decision in principle to create the ERDF taken in 1972, it was a difficult journey to final agreement two years later and came only when the Irish and Italian governments threatened to boycott the Paris Summit of 1974 unless they were promised progress on the matter. The size of the initial fund (1.3 billion EUA) disappointed the demandeur member states, but was nonetheless seen as an important breakthrough. It would provide up to half of the cost of development projects in eligible regions, with the remaining cost met from domestic sources. This principle of cofinancing was to ensure domestic commitment to projects and remained a fixture of the regional policy (and cohesion policy) henceforth.

While a regional fund was created in 1975, it was not until 1988 that this and other instruments were integrated into a cohesion policy. Up to this point, national governments prevented a more effective supranational approach. They ensured that the fund was distributed according to national quotas thrashed out by governments, rather than according to objective Community criteria. Moreover, each government demanded a quota, even though this meant that relatively prosperous regions in wealthier member states would receive funding at the expense of poorer regions elsewhere. This carve-up by governments meant funding was dispersed over 40 percent of the total EC population rather than concentrated on areas of greatest need.

At this stage, the regional policy process was generally viewed as a "virtual paragon of intergovernmentalism" (McAleavey 1992, 3). Governments not only dominated the EC-level process, but also policy implementation. In particular, they were reluctant to accept the additionality requirement that "the Fund's assistance should not lead Member States to reduce their own regional development efforts but should complement these efforts" (European Commission 1975). On this issue, the British government was particularly difficult (Wallace 1977; Bache 1998). Resistance to this rare supranational principle of regional policy remained even after the Commission became more powerful to act after 1988, and the struggle over this issue became an important barometer in measuring the relative strengths of national and supranational actors. Naturally, it became central to conceptual debate (chapter 3).

The additionality requirement apart, there was little supranational influence over regional policy principles before the 1988 reform. There were some experiments with nonquota programs after 1979, and experiments with multiannual programs after 1984 that proved to be important forerunners of later policies. Generally though, national governments shaped the broad contours of the policy and managed its effects, while supranational actors had only marginal influence. Moreover, there were no significant cross-sectoral or multilevel policy networks that were important to the later development of multilevel governance.

THE CREATION OF COHESION POLICY

In the Single European Act (SEA) of 1987, cohesion had a treaty base for the first time and the birth of cohesion policy proper followed in 1988 with a major reform of the structural funds. Both the completion of the single market program and enlargement to include Portugal and Spain provided impetus for strengthening cohesion (see chapter 3). The structural-fund reform brought together the ERDF with two other financial instruments, the European Social Fund (ESF) and the guidance section of the European Agricultural Guarantee and Guidance Fund (EAGGF). The aim was to coordinate their activities more effectively with each other and also with the activities of the European Investment Bank (EIB) and other financial instruments (European Commission 1989, 11). The Brussels European Council of February 1988 agreed to the draft regulations in principle and also agreed to a doubling of structural-fund allocations by 1993. The final details were agreed in three main regulations that came into effect on January 1, 1989.

The reformed policy had a strong regional focus, which required the EU to adopt a system for classifying its territorial units below the national level. It did this by adopting the NUTS[3] system, which provided a hierarchical categorization of different territorial units in the EU according to five levels, the largest being NUTS 1 (sections of a country grouping together basic regions).

This level was subdivided into NUTS 2 (basic regions), with subdivisions continuing through NUTS 3 and NUTS 4 to the smallest level of NUTS 5 (villages and towns). The NUTS 2 category of "basic regions," which were generally defined by member states for their own regional policy purposes, were the ones adopted for the main territorial objectives of cohesion policy.[4] For practical reasons—that is, the availability of suitable data—the NUTS categories were generally based on the existing institutional divisions within member states.[5]

The doubling of financial allocations for the structural funds in this reform was accompanied by important policy revisions. The additionality requirement was clarified and was accompanied by three new principles: *concentration* focused funds on areas of greatest need, *programming* required regions to develop strategic multiannual plans to ensure coherence between projects funded, and *partnership* required that funds be administered through regional partnerships within each state, consisting of representatives of national government, regional (or local) government, and the European Commission.

Following the principle of concentration, structural-fund expenditure was focused on five objectives, three with an explicit regional dimension (objectives 1, 2, and 5b). The bulk of spending was focused on the most disadvantaged regions eligible under objective 1 (approximately 65 percent of total structural-fund allocations). The objectives are set out below.

Objective 1: Promoting the development of "less developed regions," that is, those with per capita GDP of less than 75 percent of the community average, or just above this figure under "special circumstances" (ERDF, ESF, and EAGGF—Guidance Section);
Objective 2: Converting the regions seriously affected by industrial decline (ERDF, ESF);
Objective 3: Combating long-term unemployment: assisting people aged over twenty-five, unemployed for over a year (ESF);
Objective 4: Assisting the occupational integration of young people, that is, people below the age of twenty-five (ESF);
Objective 5: a) Accelerating the adjustment of agricultural structures (EAGGF—Guidance Section); b) Promoting the development of rural areas (EAGGF—Guidance Section, ESF, ERDF).

In addition to the "mainstream" structural funds allocated according to the five objectives, approximately 9 percent of the ERDF budget was retained for "Community Initiatives" (CIs). These were programs devised by the Commission to meet outstanding regional needs. As with the nonquota and Community programs, such as Resider (steel areas) and Renaval (shipping and shipbuilding areas), CI programs would primarily address the needs of particular categories of regions, such as those suffering from the decline of a dominant industry.

The Cohesion Fund

In between structural-fund reforms, the Cohesion Fund was agreed at Maastricht in 1991. This fund was aimed at member states with a GDP of less than 90 percent of the Community average, not at specific regions. It supported up to 85 percent of the costs of projects, a higher intervention rate than with any of the structural funds, and funded environment and transport projects. As with the structural funds, the Cohesion Fund—and the interim instrument established before the fund came into operation—was subject to indicative allocations (Greece, 16–20 percent; Spain, 52–58 percent; Portugal, 16–20 percent; and Ireland, 7–10 percent) (Scott 1995, 38). The dominant interpretations of the creation and operation of the fund were intergovernmental (Scott 1995, 38; Morata and Muñoz 1996). In particular, they emphasized the push given by poorer member states led by Spain—which would otherwise be a net contributor by 1993—for an additional compensatory financial instrument, which was necessary in the context of moves toward EMU. The key principles guiding the structural funds did not apply to the Cohesion Fund. There was no reference to partnership and the decisions on projects (not programs) to be funded were made by the Commission in agreement with the "member state" concerned. In terms of additionality, the preamble to the interim regulation stipulated that member states should not "decrease their investment efforts in the field of environmental protection and transport infrastructure," but the more tightly defined principle of additionality included in the structural-fund regulations did not apply.

The relaxed requirements on additionality and partnership, and the prominent role of governments, related to the pressures on public expenditure in the context of moves toward monetary union, which would have been experienced most strongly in the "cohesion four" member states. Moreover, that the types of projects funded were generally large-scale and few in number meant that programming had less relevance.

Subsequent Reforms of the Structural Funds

The principles agreed to in 1988 were maintained in the 1993 reform, although some adjustments were made, the most significant being to the additionality principle (for details, see Pollack 1995; Bache 1998; Allen 2000). The changes relevant here are discussed below.

In 1999, the focus of reform was on preparing the ground for the accession of countries from central and eastern Europe, with an average GDP of typically around one-third of the EU average. The challenge was twofold: securing member state agreement for a reduction in their structural-fund allocations to facilitate enlargement and agreeing to measures to develop the institutional capacity and capability in the accession states that would allow them to deal with large-scale structural funding effectively. Not without the usual horse trading, agreement was reached on the principle of large-scale transfer of structural funding away from existing member states to the new ones postenlargement. On the second challenge, a number of instruments were put in place over the post-2000 period. The Instrument for Structural Policies for Pre-Accession (ISPA) provided funding for environment and transport projects as a forerunner to Cohesion Fund allocations; the Phare (Poland and Hungary: Aid for Economic Restructuring)[6] program aimed to strengthen economic and social cohesion and to develop administrative and institutional capacity in anticipation of structural funds, while SAPARD (Special Accession Programme for Agricultural and Rural Development) played a similar role for rural areas.

COHESION POLICY AND MULTILEVEL GOVERNANCE

The guiding principles and territorial focus of cohesion policy have remained remarkably consistent since 1989. Three aspects of this policy have particular relevance for research on multilevel governance: the prominence of territorial objectives; the partnership principle; and the programming requirement. The first of these relates to the vertical dimension of multilevel governance, while the latter two have both vertical and horizontal implications. We deal with each of these aspects in turn.

Regionalization

Leonardi (2005, 30) has argued that "what distinguished the first package of Structural Funds from previous interventions was that the greatest amount of resources was concentrated on territorialized objectives" (1, 2, and 5b). This shift placed emphasis on the region as the main unit of development policy. In terms of development theory, this focus has a sound rationale: the regional level is seen as both large enough to incorporate a strategic perspective, yet small enough to allow "human factors" to work, namely "familiarity, trust

Table 4.1.   EU population covered by territorialized cohesion policies, 1989–2006 and beyond

EU Population Covered by	1989–1993	1994–1999	2000–2006	2007–?
Objective 1	22%	25%	22%	25%
Objective 2	16%	16%	18%	
Objective 5b	5%	9%		
Objective 6		0.4%		
Total	43%	50.4%	40%	

Source: ESCOLAB-LSE, reproduced from Leonardi 2005, 16.

and the flow of knowledge between actors" (Bachtler and Taylor 2003, 15). This focus led to both the adoption of the NUTS classification of territorial units below the national level in each member state and to the involvement of subnational actors in the policy-making process through regional programming undertaken by regional partnerships.

The nature of the main territorial objectives (1 and 2) remained largely unchanged until 2006, with the changes that occurred not affecting the focus of the research here.[7] Moreover, the proportions of the EU population covered by these objectives remained relatively consistent up to 2006 (see table 4.1 above).

Partnership

Partnership has the most obvious implications for the emergence of multilevel governance and its implementation has been the focus of most studies (chapter 5). The requirement has both horizontal and vertical dimensions. As a part of the structural-fund regulations, the requirement has legal status and must be complied with as a condition of funding. However, while the requirements of partnership have become more precise, there is still a role for member states' interpretation. Nonetheless, the way in which the requirement has developed in the regulation is important here. The framework regulation adopted by the Council in 1988 formally defined partnership as "close consultation between the Commission, the member states concerned and the competent authorities designated by the latter at national, regional, local or other level, with each party acting as a partner in pursuit of a common goal" (Regulation EEC2052/88).

Partnerships were to be active in the management, presentation, financing, monitoring, and assessment of structural-fund operations, including: preparation of regional development plans for submission to the Commission, implementation of the operational programs, and monitoring and assessment of measures taken.

To the extent that this requirement changed after 1988, it was to add more precision to the regulation. In 1993, the regulation referred to the extension of partnership to the "competent authorities and bodies—including, within the framework of each member state's national rules and current practices, the economic and social partners, designated by the member state" (European Commission 1993, 19). The additional reference to "economic and social partners" was in response to the practice of some member states excluding trade unions from partnership arrangements (on Britain see chapter 6), although governments were left in control of arrangements by the phrase "within the framework of each member state's national rules and current practices." However, it was a significant shift in emphasis toward greater horizontal cooperation.

In the 1999 reform, the regulation added a reference to involvement of organizations that would reflect the "need to promote equality between men and women and sustainable development through the integration of environmental protection and improvement requirements" (OJ L161, June 26, 1999, 12).

The technocratic rationale for partnership was that it improved the prospects for effective development policies by including those actors closest to the problems and priorities of targeted regions and groups. Specifically, it has three perceived benefits: it adds to specialist knowledge that improves the quality of decision making, it builds a consensus that allows program documents to be finalized more quickly, and it leads to rapid decisions at the implementation stage (Kelleher, Batterbury, and Stern 1999, 145). However, the political implications of partnership often proved controversial (chapters 5, 7, and 8).

Growing out of the partnership principle was a "local development" approach that became particularly important in some Community Initiative programs (e.g., Urban, Leader) and was also mainstreamed into objective 1 and 2 programs in some member states, including Britain (chapters 7 and 8). This was a "bottom-up" approach to development, which placed local residents and their voluntary and community organizations at the center of the decision-making process. As discussed in subsequent chapters, this approach did have precedents in Britain, but in the 1990s in particular was an important contribution to shaping local decision making. Interviews with Commission officials (author 2006) emphasized the importance of this contribution, described as "not a principle, but a method."

Programming

The switch to multiannual programming in 1989, after a decade of trying by the Commission, promised more coherence in formulating regional development strategies. This switch drew on the experience of programming pioneered in the Integrated Mediterranean Programmes (IMPs) of the mid-1980s (see Hooghe and Keating 1994), a feature of which was the incorporation of ex-ante and ex-post assessments of programs. This feature and subsequent developments in relation to monitoring and evaluation sharpened the potential for learning in structural-fund programs. The approach was inspired by the French model of Contrats de Plan État-Région and when it was adopted, it "provided a genuinely new means of organizing regional development in most parts of the EU" (Bachtler and Taylor 2003, 20).

Programming was not just multiannual, but also sought to integrate the different structural funding instruments operating in different sectors. In the first instance, objective 1 regions received funding for five years and objective 2 regions for three years. The shorter period for objective 2 programs was meant to give flexibility in case of unanticipated changes in industrial restructuring. Programming initially followed a three-stage process. First, after full consultation with the subnational implementers, national governments submitted regional development plans to the Commission. Each of these plans detailed regional problems, set out a strategy indicating priorities, and provided an estimate of required funding. Second, the Commission then incorporated member states' views in Community support frameworks (CSFs) that prioritized spending, outlined the forms of assistance, and provided a financial plan. Third, detailed operational programs were agreed to by the partners to provide the basis on which they would implement the objectives of the CSFs. These identified appropriate measures, beneficiaries, and costs.[8] Beyond this, each program was monitored and evaluated to assess whether money was being spent appropriately.

In 1993, the revised regulation laid down a six-year programming period for objective 1, 3, and 5b areas, while two three-year phases were specified for objective 2 (and objective 4 had a similar arrangement). This longer programming period brought the system into line with the broader financial perspective of the EU. The three-stage process was reduced to two stages in which member states submitted a single programming document (SPD) to the Commission, which comprised both the development plan and applications for assistance relating to it. The second stage was the setting out of funding priorities and forms of assistance in the CSFs. The programming approach was retained in the 1999 reform, although the Commission adopted a more strategic role and delegated more responsibilities to domestic actors for the day-to-day operation and monitoring of programs. Programming was a relatively uncontroversial principle of structural policy and its value was widely recognized and accepted.

UNDERSTANDING COHESION POLICY

There are two sets of related issues to unpack here: one relates to the struggle between intergovernmental and supranational forces over cohesion policy, the other alludes to the issues and values that underpin this struggle. There has been and remains much dispute over who controls cohesion policy in its various forms and at its various stages and a similar degree of contestation over the motives of the actors seeking control. While these issues cannot be resolved here, an exploration of the debates surrounding them reveals a richer perspective on the nature of cohesion policy that sets the scene more completely for the discussion in subsequent chapters.

There is little disagreement among scholars that the 1988 decision to double structural funding was an intergovernmental agreement: the more prosperous member states strongly supported the completion of the single market and wanted this market extending to include Portugal and Spain. In this context, the likely paymaster governments accepted the doubling of the structural funds as a "sidepayment" to the Community's poorer nations in exchange for their support on the internal market program (Moravcsik 1991, 62). Multi-level governance theorists generally shared this view (Hooghe 1996a), although Marks (1992, 198) conceptualized the deal in neofunctionalist language, describing it as an illustration of forced spillover "in which the prospect of breakthrough in one arena created intense pressure for innovation in others."

Consensus between scholars over other aspects of the 1988 reform is harder to find. Pollack (1995) took an "essentially intergovernmentalist" view, arguing that agreement could be explained by changes in the preferences of the various member states—in particular net contributors such as Britain, France, and Germany. The preferences of the net contributors changed in three ways. First, with the Iberian enlargement, the proportion of structural funds received by the "big three" member states decreased significantly. This meant that for these governments, "the idea of greater Commission oversight seemed less like an intrusion into the internal affairs of one's own state, where EC spending was minimal, and more like a necessary oversight of the poor member states where the bulk of EC money was being spent" (Pollack 1995, 372). Second, the Iberian enlargement made France, like Britain and Germany, a net contributor to the EC budget, thus giving the "big three" governments a common interest in the efficient use of the structural funds. Third, the spiraling costs of both the CAP and the structural funds made the level and efficiency of EC spending a "political issue" of increasing concern to the governments of France, Germany, and Britain in the 1980s (Pollack 1995, 372).

There is, however, little argument that the policy details enshrined in the regulations were shaped by the Commission, drawing on its "monopoly of initiative on the institutional design" (Hooghe 1996b, 100). Moreover, the principles advanced were ones the Commission had long advocated (Bache 1998). A good example was the inclusion of the partnership principle in the regulations, which was the major institutional innovation of the 1988 reform: "the insular drafting, the backing of Jacques Delors, the timing, and the careful selection of the negotiating team suggest that the Commission had not been acting on behalf of the states . . . and that it was not advancing partnership merely to solve the problem of value of money but had its own agenda" (Hooghe 1996b, 99). As subsequent chapters will show, there is certainly evidence that the Commission has exercised influence over aspects of regionalization, partnership, and programming both in their design and implementation. More problematic has been identification of the Commission's motivations in advancing these principles, and, in particular, an understanding of the extent to which these motivations were driven politically (either by values or rational interests) or by the search for effective policy solutions (technocracy).

On this, Hooghe and Keating (1994, 374) argued that "values were of some importance to the Commission which, under the socialist president Jacques Delors, was keen on a social counterbalance to the free market thrust of the single market programme as a whole; and was aware of the need to mobilize support for the programme in the vulnerable as well as the prosperous regions. This complex set of rationales was wrapped up in the concept of 'cohesion.'"

Alongside the emphasis on values in explaining the Commission's role, a number of technocratic arguments have been advanced for the Commission's enthusiasm for empowering subnational and nonstate actors. These arguments related to the efficacy of networks in developing policies most suited to the needs of recipients, to the need to reduce the workload at the European level, and to promote policy transfer between more and less developed regions to promote innovation in the latter (Tommel 1998, 69). Nevertheless, in this view too, it is acknowledged that separating the political and technocratic aspects is difficult in that apparently technocratic motivations had significant political implications, making subnational actors "aware of their position, their interests, and their potential allies in the context of European integration" (Tommel 1998, 67).

Critics of the EU within member states were quick to seize on the argument that the Commission was trying to bypass states and empower regions as part of a political strategy to promote integration. This view was not widely articulated in academic circles, although some acknowledged that the Commission "might be said to have an institutional interest in the development of a new level of legitimate government, as a means of by-passing the member states" (Richardson 1998, vii). Moreover, consciously political or not, the idea of a "Europe of the Regions" was embraced as a slogan by regional political actors and even by the Commission for a short while under the presidency of Jacques Delors (John 2001, 73).

Of course, the Commission has studiously avoided making counterproductive public pronouncements on such politically sensitive matters as the balance of territorial relations within member states and within the EU as whole. At the same time, the 1988 reform of the structural funds explicitly aimed to involve subnational actors in EU cohesion policy making and made subnational mobilization "crucial to its success" (Hooghe 1996b, 89). Later interviews revealed an ongoing public ambivalence within the Commission on the issue:

> In this directorate, we deal with regional policy so in this context our aim is to empower regions. We think that development is most appropriately conducted at this level, unless the state is very small. But there has never been any attempt by the Commission to try to dictate to member states. We say you have to take into account the regional or local. But we have never entered the debate about what the ideal region would look like. (DG Regio official 2, interview by author, 2006)

THE FUTURE OF COHESION POLICY

The big issue in negotiations over the post-2006 period of cohesion policy was the British proposal for a partial renationalization of the structural funds (see chapter 8). The Commission's opposition to this proposal was supported in particular by the new member states, plus Italy, Spain, Portugal, Ireland, and Finland (DG Regio official 2, interview by author, 2006). The British government's argument was that the richer member states should not be part of the common policy, but should cut their contribution to the EU policy in order to fund more domestic regional policy initiatives. This proposal was unpopular among subnational actors across the EU because it would increase their dependence on national governments for regional policy measures. Ultimately, the British proposal was rejected and the broad coverage and key principles of cohesion policy remained intact. Specifically, for the relevance of the discussion here, the key principles of partnership, programming, and additionality remained in place for the 2007–2013 programming period.[9]

The context of the reform was the Lisbon (and Gothenburg) agenda and the global economic competitiveness of the EU. The priorities of growth, jobs, and competitiveness did not sit comfortably with the more socially oriented aspects of cohesion policy. In particular, there was concern that the bottom-up approach to development might be marginalized in favor of higher-profile projects that would be more top-down. As one DG Regio official (1) (interview by author 2006) commented, "Some of these local projects are very important but in terms of creating sustainable jobs and the economic growth of the region the benefits are perhaps not so easily captured." However, it was clear that the multilevel governance dimension of cohesion policy was linked positively to this growth agenda. The Commission for Regional Policy (Hübner 2004) stated:

> Successful implementation of the Lisbon and Gothenburg agenda is impossible without the involvement of regions. In that respect I would argue that the added value of cohesion policy goes beyond the money that is invested. Cohesion policy's very specific system of governance, involving all relevant partners in the region, is as important as the financial contribution. The emphasis we have on partnership in fact allows us to do two things:
>
> First of all, it allows us to increase understanding of what the Lisbon and Gothenburg agenda is all about. Secondly it ensures that all the stakeholders involved realise that there is an enormous synergy between their interest in regional development and the EU interest in competitiveness.

CONCLUSION

As Leonardi (2005, 18) has recently argued, "what is of interest with regard to cohesion policy is that one finds the European-level 'imprint' in all of the innovative aspects of the policy." There is evidence of some uploading in the French inspiration for programming and also partnership (Benz and Eberlein 1999, 17), but the overall approach to EU cohesion policy is distinctly "European." The extent to which this approach was driven by politics or policy efficacy remains contested. What is clear is that, drawing on its own knowledge base, prevailing development theories and previous experimentation, the EU established regionalization, partnership, and programming as key themes in cohesion policy that remained constant from 1988 onward. As such, it is not difficult to agree with Leonardi (2005, 18) that "cohesion policy offers an extraordinary opportunity to examine how Europeanization affects the policy process with regard to a policy area that traditionally was national in its origin." We now turn to this task.

NOTES

1. In this categorization, distributive and redistributive policies involve public expenditure, while regulatory (rule-making) policies do not. The distinction between the

two is that while the distributive category refers to spending on a wide range of public programs and services generally aimed at particular sectors or "clients," redistributive policies are generally aimed at broader categories: "they are, crudely speaking, haves and have-nots, bigness and smallness, bourgeoisie and proletariat" (Lowi 1964, 691).

2. For an overview of the debate, see Bache 2006 and Bache and George 2006, chapter 28.

3. Nomenclature of Territorial Units for Statistics. The NUTS acronym originated from the French (Nomenclature des unités territoriales statistiques).

4. NUTS 2 for defining objective 1 regions, but NUTS 3 for defining objective 2 regions.

5. From 2004 the NUTS nomenclature was extended to the new member states, which meant that on May 1, 2004, the territory of the EU was subdivided into 89 regions at NUTS 1 level, 254 regions at NUTS 2 level, and 1,214 regions at NUTS 3 level. NUTS 4 became Local Administrative Units (LAU) 1 and NUTS 5 became LAU2. For further details on NUTS classifications, see the Europa website, http://ec .europa.eu/comm/eurostat/ramon/nuts/ (as of August 6, 2006).

6. Phare was subsequently extended to other accession states.

7. In 1993, reform objectives 1 and 2 were not changed from 1988, but objectives 3 and 4 were merged to create a new objective 3. This new objective 3 was aimed at "facilitating the integration . . . of those threatened with exclusion from the labour market" (European Commission 1993, 11). A new objective 4 was designed to give emphasis to new tasks laid down in the Maastricht Treaty to "facilitate workers' adaptation to industrial changes and to changes in production systems" (European Commission 1993, 11). Objective 5a maintained its initial goal of accelerating the adjustment of agricultural structures as part of the CAP reform, but a new fund was added to assist the fisheries: the Financial Instrument of Fisheries Guidance (FIFG). Problems arising from the decline in fishing and fish-processing activities would also be addressed through objectives 1, 2, and 5b. Objective 5b changed slightly from the "development of rural areas" to the "development and structural adjustment of rural areas" (European Commission 1993, 11). Objective 6 was created to provide assistance to the sparsely populated Nordic areas (ERDF, ESF, EAGGF-Guidance Section).

In the 1999 reform it was agreed that objective 1 would continue to assist the least developed regions, defined as those with a GDP per capita at 75 percent or less of the EU average over the previous three years. Henceforth, this criterion would be strictly enforced. In addition, the new objective 1 included the regions that previously qualified under objective 6, which were the sparsely populated regions of Finland and Sweden. Objectives 2 and 5b were merged into a new objective 2, assisting areas undergoing socioeconomic change in industrial and service sectors, and rural areas, urban areas, and areas dependent on fisheries facing difficulties. Objective 2 would be concentrated on no more than 18 percent of the EU population, with the safety-net mechanism ensuring that no member state's objective 2 population would be less than two-thirds of its coverage under the 1994–1999 program period. From 2000, objective 3 would apply across the EU, except in objective 1 regions, and would assist in modernizing systems of education, training, and employment (adapted from Bache and George 2006, 470 and 476).

8. For a detailed discussion of the planning processes for the five objectives, see Leonardi 2005, 52–54.

9. For full details, see Council Regulation (EC) No. 1083/2006 of July 11, 2006, *Official Journal of the European Union*, 31.7.2006, L210/25. For a discussion of the run-up to the 2006 reform, see Leonardi (2005, 185–90).

5

EU Cohesion Policy and Domestic Governance

In developing this cross-national comparison of the effects of cohesion policy on domestic governance, the analysis follows the distinction made between compound and simple polities (chapter 1). To recap briefly, in the former, "power, influence and voice are diffused through multiple levels and modes of governance" while in the latter, "power, influence and voice are more concentrated in a single level and mode of governance" (Vivien Schmidt 2003, 2).

In terms of presentation, it is necessary to deal with some of the case study material chronologically. Earlier studies in particular cover the mix of compound and simple polities that comprised the EU15 (see figure 1.2), before the focus of research switched to the simple polities of central and eastern Europe as both candidate and accession states.

While the basic distinction made is between simple and compound polities, there are other variables that should be noted at this stage. These are the *size* of the country (population and/or territory), the *scale* of structural funding it has received, and the length of *time* it has been in receipt of cohesion funding. We reflect on the significance of these dimensions in the concluding section. Moreover, Schmidt's (2006) argument does acknowledge that there are circumstances in which the explanatory value of the broad institutional fit can be "trumped" by a lack of fit in mandated policy-making processes.

There is not space here to systematically analyze developments in all EU member states, only to provide some flavor of the various factors that account for the role of EU cohesion policy in promoting multilevel governance alongside other explanations.[1] Where relevant, a distinction is drawn between the vertical and horizontal effects and the implications for type I and type II multilevel governance (see chapter 3) are reflected on in the concluding section.

THE EU15

Early studies on the effects of cohesion policy on domestic governance did not generally use the concept of Europeanization to frame research, but these studies were nonetheless concerned with similar issues to those later studies that did. Hooghe's (1996a) study on the effects of cohesion policy on territorial restructuring in member states considered whether partnership had led to the convergence of diverse domestic territorial relations across member states, or whether existing territorial relations had been upheld. The study revealed significant differences in the effects of partnership in different member states. A key part of the explanation in the degree of multilevel governance resulting was the preexisting balance of territorial relations within a member state. In other words, and consistent with later arguments from the Europeanization literature, the mediating role of domestic institutions was crucial.

In centralized member states where central governments actively sought to limit the territorial impact of the new arrangements, they met with considerable success (see below, and chapters 7 and 8 on Britain). There was sufficient scope within the EU requirements for strong central governments to dominate partnerships, where there was a will to do so. In these cases, subnational actors were mobilized, but not necessarily empowered. In more decentralized member states, subnational authorities—normally regional governments—were often better placed to take advantage of the opportunities provided by the partnership requirement, which also fed into pressures for regionalization in states such as Belgium and Spain (Marks 1996, 413). This study is well documented and has already contributed significantly to the development of debate on multilevel governance (see in particular Hooghe 1996a; Bache 1998). However, it is important to record here, not least because it points toward the analytical distinction between simple and compound polities in the first phase of the post-1989 effects of the structural funds.[2]

A later study, funded by the European Commission, also highlighted continuing differences in the implementation of the partnership principle and its territorial effects, emphasizing the continued importance of the intervening role of many national governments: "Member States continue to dominate and delimit partnership functioning—through their roles in negotiating program content and selecting horizontal partners, and through their provision of secretariats and managing authorities" (Kelleher, Batterbury, and Stern 1999, vi). Yet the report also suggested that governments were increasingly realiz-

Table 5.1.   The relative strength of role of regional partners (highly stylized)

Example	Central Government	Regional Government	Social Partners	Municipalities
Austria	Moderate	Moderate	Moderate	Moderate
Belgium	Moderate	Moderate	Moderate	Moderate
Denmark	Strong	Moderate	Moderate	Moderate
Finland	Strong	Moderate	Moderate	Moderate
France	Strong	Strong	Weak	Weak
Germany	Strong	Strong	Moderate	Weak
Greece	Strong	Weak	Weak	Weak
Ireland	Strong	N/A	Weak	Weak
Italy	Strong	Strong	Weak	Weak
Luxembourg	Strong	N/A	Moderate	Weak
Netherlands	Strong	Moderate	Moderate	Moderate
Portugal	Strong	Weak	Weak	Weak
Spain	Strong	Strong	Weak	Weak
Sweden	Strong	N/A	Moderate	Strong
UK	Strong	Weak	Weak	Moderate

Source: Adapted from Kelleher, Batterbury, and Stern 1999, 47.

ing the benefits of partnership working for their own agendas and were often encouraging the practice and broadening participation, an early indication of learning taking place. Here, the Commission was identified as an important force in promoting greater inclusion, although considerable variations in the inclusivity and effectiveness of partnerships across member states remained: the role of social partners was generally limited and nongovernmental organizations (NGOs) were often absent from partnerships. The strength of various partners in regional-level cohesion policy partnerships was summarized by the authors in table 5.1, above.

In this study also, domestic factors were key to understanding the nature of partnerships within member states. Echoing the Hooghe study, the report emphasized that "the degree of decentralization and the type of de-concentration occurring in the different Member States inevitably shapes the relations between key actors within partnerships and determines the competencies and composition of partnerships" (Kelleher, Batterbury. and Stern 1999, viii). Yet the report found that where member states had little experience of partnership, the EC regulation had often "kick-started" partnerships and, where member states had more experience with the principle, the EC regulation was seen to often reinvigorate their activities and promote innovation (Kelleher, Batterbury, and Stern 1999, viii). The next section reflects on these findings and subsequent research on the EU15, drawing the distinction between simple and compound polities; notions of misfit would suggest that the EU's approach to

cohesion policy would be more challenging in the former. Following the discussion in chapters 1 and 3, a distinction is drawn between vertical and horizontal governance effects in each case.

Simple Polities

Here, we reflect in some detail on developments in Ireland, Greece, and Portugal before sketching the main findings in other simple polities of the EU15.

Ireland

Ireland falls safely into the "simple polity" category, being a traditionally
centralized state with weak subnational actors and no regional tier, a feature
explained both by the (small) size of the country and its relatively homogeneous population, together preventing any strong requirement or demand for
regionalization. There was some experience of partnership at the national
level before the structural-fund requirements were introduced. Despite this,
there is a consensus that EU membership has played an important role in reshaping governance in Ireland and that the structural funds have been central to this.

In the first period after 1989, there were no obvious vertical effects from
cohesion policy: Ireland in its entirety had objective 1 status and until 1999
was the largest beneficiary of the structural funds as measured by resources
per head of population.[3] However, Ireland's economic success came to
threaten its status as an objective 1 region. So, in response the Irish government sought to maximize its structural funding opportunities by dividing the
country into two NUTS II regions. By the creative construction of these two
statistical regions, the government was able to retain objective 1 status for
part of the country, despite Commission skepticism and internal opposition to
the strategy[4] (Adshead and Bache 2000). In addition to this formal regionalization, the structural funds have had a more general effect in enhancing the
institutional capacity of local and regional governance (Roberts 2003, 39).
This change has involved a process of learning to adapt domestic institutional
structures in response to the EU, which has involved some resistance from
both administrators and politicians, but ultimately led to a shift in the way in
which intergovernmental relations in Ireland take place (Rees, Quinn, and
Connaughton 2004, 379).

Alongside the EU effects there have been domestic changes over thirty
years that were also aimed at increasing the level of subnational competence
and capability (Roberts 2003, 37). In isolating the EU contribution, Rees,
Quinn, and Connaughton (2004, 402) concluded that "within the regions

there has been evidence of innovation, mobilization and experimentation, as well as increased competence, capacity and confidence. In effect, this represents institutional realignment to cope with new demands rather than radical institutional innovation and transformation."

In terms of the horizontal dimension, there was more complementarity (or "fit") between the EU's structural-fund requirements and domestic politics. Kelleher, Batterbury, and Stern (1999, 6) noted that Ireland's approach to partnership for the objective 1 program had been "highly inclusive" and described this as being in keeping with domestic practices. National partnerships involving government, employers, trade unions, and farmers preexisted the EU requirement for partnership, although the structural funds were seen to expand this practice, not least to increase the involvement of the community and voluntary sectors at the local level. Rees, Quinn, and Connaughton (2004, 401) identified a number of nongovernmental bodies being either "generated" or "revitalized" through the structural funds, exhibiting both "single loop" and "double loop" forms of learning in the process. In some cases, "the changed organizational cultures and social norms have effected a reconceptualization of interests and identities, thereby demonstrating a logic of appropriateness within the adaptation process" (Rees, Quinn, and Connaughton 2004, 401).

The impact of the structural funds in Ireland has to be seen in the context of the perception that the scale of funding contributed significantly to the economic boom it experienced in the 1980s and 1990s. This brought legitimacy to the EU's approach. Specifically though, the process of institutional change in Ireland accelerated following an economic downturn in the early to mid-1980s and coincided with the introduction of the EU partnership principle, which then became essential to reforms in the Irish administrative system (Roberts 2003, 38). There is subsequent evidence of thick learning taking place among structural-fund participants. The overall effect of cohesion policy in Ireland has been to strengthen both the vertical and horizontal dimensions of multilevel governance and thus to move it further along the compound polity end of the Schmidt (2006) continuum.

Greece

Traditionally, government and politics in Greece are seen to have a high degree of misfit with EU governance. The political and administrative structure is hierarchical and centralized, civil society is weak, and there is an absence of a consensus-building approach among political elites. The country as a whole received objective 1 funding from 1989 and, before that, faced similar governance requirements from the Integrated Mediterranean Programmes

(IMPs). The scale of funding has remained high throughout the Greek period of membership.[5] In this context, significant adaptational pressures were generated by structural-fund requirements: "The introduction of the 'subsidiarity' and 'partnership' principles and the promotion of the integrated approach to planning totally misfit with the Greek centralized and interventionist administrative tradition, the predominance of the state and the limited participation of social and private actors" (Getemis and Demetropoulou 2004, 358). Not surprisingly therefore, the early period of membership witnessed some resistance to EU requirements. However, EU structural policy soon began to have effects on domestic governance although the picture is more mixed than with the case of Ireland.

On the vertical dimension, the most important effect of cohesion policy was the creation of a regional level of government, which followed the introduction of the IMPs into Greece in 1985. As discussed in the previous chapter, the IMPs pioneered the multiannual, multisectoral approach, which included requirements for regional partnerships to be created. In response to these requirements, Greece was initially divided into six regions, although the division was purely administrative and limited in institutional terms to the monitoring committees required to oversee the IMPs. Subsequent legislation in 1986 divided the country into thirteen NUTS 2 regions, which were to provide the basis for Community support frameworks (CSFs). These regions had a centrally appointed regional secretary supported by a small cohort of civil servants drawn from the central government. In addition, regional councils were established that were made up of appointees from central and local government and chaired by the regional secretary (Andreou 2006, 244–45).

After this initial burst of activity, decentralization halted and in some areas regressed (Verney and Papageorgiou 1993). More specifically in relation to the structural funds, Kelleher, Batterbury, and Stern (1999, 64) noted an "absence of decentralisation" in the Greek objective 1 program and only a marginal role afforded to regional bodies. Generally, regional-level networks were slow to emerge and were "mostly fragmented and controlled by the state, despite impressions of relevant autonomy" (Getemis and Demetropoulou 2004, 374). Beyond the creation of regional structures in 1986, the main features of decentralization and territorial relations that have developed in Greece during the period of EU membership have been attributed primarily to domestic factors (Leontitsis 2006, 17–18). Andreou (2006, 246) concluded that "EU cohesion policy acted as a catalyst for the creation of new institutions at the regional level. However, the structure, functions and evolution of these new entities were shaped by domestic factors."

In relation to the horizontal dimension, the legacy of authoritarian statism in Greece was a weak civil society and an abundance of political mistrust. Despite this, structural policy did stimulate horizontal partnerships by promoting the role of a number of nonstate organizations (NGOs, social groups) at the regional level, even though the state retained a pivotal role (Kelleher, Batterbury, and Stern 1999, 64). On the post-2000 period, Getemis and Demetropoulou (2004, 374) said, "It could be argued that the partnership trends of the 1990s are being re-placed by a pseudo-corporatism of state control . . . current trends do not leave much room for optimism about a more rapid adaptation at the regional level." However, Andreou (2006, 250) suggested that the relative failure of meaningful partnerships to develop in Greece was partly a consequence of subnational and nonstate actors lacking the necessary capacity to engage effectively. In this context, centralized programming and management of the funds was probably a "necessary evil" in the short term at least, an argument that has resonance with developments in the accession states of central and eastern Europe (below).

Overall, the picture of cohesion policy effects in Greece is one of some decentralization occurring, but with a subsequent clawing back of control by the center, leaving the regional level remaining weak within the Greek system. Similarly, horizontal partnerships were established in the regions, but central government retained a key role in decision making. Clearly, the central state had to adjust to the new realities of multilevel governance generated by the structural funds, but did so in a strategic way. To the extent that there was learning, it was generally "thin" learning. Getemis and Demetropoulou (2004, 371) concluded that "the structure and the administrative tradition of the Greek state, the peculiarities of Greek centre–periphery relations and the traditional weakness of Greek civil society have considerably limited the capacity of the regional institutional infrastructure for learning and adaptation." As such, the Greek case most closely approximates to the category of accommodation set out in chapter 2 (Andreou 2006, 253), and it has not moved very far toward the compound end of the Schmidt continuum as a result of Europeanization.

Portugal

Before EU membership, Portugal was a traditionally centralized state with the only notable exception to this tradition being the creation of regional governments for the nonmainland territories of Madeira and the Azores in 1976. Like Greece, the horizontal dimension of governance was weak following a period of authoritarian statism. Portugal acceded to the EU in 1985 and its territories as a whole qualified for objective 1 funding from 1989. It continued to receive large sums of structural and cohesion funding subsequently.[6] As such, this was also a case where cohesion policy provided significant pressures for vertical and horizontal change.

In Portugal, EU cohesion policy has been seen as important in relation to stimulating the institutional and administrative change necessary for undertaking regional development programs, specifically through the creation of five new administrative regions on the mainland. However, while there has been formal conformance with policy requirements, "the direction has been to decentralize the ministerial structure while maintaining a high degree of central control, with the exception of the two autonomous regions of the Azores and Madeira" (Nanetti, Rato, and Rodrigues 2004, 410). A 1998 referendum on strengthening the role of the mainland regions by creating elected bodies was rejected. Leonardi (2005, 207) suggests this was because the regions proposed were not coterminous with those that had been created for cohesion policy purposes and which had become established: "The government proposed to create 10 regions that would have cut up many of the existing administrative regions, which had already begun to root themselves into popular political consciousness."

If the territorial dimension in Portugal is characterized as decentralization within central control, horizontal change relating to the role of nonstate actors might be characterized as limited, incremental, but not insignificant (Nanetti, Rato, and Rodrigues 2004, 412). Civil society participation started from a low base in 1989 and while remaining largely consultative in relation to EU structural policy making, did improve over time.

The case of Portugal more closely resembles the experience of Greece than that of Ireland. Despite incremental shifts toward greater subnational and nonstate participation and the creation of new regional structures, the central government retained a firm grip over much of the important decision making. This weak multilevel governance was seen as detrimental to policy effectiveness: "The rather efficient Ministry-based institutional structure, including its regional Commissions, is no substitute for regional autonomy and a bottom-up and pro-active, integrated approach to development strategies which would be territorially specific because it would be designed and carried out by regional and local institutional actors" (Nanetti, Rato, and Rodrigues 2004, 428). So again here there is accommodation and some movement along the continuum from simple to compound, but not much.

Other Simple Polities

The picture that emerges from this overview of developments in three simple polities is one of slow and incremental change, but change that can be very significant, as in the case of Ireland. Change occurs when domestic and EU preferences, practices, or policies converge, either from a process of learning—as is partly the case in Ireland—or through a change in domestic circumstances. By contrast, where there is divergence between EU and domestic preferences, the evidence from Greece and Portugal, in particular, continues to confirm the findings of earlier studies that national actors play a major role in constraining and containing the governance effects of cohesion policy. This observation is reflected in studies of other simple polities. In France, Steclebout (2002, 10) concluded that while there was a political discourse in favor of decentralization, "the French central state remains very much centralized and insists on managing the projects directly and spending money according to its own objectives." A later study by the European Commission (2005b, 20) reported that while multilevel partnerships had been established in France and in some cases the "interconnection of partners also extends beyond the management of the Structural Funds to other areas of public action," the participation of partners who were not from the public institutions remained limited.

The discussion of simple polities continues in the section on central and eastern European countries below.

Compound Polities

Here we reflect on developments in Germany, Spain, Sweden, and Finland.

Germany

Germany is an important point of contrast for the study of simple polities generally and of Britain in particular. Helen Wallace (2003, 5) has suggested that the two states are "arguably at opposing ends of the range in terms of the 'goodness of fit' between the country and the European arena, in so far as the European arena is EU-defined." A similar observation was made by Bulmer (1997) and by Bulmer, Jeffery, and Paterson (2000), who spoke of Germany "shaping the regional milieu," with the result that EU governance fitted well with German governance. In Schmidt's (2006) terms, it represents the epitome of the compound polity, having a federalized state, corporatist structures, and proportional representation. However, research on Germany comes to some counterintuitive conclusions in relation to the governance effects of cohesion policy and particularly highlights the value of investigating specific member state cases rather than making generalized assumptions.

Historically, Germany was not a major recipient of EU funds, but received significant amounts following unification in 1990 when all of the regions in the former East Germany qualified for objective 1 funding.[7] While theoretically a good "fit" existed between the multilevel partnership requirement and the main features of the federal system, in practice there were tensions. The regional governments (Länder) had a prominent role in domestic regional policy in West Germany before 1989 and were keen to protect this role subsequently, even where the partnership requirement pointed to a greater role for subregional and nonstate actors. On the vertical dimension, Länder were generally reluctant to devolve policy making below the Land level, although Thielemann (2000, 21) noted that the Social Democratic government of North Rhine-Westphalia was an exception to this.

Horizontally, there was considerable variation in how the partnership principle operated across Germany according to different regional traditions. Thus, for example, where there was a tradition of including social partners in public policy making they were included in the structural-fund processes (Bremen, North Rhine-Westphalia); where they were traditionally excluded, they were similarly excluded for structural-fund purposes (Lower Saxony, Bavaria). This issue of the role of social partners proved to be particularly contentious in Germany, with the European Commission (1997, 137–38) critical of their exclusion in a number of regions and particularly in the eastern Länder, which were the biggest recipients of structural-fund assistance. Within Germany, there was suspicion that the then regional policy commissioner, Monica Wulf-Mathies, who was formerly a trade union leader in the country, was advancing a political agenda.

Eventually, trade unions were reluctantly introduced into more structural-fund partnerships, although they were not always able to have a significant input. Kelleher, Batterbury, and Stern (1999, 47) concluded that "the role played by the social partners is marginal and at best they have a role as consultees prior to the development of the programmes. Their role in the Structural Fund partnerships is one which is situated at the periphery of the partnerships and, on occasions, they lend only an illusion of inclusiveness to partnership operations." The same report also found that the federal government had been particularly involved in the administration of the structural funds in the eastern Länder, which may have been necessary in the absence of more established regional structures (as observed elsewhere—for example, Greece) but limited wider participation and constrained the potential for organizational learning (Kelleher, Batterbury, and Stern 1999, 105).

While ostensibly a "good fit" with cohesion policy principles, the particular tradition of cooperative federalism in Germany did not sit well with the EU's partnership requirements, with its implications for subregional and nonstate participation. The issue of the role of the social partners was a good illustration of this and this issue proved also to be a key test for partnership in the very different institutional context of Britain (chapters 7 and 8). The explanation for this apparent misfit between EU partnership requirements and the German polity lay in the detail of Germany's cooperative federalism, which revealed less compatibility than might superficially be assumed. Traditionally, the German federal government had dominated relations with the EU, and EU policy implementation was seen as a task for public authorities. Thus, as Thielemann (2000, 21–22) argued, partnership challenged cooperative federalism in two ways: first, by legitimizing direct contacts between the Länder and EU officials and thus undermining the gatekeeping role of the federal government; and second, by formalizing the policy-making role of the economic and social partners, who traditionally had been restricted to "rubber-stamping" decisions taken by public actors.

Yet over time the partnership process in Germany was seen to improve, with the European Commission (2005b, 23) acknowledging that while partnership developed "relatively slowly" up to 1999, "a much more developed situation can be found since 2000. It has brought together a wide range of partners with more experience and commitment, participating early in the process." As one Commission official (DG Regio official 1, interview with the author, 2006) put it, "It [partnership] is not a question any more, so that is evidence of progress." Thus, while there may have been a general consolidation of Germany's place on the simple-compound polity continuum, adaptation to the requirements of cohesion policy was not as easy as anticipated, not least because of the misfit with the practices of Länder that mimic those of simple polities.

Spain

The end of the Franco era in 1976 did not signal the end of strong centralized government in Spain, since this was also a feature of the 1978 Constitution. However, a process of devolution began in 1979 and the Spanish system is now generally accepted as one characterized by asymmetric federalism, in which some regions (Andalucia, the Basque Country, Catalonia, and Galicia) have "full" autonomous status, while the remaining thirteen regions have lesser degrees of devolution. The degree of devolution varies according to a range of political and institutional factors (for an overview, see Morata and Muñoz 1996, 197–98). In Schmidt's (2006) terms, Spain is best understood as a "regionalized" state because its central state is still formally unitary and still expects to exercise power over the periphery, even though the regions have a high degree of autonomy.

Spain as a whole qualified for objective 1 funding from 1989.[8] Before 1989, only a minority of the stronger regions, such as the Basque Country and Catalonia, sought a significant role in the administration of EU funds and in cultivating direct relationships with EU actors. Others were generally more concerned with maximizing their receipts than in shaping the policy process.

After 1989, this began to change, with more regions seeking to play a role in policy making. The partnership principle intensified contacts between regions and the center, although in the first programming period the speed with which programs had to be developed limited regional influence (Jones 1998, 143). The role of regions was limited further by the insistence of national government on submitting national plans for each of the three relevant objectives (1, 2, and 5b), rather than for each region. The emphasis on nationally determined infrastructure projects in these plans strengthened central control further. The center also retained key controls over budget setting for each region and sought to monopolize relations with the Commission when negotiations took place over the distribution of funds between regions (Bache and Jones 2000, 6). In the first phase of structural programming, central government's reaction to the partnership requirement was negative: "the ministries were very much upset because 'those guys from Brussels were coming to discuss regional problems,' which meant money out of the ministries to the regions" (DG Regio official 3, interview with the author, 2006).

In short, despite the provisions of the 1988 reform, the effects on domestic governance in Spain in the first programming period were negligible. As Morata and Muñoz (1996, 217–18) put it, "The new Community procedures and changes in the distribution of territorial power did not prevent the central government from programming regional development and allocating a substantial amount of shared funds according to its own preferences."

After 1993, a more significant role for the regions emerged. The autonomous communities became more involved in setting priorities for the next objective 1 plan and direct exchanges with the Commission became more frequent. There were still evident limits to the role of the regions in this context, though: meetings with the Commission generally took place with a national official present, and central government continued to exclude regional representatives from the committees of Interreg, a Community Initiative program aimed at promoting interregional cooperation. So while the regions participated more after 1993, this did not amount to a transformation of relations with the central government, nor in fact did it have a direct impact on the share of funding managed: in both the 1989–1993 and 1994–1999 program periods, the regions managed approximately one-third of the ERDF expenditure (Conejos i Sancho 1993, 336; Ministerio de Economía y Hacienda 1995, 89). Moreover, even the stronger regions remained dissatisfied with their role in the process and continued to press for more influence (Bache and Jones 2000, 8). However, one notable outcome from their growing role was that the autonomous communities that had gained influence sought to play a gatekeeper role at the regional level, limiting the role of municipalities and nonstate actors (Kelleher, Batterbury, and Stern 1999, 88).

In the programming period 2000–2006, the European Commission reported an improvement in the operation of partnership between the regions and central government and also a greater involvement of the social partners than had previously been the case. This improvement was reflected in a more integrated view of regional development in the country, which produced higher quality development programs and more effective implementation (European Commission 2005b, 35). However, there were observable variations across regions: "All regions have their partnership meetings. Some of them do it because they have to and they don't want them to have an important effect. Others do it properly. It really depends on the persons and the political party that is in the government" (DG Regio official 3, interview with the author, 2006). Overall, cohesion policy has had limited effects on both the vertical and horizontal dimensions in Spain, signifying only a marginal EU-induced shift along the simple-compound polity continuum in a state in which domestic factors dwarf the EU's effect.

Sweden

Sweden is categorized as a "compound polity" but is not a straightforward case because while it has a corporatist history, the regional level has traditionally been overshadowed by national and local levels and has operated as "a state instrument of control and administration" (Olsson and Astrom 1999, 3). Specific regions became eligible for structural funding upon entry to the EU in 1995[9] and, while Sweden has not been one of the major recipients of the structural funds, it has nevertheless experienced significant governance effects as a consequence.

It is in relation to the vertical dimension, where there was greatest misfit with EU requirements, that the effect has been most significant. Following accession, there was talk of a "new Swedish regionalism" in which the EU was seen as "an important driving force in the process of regional self-government" (Olsson and Astrom 1999, 14). There were considerable variations across regions, which were in part ascribed to how much structural funding had been allocated to them. Kelleher, Batterbury, and Stern (1999, 67) argued that the partnership requirement for the objective 6 program had "provided a driving force toward progressive decentralisation" and that its monitoring committee was the first ever formal arena for discussions in northern Sweden that involved all tiers of government, the social partners, and the voluntary sector.

Adaptation to the horizontal requirements of cohesion policy was perhaps less straightforward than might have been assumed, given Sweden's corporatist traditions. In general terms, the partnership requirement was accepted as an "old corporatist friend" but there were "important differences in kind

between cooperation as partnership and cooperation in the form of corporatism (such as co-financing rules and the size of the network)" (Bache and
Olsson 2001, 229). However, unlike other member states discussed, there
were no problems in relation to including the social partners or local politicians, and the mode of decision making on partnership bodies was generally
consensual.

In evaluating the effects of the structural funds in Sweden, the European
Commission (2005b) pointed to an "intensive learning process" in the first
programming period after membership (1995–1999), which had stimulated
important governance effects. These included the creation of new networks
and public interest groups as well as promoting an increased sense of responsibility for policy making. More specifically, the structural funds had been
seen to "break down administrative barriers within the Swedish public administration, thus enhancing its effectiveness and leading to new and intensive co-operation and networking across administrative and national bor-
ders," and had "brought the EU and also the national government closer to the
citizens through the decentralisation process" (European Commission 2005b,
66). So Sweden, a somewhat compound polity, has become even more so
through the effects of EU cohesion policy.

Finland

Like Sweden, Finland is categorized as a compound polity, but for similar
reasons is not a straightforward case. It has traditionally been centralized, but
with corporatist processes and a proportional representation system that tend
toward consensus politics. Although eligible for structural funding upon entry, its receipts have been relatively limited.[10] However, and again like Sweden, the effects on domestic governance have been significant.

In the period between 1990 and 2003, regional structures in Finland underwent a transformation, which was largely attributed to EU accession in
1995. Change began in anticipation of membership, with regional reform beginning in 1993 with the transfer of some regional development responsibilities to regional councils and a programming approach to regional development mirroring that of the EU introduced in 1994. Further changes in the late
1990s involved reducing the number of provincial governments from twelve
to five, and a corresponding reorganization of the regional offices of the central government. These changes were seen to "correspond to the demand of
Europeanization," with the structural-fund requirements of partnership and
subsidiarity being crucial (Kettunen and Kungla 2005, 369). A decade after
their creation, the new regional organizations remained weak, with central
government outposts determining the expenditure of up to 90 percent of the

structural funds. However, the structural funds were seen to have triggered changes, the full potential of which had not been realized at this stage: "even though the direct influence of the EU did not lead to a full-powered regional policy making, the regional councils, even in their limited form, have acted as a catalyst. There have been a number of reform proposals which have put forward a variety of ideas on how to strengthen the regional councils" (Kettunen and Kungla 2005, 370).

In terms of the horizontal dimension, the situation was not so clear-cut. Partnerships were established that included actors from different levels and sectors and the programming approach was adopted. Moreover, the European Commission (2005b, 18) suggested that the introduction of the structural funds had "revolutionalised the traditional Finnish national set up for regional development" and had "introduced multi-annual, strategic, and widely consultative processes in the national context, improving the targeting of policy and the quality of interventions." The partnership approach in particular became seen as an "indispensable" part of regional development policy making in Finland. However, as in other member states, some commentators were critical of the extent to which participation through the partnership principle led to influence. Kettunen and Kungla (2005, 379) found that representatives of municipalities, local business, and others had "not been able to challenge the state regional offices and, in the worst cases, simply ratify the funded projects, avoiding any strategic or future oriented discussion."

The case of Finland resembles that of Sweden. They have similarities in terms of institutional and political traditions and have adapted to structural policy requirements similarly. Despite a more obvious a priori "fit" with the horizontal requirements of structural policy, the most significant effects have been vertical in relation to strengthening the regional level. Moreover, while these effects are already tangible, there is a suggestion that more is yet to come.

Other Compound Polities

Aside from the compound polities discussed above, the case of Italy has featured most in the literature on cohesion policy. Gualini's (2003, 633) study of the implementation of the structural funds in Italy emphasized the constraints facing central government actors, both in relationships with the Commission and with subnational governments, which hindered its ability to play the gatekeeping role over the domestic effects. However, Leonardi (2005, 149) found evidence of learning among regional and government actors in relation to cohesion policy, a process which was seen to depend on two elements: "the technical and administrative capacity of each region to adopt the rules and

procedures governing EU policies and the political will to undertake the necessary institutional reforms to connect actors in the centre and the periphery
through an effective multi-level form of governance."

Analysis of the EU15

The findings on the EU15 reveal the importance of national institutional and
political traditions and, in relation to understanding this, the simple or compound polity distinction is broadly instructive. For example, in relation to the
vertical dimension, it was clear that states with strong centralized traditions
tended to be more vigilant and more effective gatekeepers over the implications of cohesion policy for regionalization. The findings in relation to the
horizontal dimension also illustrated the usefulness of the simple or compound distinction and, in particular, the refinement to the Lijphart model provided by the statist-corporatist continuum (see figure 1.1).

Thus, here, there is a clear example of corporatist traditions in Ireland,
Sweden, and Finland leading to a degree of fit with the horizontal requirements of cohesion policy, although this is less straightforward in the latter two
cases. Best illustrating that the devil is often in the details when it comes to
issues of fit and misfit was the case of Germany, where there were variations
according to regional traditions and political preferences, as well as a more
general challenge to the broadly perceived fit between the EU and German
systems. The complementary hypothesis relating to statist traditions is generally upheld, with the horizontal dimension remaining weak in Greece, Portugal, and Spain, although there is evidence in each case of this position changing, albeit slowly.

Or course, variations in effects are anticipated by the Europeanization approach, as EU inputs are refracted by domestic politics. That Ireland was a centralized state influenced in the direction of greater local influence by the EU
demonstrated that no easy assumptions could be made about the "fit" between
the multilevel partnership principle and established territorial relations within
member states. Germany provided another case counter to this assumption.

The Kelleher, Batterbury, and Stern (1999, 159) study concluded that cohesion policy had had significant effects on institutional reform and capacity
building across the EU15, and particularly where key domestic actors were
able to associate the EU's requirements positively with notions of "modern-
ization" or the need to be "European." They found the territorial programs
had provided a stimulus toward decentralization and in some cases the "virtual invention" of a regional tier of coordination, although this had taken
many forms (Kelleher, Batterbury, and Stern 1999, 71). In addition to identi-

fying variation in the territorial effects across states, a number of studies found variations across regions within states. This was observed not only in the Hooghe study discussed above, but also in comparative research on France and Italy. Here, Smyrl (1997) related different degrees of regional empowerment within these states to the presence in empowered regions of regional political entrepreneurs and/or the preexistence of a territorial policy community for regional development, both of which allowed regions to make the most of the EU opportunities offered.

The more recent studies of cohesion policy effects in the EU15 have placed a greater emphasis on the process of learning. Kelleher, Batterbury, and Stern (1999) suggested that one outcome of such learning had been evidence over time of less resistance to the partnership principle. On Greece, one of the more unlikely cases for learning to take place because of the centralized state structures and weak civil society, both of which act as impediments to social learning by limiting scope for collective action, Paraskevopoulos (2001, 276) found that cohesion policy had stimulated a learning process:

> Even in cases where these qualitative features are missing and consequently the local institutional infrastructure is poor, the Europeanization process constitutes a positive external shock that initiates the processes of institution-building and social capital formation. This is achieved through the transformation of the local governance structure (local networks), by challenging the balance of power and hence established interests and patterns of behaviour of the actors.

CENTRAL AND EASTERN EUROPEAN COUNTRIES

Eight central and eastern European countries (CEECs) entered the EU in 2004. They shared a history of "democratic centralism" under communism, during which time regional imbalances were addressed by the central direction of investment. Moreover, as Glowacki (2002, 105) said of Poland, "the life of society was organized around the place of work rather than around the place of living: hence the increasing importance of industrial sectors relative to regions of the country." Postcommunism, there were attempts to introduce regional development measures before the EU accession process began, but these were piecemeal. Most regional units remained part of the central state administration, although in some cases local self-government became relatively well established (European Commission 1999, 61–62). The dominance of the communist state had also meant that, in most instances, where civil society organizations existed they were weak and levels of social capital were low, with trust in political institutions particularly low. Against this

background the requirements of EU cohesion policy, including the preaccession instruments,[11] presented obvious challenges and adaptation pressures
were high. The suggestion was that in the postcommunist institutional flux,
the challenges posed by the EU should "allow for more flexible strategies
than compared to the current EU member states, where institutions and networks are more firmly entrenched" (Dieringer and Lindstrom 2002, 4) and
thus produce a higher degree of change.

Paralleling much of the early literature on the EU15, the main focus of research on the CEECs to date has been on the impact of EU requirements on
the regional level. Again, this focus reflected the more significant early effects of cohesion policies on the vertical rather than horizontal dimension.

The role of the Commission in advancing multilevel governance has been
brought under particular scrutiny in this literature. The desire of the central
and eastern European (CEE) states for membership of the EU led to assumptions of high asymmetries in their relationship with EU institutions and thus
the possibility of significant EU influence on domestic change. The Commission had a number of tools at its disposal, both generally in relation to accession and specifically in relation to cohesion policy. In particular, it set a reform program and timetable for applicant states in 1997, which it monitored
and reinforced in its regular reports on progress. Chapter 21 of the acquis
dealt with the requirement for accession states to have the administrative capacity necessary for the delivery of EU regional policy.

To avoid political controversy, the Commission studiously avoided making pronouncements on what type of regionalization it favored in the
CEECs: one participant reported, "I remember, while [I was] a mayor, we
expected something very clear from the European Union about local and regional government. In fact that was not the case. The European Union ab-
solutely avoids any comments on this. We got very weak expressions like
'regions should be in partnership within the member state'" (former CEEC
mayor, interview with the author, 2006). However, it has been claimed that
at an early stage of the accession process the Commission appeared to pre-
fer democratically elected regional self-governments with a degree of financial and legal autonomy (Brusis 2002, 542). This argument has logic in
relation to the requirements relating to democratic stability and the rule of
law in the Copenhagen criteria for EU membership (Brusis 2002, 544) as
well as in meeting cohesion policy requirements. Time does appear to play
a role in explaining how and what the Commission conveyed in terms of cohesion policy requirements. Closer to accession the Commission's priorities
became more sharply focused on efficiency and with completing enlargement, with the building of multilevel governance relegated in importance
(below).

Poland

Poland was the largest of the 2004 entrants to the EU, with a population of approximately thirty-eight million people. In the period up to accession it received EU funding through Poland-Hungary: Actions for Economic Reconstruction (Phare), the Instrument for Structural Policies Pre-Accession (ISPA), and the Special Accession Programme for Agriculture and Rural Development (SAPARD). On acceding, it became eligible for the Cohesion Fund and all of its regions gained objective 1 status for structural funding.

After the end of the communist period in 1989, Poland embarked on a process of territorial restructuring. While Poland remained a unitary state, the result of this restructuring was a distinct three-tier structure, with national, regional, and local government units. There were two major reforms: the first was the 1990 Territorial Self-Government Act, which aimed to reduce central power by creating local self-governments (approximately 2,500 *gminas* or communes)[12]; the second reform took place in 1998, and came into effect in January 1999. In this reform, the country was divided into 16 voivodships (NUTS 2), 45 subregions (NUTS 3), 315 (as of April 19, 2002) poviats (districts), 65 cities with the poviat status (NUTS 4), and 2,489 communes (NUTS 5) (Chroszcz 2005, 68). This fit with the EU designation of NUTS 2 regions was unique in the CEECs (Marcou 2002, 22).

There is consensus that the prospect of EU membership and the role of the Commission in the accession process have played an important role in territorial restructuring in Poland (Baun 2002; Glowacki 2002; Ferry 2003; Czernielewska, Paraskevopoulos, and Szlachta 2004; Jewtuchowicz and Czernielewska-Rutkowska 2006). However, it is also agreed that while the EU's effect was very strong in relation to the 1998 territorial reform, it was at best marginal in relation to the one undertaken in 1990. Moreover, while there was an eventual willingness to swim with the EU tide, the process was not without some hesitation within Poland: there were concerns that strong regionalization could lead to the loss of control over some border regions (Silesia and Pomerania), which had close historical ties to Germany (Baun 2002, 274).

In 1990 there was a general acceptance within Poland that some reduction of central power through decentralization was necessary to democratize the country postcommunism. Thus, the 1990 reform was primarily driven domestically. One participant in this process commented, "There is a stereotype that we organized many things in Poland because of the European Union. It's a mistake. We reconstructed the local authorities because we wanted to change the country. At that time [1990] we didn't think about the European Union much" (Polish MEP, interview by author, 2006). In relation to the changes instigated in 1998, the EU influence was much clearer. Adaptation pressures for regionalization, arising from the requirements of EU funding that applied across the CEECs, were seen as particularly intense in the Polish case because of the size of the country. This had caused some initial problems in the management of preaccession aid. The 1998 reform was in large part designed to address these issues.

The horizontal dimension of governance in Poland had been weak under communism, with the church, and the associations surrounding it, the only significant civil society organizations emerging posttransition. After 1989, this dimension remained weak, despite aspirations of acceding to the EU and its subsequent accession requirements. Jewtuchowicz and Czernielewska-Rutkowska (2006, 167–68) found that participation of NGOs was limited and that "social dialogue is considered as 'soft,' non-binding, putting an emphasis on information and consultation provision and, hence, the institutionalized forms of dialogue are limited." Lack of trust pervaded partnership relations. This was evident in the mutual distrust in vertical relations, but also horizontally. One interviewee (Polish MEP, interview by author, 2006) suggested that this mutual distrust was particularly acute in relations between politicians and NGOs: "Both think they are the real representatives of the people." Despite these problems, a change was perceived over time, although commentators perceived the EU to be only part of the explanation. There was a general "awakening" of civil society after communism and the creation of local self-government in 1990 was seen to assist this: a clear connection between the vertical and horizontal dimensions.

While the EU's impact on governance change in Poland in the late 1990s was significant, there was later evidence of some recentralization in the approach to structural funding (Czernielewska, Paraskevopoulos, and Szlachta 2004; Chroszcz 2005). Ferry (2003, 1110) suggested that "paradoxically, the administration of the Structural Funds, designed to foster the development of regional capacity in preparation for Poland's accession contributes to the continuing dominance of the center over the regional tier in Poland." The weakness of the new institutional structures at the regional level and central control over local finance was seen to strengthen the "gatekeeping" role of the state in relation to regional policy making (Jewtuchowicz and Czernielewska-Rutkowska 2006, 170). The ongoing weakness of the regional level was ascribed in part to the EU's failure to "take into account crucial aspects of state-society relations" when promoting the development of institutional capacity at national and regional levels (Czernielewska, Paraskevopoulos, and Szlachta 2004, 492). Moreover, the future prospects for regionalization looked uncertain, with Chroszcz (2005, 68) suggesting that "a choice between a decentralized or centralized system [for managing the funds] belongs to the European Commission, who may decide on the latter due to its good functioning in the current programming period 2000–06. In this case, the status of the regions and the political importance of the self-government units would be seriously diminished."

In terms of the horizontal dimension, wide and effective participation remained constrained by legacies of democratic centralism: a weak civil society, low levels of social trust and trust in political institutions, and a high level of political clientelism and corruption in a system dominated by political parties at all territorial levels. These features were significant impediments to processes of learning and adaptation (Jewtuchowicz and Czernielewska-Rutkowska 2006, 169–71).

Czech Republic

The Czech Republic entered the EU in 2004 with a population of just over ten million people. It had immediate eligibility for objective 1 funding, having previously been a recipient of Phare, ISPA, and SAPARD. The adaptational pressures from EU requirements were strong in the case of the Czech Republic, particularly because there had been little attempt to instigate domestic regional policy measures in the final years of communism (Jacoby 2005, 94), as there had been in other CEECs such as Hungary (below). Similarly, in the postcommunist period before accession started, the Czech government did not take an interest in the developments in European regional policy, unlike its counterpart in Hungary.

Thus, structures for regional development were subsequently slow to emerge in the Czech Republic, relative to other CEECs. When it applied for membership in 1996, domestic regional policy was largely absent. The Commission was quick to draw attention to this absence and pointed to the "functional necessity" of appropriate bodies for formulating regional development measures. The Commission used its regular progress reports to highlight this deficiency and reinforce the need for remedial measures. Despite this pressure, the timing of reform is explained primarily by domestic factors and particularly by the replacement of the centralist government of Václav Klaus with the social democratic government of Mikloš Zeman in 1998. This change accelerated the reform process, with the new government setting out its aspirations for decentralization in EU-friendly language in the document *The Principles of the Government on Regional Policy.* The newly created Ministry for Regional Development subsequently established management and monitoring committees to oversee administration of the structural funds in eight NUTS 2 regions.

Subsequent political wrangling over the number and composition of regions that would make up a formal system of subnational government meant

that fourteen regions were eventually created. Thus, unlike Poland, the regionalization that occurred in the Czech Republic in the preaccession period
did not map neatly onto the EU's NUTS classifications (Adshead and Bache
2000; Novotny 2000). The explanation for this difference lay in domestic politics: it was partly because local and regional politicians wanted to create a
greater number of regions than was necessary for purposes of EU structural
policy in order to maximize the number of new political positions available,
and partly because opponents of decentralization wanted to maximize the
number of regions to limit their potential for creating a power base beyond
the center. The outcome was a territorial division that cut across some strong
historical regions (Baun 2002, 269).

In assessing the specific EU effects on regionalization, Jacoby (2005, 101)
suggested that "a more competent regional political layer is emerging in the
Czech Republic—a development difficult to imagine without the external incentives from the EU." However, a combination of factors ultimately contributed to the nature and timing of change in the Czech Republic, which included the Commission thresholds, funding incentives, and a change of
government (Jacoby 2005, 99; Marek and Baun 2002).

Hungary

In terms of population, Hungary was a similar size to the Czech Republic,
with just over ten million people when it entered the EU in 2004, but with a
level of development higher than most of the other entrants (European Commission 2005a, 28). Despite this, the whole of the country was eligible for objective 1 funding from 2004, having previously been a recipient of Phare,
ISPA, and SAPARD.

Hungary is another case where the EU pressures have been significant and
have prompted change, but where an understanding of domestic processes is
crucial. Jacoby (2005) highlighted shifts in the Hungarian approach to regions
and regional policy before the end of communism, with programs aimed at rural villages in the 1970s and a decree creating systematic regional policies in
1985. In the late 1990s, Hungary began to develop the kinds of devolved regional structures sought by the Commission, with the Law on Regional Development and Physical Planning of 1996 a landmark measure. The Phare program, with its focus on subsidiarity, partnership, and programming, had
influenced the design of this law. In the same year, regional development
councils and regional development agencies were established and given a
prominent role in the implementation of EU programs. The EU effect had been
strong in relation to formal institution building and in promoting a culture of
coordination (Pálné Kovács, Paraskevopoulos, and Horvárth 2004, 457).

Jacoby (2005, 95) noted that while there was a clear and substantive response to EU requirements and incentives, "behavioural changes still lagged behind the formal adoption of EU rules." A similar observation was made by Pálné Kovács, Paraskevopoulos, and Horvárth (2004, 457), who suggested that "the formal institutional arrangements may Euro-conform, but the content is rather similar to the 'eastern political culture,'" by which they meant central control and clientelism. Consequently, the learning that had taken place in Hungary was of the "single loop" variety, in which strategies changed but preferences did not. From the Commission's perspective, Hungary was viewed as well organized and effective in relation to cohesion policy administration, even if the decisions taken were not always the ones the Commission favored. The explanation offered for these qualities was historical: "Hungary is an ex-empire, so there is a culture there of people who know how to run a society. This is a country that is able to take decisions. . . . But effective governance cannot guarantee that things are going to be done as you would want: only that things are going to be done" (DG Regio official 3, interview by author, 2006).

Other CEE States

In the case of Lithuania, regional policy was relatively underdeveloped until 1996 and preaccession aid was important in stimulating regional participation. However, there was a subsequent move toward centralization encouraged by the European Commission, as it sought to ensure effective use of the funds in the run-up to accession. The end result was a "highly centralized and complex system which completely eliminates regions" (Maniokas 2005, 12). Slovenia had a similar experience, with the Commission initially critical of the lack of decentralization in the country and prompting the creation of a set of regional development agencies. However, during the final months of negotiations over the regional policy chapter of the acquis, the Commission decided that it would be most efficient for Slovenia to be treated as a single region (Faro 2004, 4). Estonia too reflected tensions between centralizing and decentralizing tendencies, with subnational authorities becoming involved in cohesion policy making, but remaining weak: "central government ministries, especially the Ministry of Finance, clearly dominate all phases of the regional policy decision-making, assigning local and regional actors only a subordinate role" (Kettunen and Kungla 2005, 367).

In Slovakia, the EU was identified as important in influencing the process of regionalization, with self-governing regions established in 2002. Again the Commission had been instrumental in highlighting the deficiencies at subnational level in relation to accession and funding opportunities. The prospect that inadequate regional structures might scupper the prize of membership was also an important force in motivating national politicians. Buãkek (2002, 144) concluded that "without this integration context there would be only a minimal shift towards regionalization within recent years." More specifically, Brusis (2002, 548) noted that in the context of internal party differences over decentralization, the government referred to the subsidiarity principle in the EU treaty in justifying the decision to decentralize.

The study by Bailey and De Propris (2002) compared the extent to which the preaccession instruments promoted a shift to multilevel governance in five CEECs: the Czech Republic, Estonia, Hungary, Poland, and Slovenia. Generally, they identified the Commission as the "dominant player" in the use of the funds in relation to determining the institutional changes required, the size of territorial units, and so on. However, their empirical study suggested that national government "gatekeepers" remained "firmly in control" of subnational actors, who were able to participate in but not significantly influence the policy process (Bailey and De Propris 2002, 319–20). Here, a key part of the explanation was the distinction between the development of institutional *capacity*, such as offices, staff, and buildings, and institutional *capability*, which referred to the ability of institutions to carry out the functions assigned to them.

Other research (Hughes, Sasse, and Gordon 2004, 2005) assumed a high degree of asymmetry in the relationship between the EU and the CEECs and framed the research in terms of "conditionality," the inference being that in such circumstances the Commission would have "unprecedented scope" for influencing domestic developments. The research compared developments in four accession states (Estonia, Hungary, Poland, and Slovenia) and, in line with other studies, emphasized the importance of historical institutional traditions in each state. Despite the perceived asymmetries, domestic factors remained important partly because the formal requirements for compliance with cohesion policy were seen to lack detail, but also because "the Commission lacked a repertoire of legal instruments to force a particular institutional model on the candidates" (Hughes, Sasse, and Gordon 2004, 547). In addition, the Commission's position (informally) on what the important requirements were changed over time. Initially, there was a preference for regionalization, inspired by Commission ideals of multilevel governance. Closer to accession, though, the Commission became more concerned with the efficient management and disbursement of funds, even if this meant they were managed centrally through national ministries (Marcou 2002, 25). The resignation of the Santer Commission in 1999 over issues of financial mismanagement was seen as important in this shift (Hughes, Sasse, and Gordon 2005).

Analysis of CEECs

EU cohesion policy requirements provided particularly strong adaptational pressures in the former communist states. Maniokas (2005, 2) argued that Europeanization, understood as the impact of the EU on the domestic structures of candidate and member states, has "transformed the nature of the state in central and eastern Europe." At the same time, he suggested that the main conclusions of the Europeanization literature are barely applicable to the CEE states because as candidate countries they could not shape EU decisions (i.e., no uploading) and, because domestic institutions were weak, there was less of a domestic refraction of EU pressures and thus a greater convergence of institutional structures across states than in the EU15. This may be a useful general observation, but conceals detailed variations in the institutional structures that have emerged, differences in the timing and scope of decentralized structures, and the variety of mediating factors that come into play in explaining developments. Thus, while there has been movement toward the compound end of the Schmidt continuum generally, this has varied both by degree and over time.

Jacoby's (2005) portrait of the different developments in regions and regional policy in the preaccession Czech Republic and Hungary pointed to the importance of not simply attributing domestic change to EU incentives because some of the changes that converged with EU requirements took place (in Hungary) before the end of communism. Hughes, Sasse, and Gordon (2004, 547) found "asymmetrical" regionalization in the CEECs, a finding convergent with "the diversity of regional government in the Member States." Marcou (2002, 21) suggested that the NUTS classification system "played almost no role in the political debates in those CEE countries that have recently established an intermediate level of government vested with self-governing rights." As noted above, only in Poland did the intermediate level of government correlate with the NUTS 2 classification. The issue of size is also important here, with the logic of scale for development administration only being strong in the largest four of the eight CEECs.

The issue of size had another effect, however, as one Commission official (DG Enlargement official 2, interview by author, 2006) stated that "small countries are always aware that their best strategy is to work within the system, within network of relations." Not unrelated to this dimension was the importance of a sense of history and of statehood. In interviews, officials contrasted their current dealings with Turkey—a country with a long tradition of statehood—with those of the Baltic states or those that came out of the dissolution of Yugoslavia: "Those countries are constructing their statehood, the apparatus of a state. You can expect them to be much more receptive to suggestions because they are inventing their system from scratch" (DG Enlargement official 2, interview by author, 2006).

Equally, assumptions over the degree of asymmetry do not match with the degree of resistance to EU pressures in the CEECs. The institutional barriers to change have been well documented, with the legacy of democratic centralism and the corresponding absence of local and regional self-government being particularly important. However, resistance to EU requirements was also partly political (and often party political); as Ferry (2003, 1097) argued, "being in the flux of post-communist systematic transformation does not mean an absence of domestic interests and pressures when it comes to reform." In particular, the new political elites, who had long struggled to displace communist elites, were reluctant to pass on their newly gained power quickly to subnational actors. Further, there were fears of strong decentralization stoking long-dormant regionalist sentiments in some territories, a fear not helped by developments in former territories of Yugoslavia and the Soviet Union (Baun 2002, 274).

Time was also a key dimension in explaining developments in the CEECs. Partly, a lot of reforms that were introduced in Poland and other eastern countries were undertaken quickly because the Commission and the EU15 recognized there was a window of opportunity not to be missed in terms of enlargement. Moreover, as accession came closer, the Commission became less concerned with building multilevel governance and more concerned with the programs being delivered and enlargement completed, even if this meant relying on centralized administration of cohesion policy (see also Leonardi 2005, 164).

While there have been significant, albeit varying, cohesion policy effects on territorial relations within CEECs, the impact on horizontal relations has been less marked. This reflects the general underdevelopment of civil society in the CEECs, but arguably also, the priorities of the EU advanced by the Commission. While both horizontal and vertical partnership has been a requirement of funding to the CEECs, addressing the lack of subnational institutional capacity was prioritized. Yet, this prioritization was not without implications for horizontal engagement: as the case of Poland in particular demonstrated, the emergence of local self-government in 1990 stimulated local civil society activity. Later, following the problems of the Santer Commission and particularly as accession moved closer, the Commission prioritized efficient administration, even if this did not strengthen partnership vertically or horizontally. Of course, postaccession, the partnership principle remained a central feature of structural funding and the story of the relationship between EU cohesion policy and nonstate actors is far from concluded at this point. This is not a facile observation, given that time emerges as an important dimension in distinguishing the experience of the EU15 from the CEECs, a point discussed further in the concluding section.

CONCLUSION

This chapter has distinguished between the simple and compound polities of the EU15 and made a further distinction between these and the simple polities of the CEECs that joined the EU in 2004. Overall, there is an evident trend toward greater domestic multilevel governance that has been encouraged and incentivized by EU cohesion policy (see table 5.2).

Beyond this general observation are a number of important differences that relate primarily to domestic politics, broadly defined. In teasing out

Table 5.2. The effects of EU cohesion policy on domestic governance: Comparative analysis of simple-compound polities

	Polity/Politics before the impact of EU cohesion policy	Vertical Misfit/ Horizontal Misfit with governing principles of EU cohesion policy	Domestic Change 3 = transformation 2 = accommodation 1 = absorption
Simple			
Ireland	Unitary (polity)	High (vertical)	2+
	Corporatist (politics)	Medium (horizontal)	2
Greece	Unitary	High	2
	Statist	High	1+
Portugal	Unitary	High	2
	Statist	High	1+
Poland	Unitary	High	2+
	Statist	High	1
Czech Rep	Unitary	High	2
	Statist	High	1
Hungary	Unitary	High	2
	Statist	High	1
Compound			
Germany	Federal	Low	1
	Corporatist	Low	1+
Spain	Regionalized	Medium	1+
	Statist	High	1+
Sweden	Unitary	High	2+
	Corporatist	Low	1+
Finland	Unitary	High	2
	Corporatist	Low	1+

these differences, the simple or compound polity distinction is useful in terms of highlighting the importance of both vertical and horizontal traditions and preferences within states. It is also useful to distinguish between the simple polities of the EU15 and those of the CEECs, in particular because time of engagement with EU cohesion policy emerges as an important explanatory variable. Not surprisingly, the time variable relates closely to the learning variable, in that deep learning is in part a function of the length of engagement. But internal dynamics are also important and, particularly where internal pressures for reform were already evident, Europeanization pressures simply added to these.

Thus, while the early period of research on the EU15 found primarily rational responses and learning only of the shallow and strategic type, deeper learning appeared as a feature in later research. In relation to the CEECs, learning was primarily strategic: a rational response to conditionality mechanisms. Schimmelfennig and Sedelmeier (2005) came to similar conclusions. Mutual suspicion between politicians and civil society organizations remains common in the CEE member states and compromise and consensus is not deeply embedded in postcommunist societies. These characteristics constrain social learning.

What is also important here is that while the relevant formal requirements for EU cohesion policy have stayed relatively constant over time, the force and nature of the ways in which the Commission has sought to promote them have not remained constant. Particularly notable here was the scale and significance of the 2004 enlargement in shaping the pragmatism with which the Commission appeared to deal with cohesion policy requirements within CEECs as accession moved closer. There was a feeling within the Commission and the governments of the EU15 that the window of opportunity for this type of enlargement might not be open again and that the momentum could not be risked. In this context, Commission preferences for regionalization and partnership had to take a backseat. Moreover, there were precedents for the Commission advocating centralized administration in the EU15 where regional institutions were weak, the East German Länder being a case in point.

The point about centralized administrative structures also relates to the issue of size. There is little doubt that this is a key dimension in mediating the degree of multilevel governance promoted by cohesion policy. In essence, there is less logic in smaller states developing strong regional structures and while there have been instances where the Commission has sought initially to promote some regionalization in smaller states, this has generally receded. Ireland, of course, provides the exceptional case of a small country that sought to regionalize itself to maximize structural-fund receipts, which is a significant if not conventional EU effect.

Two Types of Multilevel Governance

The evidence above suggests that both the vertical and horizontal dimensions of multilevel governance have been strengthened by cohesion policy, albeit to different degrees in different circumstances. Generally, it remains the case that in centralized systems, there is evidence that central governments can be effective gatekeepers. Thus the extent to which cohesion policy can promote type I multilevel governance at the regional level, where it is most likely to have such an effect, is very much dependent on its requirements converging with the preferences of key domestic actors. This is no less true in the CEECs than anywhere else and, in particular in those former communist states where there is fear of reigniting the flames of long-suppressed regionalist sentiments, as happened in postcommunist Russia and Yugoslavia. However, even in the more extreme cases of gatekeeping, regionalization has at least been put on the agenda and some structures were established, however flimsy. In regionalized or federalized states, cohesion policy has generally served to intensify multilevel interactions and promote interdependence without there being a transformative effect.

In relation to type II multilevel governance, the promotion of task-specific bodies, the changes are generally more marked and in some cases highly significant. Horizontal partnerships at subnational level have become an established part of the landscape in the EU15, whether the domestic traditions have been statist or corporatist. The difference generally is that in statist countries, partnership has been embraced slowly and reluctantly and often exists in name only, with participation a more accurate depiction of the role of most partners than influence. In the statist polities of CEECs the situation is understandably less advanced still, with civil society generally remaining weak after the fall of communism and social and political mistrust remaining high. In more corporatist states, horizontal partnership has often been embraced, but there are many variations. In some states, such as Germany, the particular tradition of corporatism did not fit well with the EU's requirements, while both in Germany and other states there were also important variations according to regional rather than national political traditions.

Discovering these variations within the broad categories of "simple polities" and "compound polities" in no way discredits the value of this categorization. The categories are inevitably broad and, as Schmidt (2006, 35) recognized, the "micro" patterns of policy making in a specific sector may not always conform to the "macro" patterns of states because of specificities in particular sectors at either or both EU and national levels. What is argued here though, is the value in placing these macro categories alongside sectoral-level developments. In the long term, developments in a specific policy sector can shape macro patterns and characteristics and there is evidence here that, in a small way at least, EU cohesion policy has influenced the macro characteristics of some states. This point is reflected on further in the concluding chapter, in light of developments in Britain. At this stage we turn to the case study of Britain to explore these issues in more detail.

NOTES

1. The selection of cases here depended primarily on the availability of secondary data, although original data were collected on developments in some states and on the pan-EU picture during 2006.

2. This study focused on the period 1989–1994: the first full round of programming and the start of the second round.

3. Between 1989 and 1999, Ireland received €10.7 billion from the structural funds and the Cohesion Fund (European Commission 2005b, 31).

4. For 2000–2006, Ireland was split into two regions for structural fund purposes: The Border, Midlands, and West region retained objective 1 status; objective 1 funding was phased out in the South and East region (European Commission 2005b, 31).

5. Over the period 1994–2006, structural and cohesion fund transfers to Greece were €41 billion. Between 2000 and 2006 they represented almost 3 percent of GDP and almost 8 percent of the total investment budget. In terms of aid intensity, Greece was the largest beneficiary of structural and cohesion funding in this period (European Commission 2005b, 25).

6. Portugal in its entirety continued to receive objective 1 funding up to and including the 2000–2006 programming period, although in this period the Lisbon region and the Vale do Tejo received only transitional aid. Between 1989 and 2006, it received almost €50 million of structural and cohesion funding: €9.4 million between 1989 and 1993, €17.6 million between 1994 and 1999, and €22.8 million between 2000 and 2006. In the latter period, EU transfers accounted for an average of 3 percent of GDP and 7 percent of the country's total investment (European Commission 2005b, 52).

7. By 2000–2006, Germany was the third largest recipient of objective 1 funds, with an allocation of €20.7 billion. For the same period it also received €3.6 billion in objective 2 funding, 51 percent of which was focused on two regions: North Rhine-Westphalia and Lower Saxony (European Commission 2005b, 23).

8. In 2005, it was the main beneficiary of the structural funds, accounting for 23.4 percent of the total allocated. It also received 62 percent of the Cohesion Fund. Taken together, in 2005 Spain accounted for 26.6 percent of all structural and cohesion funds (European Commission 2005b, 61).

9. Sweden received €1.072 million from 1995 to 1999 and €2.115 million for the 2000–2006 programming period. Support is targeted toward diminishing the structural peripherality of the sparsely populated northern areas, job creation, and developing a competitive business sector (European Commission 2005b, 64).

10. Finland received around €1.650 million for 1994–1999 and around €2.090 million for 2000–2006, which translated into 0.4 percent of GDP in the first period and 0.2 percent in the second. In the 2000–2006 periods it had two objective 1 programs, three objective 2 programs, and one objective 3 program.

11. As discussed in chapter 4, the following financial instruments were available to the application states of central and eastern Europe: ISPA (Instrument for Structural Policies Pre-Accession) provided funding for transport and environmental projects, SAPARD (Special Accession Programme for Agricultural and Rural Development) provided assistance for agriculture and rural development, and the Phare (Poland and Hungary: Aid for Economic Restructuring) program aimed to strengthen economic and social cohesion and administrative and institutional capacity in the accession states. These three programs alone were worth €3 billion each year from 2000 to accession and continued for the period 2004–2006 at the rate of €1.6 billion per year. In this period, Bulgaria and Romania also became eligible for this funding. In addition, the new member states were eligible to claim up to €21.8 billion of structural funding between 2004 and 2006 (European Commission 2004, xxii–xxiii).

12. These communes had varying degrees of spending and revenue-raising responsibilities and there were direct elections to the city councils (Jewtuchowicz and Czernielewska-Rutkowska 2006, 141).

6

The Changing Nature of British Governance

> The UK case is very different. Here, we have an old polity, with different traditions and experience, as well as significantly different operating norms and practices, struggling to come to terms with European integration, managed through an institutional framework which bears rather few imprints of British political methodologies.
>
> —Helen Wallace[1]

As noted in chapter 1, British governance has experienced significant change in recent decades. Some of these developments are formal and high profile, such as devolution to Scotland, Wales, Northern Ireland, London, and the English regions. Other changes are often informal and lower profile and relate to the proliferation of governance through agencies, networks, and partnerships. While the full implications of these vertical and horizontal changes are yet to be realized and understood, they have been deemed significant enough for an increasing number of commentators to describe Britain as a multilevel polity (e.g., Gamble 2000; Pierre and Stoker 2000; Bulmer and Burch 2002; Hay 2002; Wilson 2003) and, as suggested in chapter 3, some scholars suggest that "multilevel governance has become a new mantra" in British politics (Marsh, Richards, and Smith 2003, 314). Following the arguments developed earlier (chapters 1 and 3), a distinction is drawn here between vertical and horizontal governance in characterizing these changes. It is evident that these changes originate from a variety of domestic and international sources and it is important not to overstate the EU role, but to put it in its proper place alongside other explanations of change.

In Schmidt's (2006) terms, Britain is a clear case of a simple polity, being both centralized and statist. However, on the former, there is evidence of a shift in the past decade (see figure 6.1):

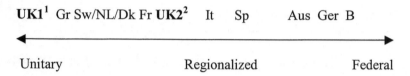

Figure 6.1.   The vertical dimension
Source: Schmidt 2006, 50 (bold added).
[1]UK1 under Thatcher.
[2]UK2 beginning with the devolutionary reforms of Blair.

On the latter category, Britain is not the most extreme case of statism, but is clearly at the statist end of the continuum (see figure 6.2).

This situation requires further explanation and, in particular, analysis of developments over time. Following the conventional take on British politics, a temporal distinction is drawn here between the post–World War II period up to the middle and late 1970s and the period that followed, in particular under the Conservative governments of 1979–1997. The conventional wisdom has it that the earlier period was marked by consensus politics and a robust welfare state, while the latter period was characterized by greater partisan conflict and an attempt at rolling back the frontiers of the (welfare) state. Beyond this established distinction is a further question relating to the impact of the post-1997 Labour government, over which there is greater dispute. For some, the Labour government represents continuity with the years of Conservatism, albeit with an often different rhetoric; for others it represents a more substantive change in values at the heart of government. We explore these issues here in relation to both the vertical and horizontal dimensions of governance.

Figure 6.2.   The horizontal dimension: Member states along a continuum from statist to corporatist processes
Source: Schmidt 2006, 108.

THE TRADITIONAL FEATURES

Most commonly, the nature of British governance has been understood through the lens of the *Westminster model*: a term referring to the concepts and narrative that have long captured the core features of British government, and which remain deeply embedded in its institutions and practices and continue to shape many aspects of contemporary politics (see Bevir and Rhodes 2003, 25). There is no definitive version of this model, but a shared understanding that parliamentary sovereignty underpins a system that operates on the basis of two related characteristics: a first-past-the-post electoral system that generally provides single-party government, and tight party discipline that ensures strong cabinet government and executive dominance of the legislature (see Richards and Smith 2002, 4). The model generally prioritizes a focus on formal institutions and particularly those located in Westminster and Whitehall. Power is conceived as zero-sum and, in formal terms, is concentrated in Parliament, which can make or remake law without fear of legal challenge. In practice, though, the electoral system ensures that effective sovereignty is exercised by the government of the day through Parliament.

Notwithstanding this practical distinction, the doctrine of parliamentary sovereignty is essential to the centralization of British politics and has led to the "focusing of all the key political, financial, administrative, and cultural networks on London" (Gamble 2003, 47). This doctrine is equally important in understanding Britain's relationship with continental Europe, being "imbued with deep, historical meaning that can be seen as fundamentally anti (continental) European" (Schmidt 2006, 191).

The importance of sovereignty to both Britain's development as a centralized state and its difficult relationship with Europe makes it a key concept for understanding how and why Britain is developing into a multilevel polity and how EU membership may have influenced this development.

Sovereignty in British Politics

The notion of parliamentary sovereignty is an emotive concept in British politics, "combining a sense of power, authority, influence, independence, and individualism, plus a sense of national determination, at the same time that it has been a symbol of 'liberty' and 'Britishness'" (Schmidt 2006, 191). It has been essentially a notion of *undivided* sovereignty, a zero-sum conception, which has made it difficult for political elites to come to terms with features of the EU, in particular that cooperation between states and international institutions can take place without national identity being compromised and with neither controlling the other (Bogdanor 2005, 699). Yet the traditional British de jure conception of sovereignty contrasts with the de facto interpretation, which is more flexible and sees international cooperation and supranationalism as a way to maximize effective state influence in a context where economics, politics, and security issues are largely internationalized (Schmidt 2006, 191–92).

A number of historical explanations are offered for the nature and persistence of the British conception of sovereignty and its importance to external relations:

> the continuity of institutions since the English Civil War; former world-power status; the successful avoidance, as an island, of full-scale invasion; the position of having "stood-alone" in 1940 together with the prestige gained as a victor; the myth of parliamentary sovereignty; pride in national identity as an aversion to "homogenization" by European social integration (arguably a variant of public concerns about immigration); and perhaps even popular loyalty to the Crown. (Bulmer 1992, 9)

However, it has been acknowledged that the more sensitive issue in British politics is not the erosion of sovereignty per se, but the formal and visible transfer of sovereignty. On less visible transfers of power, successive governments have been more pragmatic (see Wallace 1986, 367). This paradox is central to understanding Britain's relationship with the European Union, in which it has generally been seen as the "awkward," "reluctant," or "semidetached" partner.

Britain and the British have often defined themselves in distinction from their continental counterparts. A zero-sum conception of sovereignty means that transfer of power to Brussels is, by definition, a loss to Westminster. Of course, as suggested above, this conception of sovereignty has not prevented British political elites from all parties accepting aspects of supranationalism in exchange for greater effective leverage over key areas of the economy in particular. But for purposes of domestic consumption, British political elites have largely been in denial about the positive-sum nature of (at least some aspects of) European integration and have sought to construct a narrative that, on the one hand, seeks to validate and legitimize the mainframe of the Westminster model, and on the other blames the seepage of authority to "Europe" for inconvenient policy failures. The effect is to further obscure lines of accountability in already complex decisional arenas and adds to public alienation and antipathy not only toward the EU, but also in relation to politics more generally. The capacity for effective governance at either the domestic or international level, and particularly at the interface between the two, thus becomes more difficult to achieve.

THE TEMPORAL DIMENSION

The discussion of the "traditional features" of British governance is broad and requires some finessing. Two dominant themes arise from conceptualizing Britain as a simple polity: centralization and statism. Centralization relates to what we have described as vertical governance, and statism to horizontal governance. These themes are addressed historically, with a distinction drawn between the postwar period, the period of Thatcherism, and the period of New Labour. Inevitably, perhaps, the distinction between these periods is less clear-cut and more controversial than might superficially appear to be the case. The interest of this study in the role of domestic political change in explaining Europeanization effects, and particularly the impact of the change of government in 1997, explains the need to distinguish between Thatcherism and New Labour. However, it is necessary to have some discussion of the postwar period before Thatcherism to understand the extent to which the period of Thatcherism and/or New Labour is more or less in line with established traditions of postwar British politics.

The Postwar Period

Despite the first-past-the-post electoral system and executive dominance of the legislature, the period after the end of World War II to the 1970s was marked by a high degree of political consensus between the major political parties. Thus, whichever party was in power, policies in key areas remained relatively stable. This was particularly true in relation to the welfare state, full employment, and the nationalized industries. Much of the explanation for the consensus lay in the history of the commitment of the British people in two world wars. Following World War I, the spoils of victory for the people was a period of economic depression and poverty. This period strengthened the labor movement and ensured that no party could govern in the immediate aftermath of World War II without a commitment to the public of a different kind. Thus, the informal contract developed in World War II between the people and its political elites demanded a new kind of society after the war. The creation of a welfare state with the National Health Service at its center, the commitment to full employment delivered through Keynesian demand management techniques, and the nationalization of major strategic industries, such as coal, steel, and the railways, were central to this postwar settlement.

When governments changed, policy change took place at the margins. For example, some industries went in and out of nationalization according to the party in power. However, core features of the consensus remained and no party could win a general election without a commitment to maintaining these core features. It was a period characterized as "Butskellism"—a contraction of the names of the Conservative politician Rab Butler and the Labour politician Hugh Gaitskell.[2]

The period was heavily statist—both in terms of the reach of state action and in relation to the dominance of the center. Politicians were keen to retain policy-making power in Whitehall and Westminster to deliver on the promises made to a public with ever-rising expectations. Devolution of the type that came in the 1990s was not on the agenda in the early postwar period, although this was a period in which local government was relatively strong, armed with the responsibility for the management and delivery of key services, such as education. In addition, regional and area boards were set up to manage and deliver other goods and services, such as electricity, gas, and water. Moreover, in this statist context corporatist structures emerged, most notably the National Economic Development Council (NEDC, or "Neddy" as it became known) introduced by the Conservative government in 1962. This created a formal arena in which government met with leaders of industry and trade unions to improve economic cooperation and promote stable growth. Subsequently, many "little Neddies" were created to perform a similar function in relation to specific industries. The NEDC survived in formal terms until 1992, but it was effectively dead long before then (below).

Accompanying this raft of initiatives were spatially targeted measures, such as an emerging regional policy, which led to the creation of regional planning councils and boards under the Labour governments after 1964. Council members were appointees of the central government. The momentum for this development came from the problems of the northeast of England (Rodgers 2004). The minister responsible for overseeing the creation of these bodies said later:

> I was allowed a good deal of freedom to put the regional structure together and commend the appointments of the economic and planning councils. Within 18 months, my task was almost complete, despite the scepticism of the Treasury, the hostility of the Board of Trade and the jealousy of the Ministry of Housing and Local Government. They had virtually no executive powers, and there was no absence of democratic accountability; but it was, I thought, the tentative beginnings of regional government, and the north-east would always take the lead. (Rodgers 2004)

These comments are particularly apposite in the context of subsequent developments (below). However, this early experiment with nascent regional government in England (Scotland and Wales made their own arrangements) was short-lived. The focus shifted to acute cases of urban deprivation and with the election of a Conservative government in 1970, momentum for developments at the regional level dissipated further.

The election of a minority Labour government in 1974 did not reignite debate on the regional dimension in England, although the issue of devolution to Scotland and Wales was very much on the agenda. By now, Britain had joined the European Community, but this was not a factor in the rise of devolution up the political agenda leading to referendums in 1979. These developments were domestically driven and were in particular a response to growing support for greater autonomy in Scotland and Wales. The government's responsiveness to these demands was at least in part connected to the electoral threat posed in Labour's heartlands (Bradbury 2006, 575). The failure to deliver devolution in both cases[3] came at a time when the unpopularity of an unpopular government was at its peak.

The 1974–1979 Labour government found itself at the center of an economic and financial crisis: the culmination of Britain's long relative economic decline (Gamble 1981). The consequence was that by midterm, the government found itself borrowing money from the International Monetary Fund and instigating a series of cuts to public services and tightening of budgetary controls that, notwithstanding the impact of Thatcherism that was to come, signaled the beginning of the end of the postwar consensus. Ongoing improvements in the welfare state and full employment could no longer be guaranteed. The corporatist structures that had been accepted by both parties and strengthened by Labour came apart. By 1979, unemployment was on the rise and consensus politics was fast becoming a thing of the past. Following the failure of the 1979 referendum to deliver devolution, the Scottish National Party withdrew its parliamentary support for the minority government and a subsequent vote of no confidence sent Labour to the polls and into opposition for a period of eighteen years.

Thatcherism

Thatcherism has been conceptualized in many ways, but there is no better shorthand than Gamble's (1988) description of it as "free economy, strong state." This summary reflection here cannot do justice to the mountain of literature that exists on the subject: the purpose is to reflect briefly on the themes relevant for this study.

The first point is that while the Labour government reluctantly began to dismantle key features of the postwar consensus, the Thatcher government embraced this challenge with zeal. Thatcherism rejected consensus politics in principle and presented the case for an unambiguous approach that prioritized markets over the state in most domains. This included a major program of privatization of nationalized industries; the gradual marketization of aspects of the welfare state; the transfer of some competences to special-purpose agencies, quangos, and/or the private sector; and a related reduction in the power and competences of local government. It meant an explicit rejection of full employment as a government goal; employment would henceforth find its "natural level" according to market forces. In this worldview, interventionist regional policy was not even on the radar, although there were excursions into interventionist urban policy that began soon after inner-city riots took place in a number of English cities in the early eighties (see Hill 2000, 26–27; Catney 2005, 97–98.). For a governing party that remained the Conservative and Unionist Party, in both name and outlook, devolution to Scotland and Wales was off the agenda. Corporatism was seen as an unhealthy and artificial construction that impeded the operation of market forces. In particular, strong trade unions and their deleterious effect on productivity and thus national competitiveness were seen as the root cause of Britain's relative economic decline. In short, Thatcherism stood in opposition to most of what the postwar settlement had rested on.

While there was no great public affection for the outgoing Labour government, the level of hostility and conflict generated by the policies of the Thatcher governments was unprecedented in postwar British politics. In most accounts, the pivotal conflict was that between the Thatcher government and the National Union of Miners (NUM) over the issue of coal mine closures in 1984–1985. It was a symbolically important conflict on a number of fronts: the NUM was the strongest union in the country and the coal industry a bastion of nationalization. To win this battle would not only undermine trade union power generally, but would prepare the ground for the privatization of the coal industry and others. It was a battle that the government anticipated, prepared for, and executed with the full force of the central state. It was a year before the NUM returned to work en masse, but the outcome ultimately broke the spine of trade union resistance to the Thatcher governments, and with executive dominance of Parliament there were few other meaningful forms of organized opposition to the restructuring of the British economy.

While there were signs of a more consensual style under the 1992–1997 Conservative government led by John Major, these signs led to little change of substance. Major's election by the Conservative party was largely a signal of continuity with the thrust of Thatcherite policies (he had been her chancellor of the exchequer), but with a less objectionable figurehead. In contrast to Thatcher's image of the iron lady, Major was generally portrayed as the gray man of British politics. Moreover, he inherited a party that was deeply divided over Europe (a key element in Thatcher's downfall) and, after over a decade in government, appeared increasingly tired and susceptible to corruption. It was a surprise to many that the Conservatives won the 1992 general election, even to many in the party itself. In retrospect it may have been one victory too many for its own good: by the time the disunited Major government suffered a landslide defeat in 1997, it had condemned the Conservative party to a long period in opposition.

Yet in terms of the vertical dimension of governance there was one significant development in the last term of the Conservative government: the creation of integrated government offices (GOs) for the regions in 1994. The GOs integrated the previously separate regional outposts of the departments of employment, environment, trade and industry, and transport under a single regional director. This move was widely seen as a central government attempt to improve its coordination of the regional sphere at a time when the structural funds in particular were proliferating regional actors and networks. The GOs would take the lead role in administering the structural funds (chapter 7).

CHANGE UNDER NEW LABOUR?

In its eighteen years of opposition, the Labour party reinvented itself. To distance itself from the failures of the 1970s was a long and difficult journey that involved massive electoral defeats in 1983 and 1987 and a shock defeat in 1992, when it thought the journey back to government would be completed.

After 1979, the divisions in the party led to a significant splintering that resulted in the creation of a new Social Democratic Party (SDP) led by four moderate former Labour cabinet ministers. Others on the right wing of the party stayed to fight against the shift to the left. The moderate James Callaghan was replaced as leader by the left-wing Michael Foot.

Fissures opened up over two main issues: the left supported and the right opposed unilateral nuclear disarmament, while the party was also split over continued membership of the EEC. On this issue, the left generally supported withdrawal and the right generally opposed it, but the dimensions explaining positions taken were multiple and not confined simply to right-left positions. The result, however, was an election manifesto committing a future Labour government to unilateral nuclear disarmament and withdrawal from the EEC. The outcome was the biggest electoral defeat in Labour's postwar history. By the 1987 general election, both of these policies had been dropped and Foot was replaced by Neil Kinnock, a politician previously close to Foot and known in his younger days as a "firebrand" of the left, but one speaking the language of "new realism" and compromise within the party. His deputy, Roy Hattersley, was very much from the moderate wing and had been politically close to most of those who had left to head up the SDP. Labour worked on its presentation, symbolized by the replacement of its emblem of the red flag with that of a red rose. Despite these changes, the electoral gap between Labour and the Conservatives remained large and heavy defeat was experienced again in 1987.

After 1987, the electoral gap closed. Kinnock and Hattersley continued to drag Labour back toward the center of British politics and the Thatcher government became more unpopular. The attempt to introduce a poll tax for financing local government proved extremely unpopular and led to mass opposition. On Europe there were public splits between Thatcher and senior cabinet members. The nature of her demise was neither graceful nor dignified and reflected badly on the government of the day and the Conservative party. Her replacement by John Major and the failure of the Labour party to convince the electorate of its suitability to govern combined to see the Conservatives reelected by a narrow margin in 1992.

Labour's response was to thank Kinnock, who had done much, but to select a successor whom many thought should have been leader for the 1992 election. However, John Smith was leader for only two years before his death in 1994. In replacing Smith, the party looked to a "new generation" in choosing Tony Blair. Not only was he significantly younger than most previous Labour leaders, but also his background in the party was not one associated with the failings of the 1970s. He had no significant history of links with the trade unions, came from a middle-class background, and had been privately educated. He emphasized his break with the past by christening the party "New Labour" and subsequently persuaded the party to drop its commitment to common ownership of the means of production in clause 4 of the party's constitution. He was the leader who would reassure the marginal constituencies of "middle England" that Labour was once again suitable for government.

Labour's victory in the May 1997 general election was on a similar scale to that of the Conservatives in 1979. Labour came into office with a similar zeal and an explicit desire to "hit the ground running." As part of this zeal, it made a rapid start on its plans for constitutional reform generally[4] and devolution specifically. Here we again distinguish between the vertical and horizontal dimensions, with change in relation to the former being notably more formal and visible.

Vertical Change: Devolution

Within six months of taking office the government had held successful referendums on devolution in Scotland and Wales, introduced a power-sharing assembly for Northern Ireland, a Greater London Assembly for the capital and advanced plans for the creation of regional development agencies (RDAs) in the English regions. From the outset, the devolution of powers to the constituent parts of the UK was explicitly uneven, or "asymmetrical" like the decentralization process in Spain in the 1980s and 1990s (see chapter 5). This section summarizes developments in relation to Scotland, Wales, and the English regions.[5]

Scotland

The Scottish people voted overwhelmingly for devolution in September 1997.[6] That the referendum took place so soon after the general election demonstrated the high priority of devolution for the new government. In the eighteen years of Conservative government, support for devolution and/or independence grew as Scotland, along with Wales and the northern regions of England, suffered disproportionately from the effects of Thatcherism. The extent of disaffection with the Conservative government based in London was reflected in there being not a single Conservative MP elected to a Scottish constituency seat in the 1997 general election; in 1987 there had been eleven (from seventy-two) and even this had been a low point for a party that had held the majority of seats in Scotland in 1959.

In this context, there was increasing public sympathy in Scotland for the nationalist argument that it was being governed by what had become in essence an English party. Important for what followed is that this period transformed also the position of the Labour party on the issue, partly through changing the positions of key individuals within the party, but also because by 1997 a number of prodevolutionists (most obviously from Scotland) were central to the New Labour project. The consequence was that, irrespective of Blair's position on the issue, the policy of referenda on devolution after 1997 became nonnegotiable for the Labour government (see Bradbury 2006, 575–76).

Following a positive referendum vote, the Scotland Act 1998 outlined the division of competences between the new Scottish Parliament and Westminster. The new Parliament would be given responsibility for primary legislation in some areas[7] and also some tax-varying powers. Unsurprisingly, Westminster retained a formal monopoly of power over foreign affairs.[8] More generally, the Scottish Parliament was given the authority to debate any issue, whether devolved or reserved by Westminster, thus providing Scotland with a more legitimate and thus more influential voice in all matters of interest. Relations between the Scottish Parliament and Westminster were to be governed formally through a series of concordats, but less formally, it was widely understood that effective relations demanded a more federal than unitary political culture in which the center would be more pluralist in outlook (Bache and Mitchell 1999).

Wales

The referendum on the creation of a National Assembly for Wales took place a week after the referendum in Scotland. This timing was deliberately aimed at creating a "domino effect": the anticipated success in Scotland would have a positive knock-on effect in Wales, where success was far from certain. This strategy may have been decisive, given the narrowness of the vote in favor of devolution in Wales.[9]

The powers of the National Assembly for Wales, as set out in the Government of Wales Act 1998, were less than those given to its Scottish counterpart. While the Scottish Parliament was granted tax-varying and primary legislative powers, the Assembly was granted no power to pass primary legislation but the ability to exercise powers previously delegated by the UK Parliament to the secretary of state for Wales and to pass secondary legislation. Further, while the Assembly was given discretion over its budget, it had no tax-varying powers.

In Wales, the nationalist wave was less strong than in Scotland and the argument for devolution rested heavily on the need to democratize the "quango state" that had emerged. While in Scotland the public mood filtered through to change in the Labour party, in relation to Wales the impetus within the Labour party came less from public pressure and was more part of a broader strategy for renewing the regions. Even when the British Labour party adopted the policy, the Wales Labour party remained cautious and only accepted the proposal for a Welsh Assembly in 1986 as part of a package that included local government reform and plans for English regional assemblies (Jones and Scully 2003, 4).

The English Regions

New Labour's policies for the English regions were explicitly connected to their need to compete more effectively in an internationalized economy. Again moving quickly after the 1997 general election, the Regional Development Agencies Act 1998 was the centerpiece of Labour's plans, creating RDAs in the eight English regions[10] and a separate development agency for London. Elected regional governments were not part of the package and would only be introduced as and when popular support for them was demonstrated through regional referenda. Until that point, the oversight and scrutiny of the private sector-led RDAs would be undertaken by regional chambers consisting predominantly of members appointed by local authorities.

While initial functions devolved to the English regions were limited primarily to matters of economic development, there was anticipation within government that this might lead to more, with a white paper suggesting the government's belief that "the creation of RDAs will help foster a sense of regional identity and develop a regional capability. In time this may lead to further transfer of functions and responsibilities to regional structures" (Building Partnerships for Prosperity, Government White Paper, Cm 3814).

While to varying degrees there was popular demand for devolution in Scotland and Wales, devolution to the English regions was unambiguously top-down. The policy came from the Labour party, in which it had gathered momentum during the period of opposition as free-market policies hit its industrial heartlands of support hardest. Despite this, the party was not unequivocally committed to such a strong regional policy: Blair and his supporters in particular were more concerned to focus policies on relatively prosperous groups in the marginal constituencies: strategically, it made little sense in electoral terms to prioritize policies for safe seats. On the English question, Blair was said to have "inherited a commitment, not a policy" (Tomaney 1999, 83) when he became Labour leader. The champion of the regional agenda within the party was Blair's deputy leader, John Prescott. In opposition, Prescott set up a regional policy commission within the party chaired by the former EU regional policy commissioner (and ex-Labour minister) Bruce Millan. This body developed the proposals for the English regions that were acted upon in government, with Prescott as the responsible cabinet minister. The nature and functions of the English RDAs were modeled on the existing RDAs for Scotland and Wales that had been set up by the Labour government of the 1970s.[11]

Having sought to build support for strengthening the position of the English regions in the British constitutional system, Prescott pushed for and secured referendums on democratizing the regional tier in the three strongest regions: the North East, Yorkshire and Humber, and the North West. However, a decisive vote against an elected regional government in the North East in November 2004—the region deemed most likely to vote in favor—led to the cancellation of the referendums in the other regions. The issue subsequently fell from the agenda, although it did not disappear entirely. Within two years, there were moves within the government toward the creation of elected mayors for "city regions" and a response from those who favored building on the established regional structures (Wintour 2006).

Horizontal Change: Agencies, Networks, and Partnerships

In relation to the horizontal dimension, two things became clear in the early period of the Blair government. The first was that features of governance that became prominent under the Conservatives—privatization, agencification, and quangoization—would remain. The second was that mechanisms that would make structures of governance more democratic and more inclusive would be sought out. This latter point is particularly relevant for our discussion of partnership here.

Unlike Thatcher, Blair was more pragmatist than ideologue. His view on governance was "what matters is what works." In a range of fields, Labour experimented with different modes of governance for policy delivery. It was generally seen as a masterstroke that within days of coming into office, the government announced independence for the Bank of England, shielding itself from future criticism over unpopular decisions on interest rates. Part of Labour's strategy was to focus on its key goals and delegate governance in areas of lower priority or where delegation could be trusted to deliver central objectives. Thus, matters of "high politics" remained the reserve of central government, but beyond the central state there was much experimentation in governance in search of "what works."

An example of Labour's experimentation in governance came in the field of education, explicitly the top policy priority of the incoming government. Here, the government audited the local education authorities (LEAs) responsible for the delivery of education. Subsequent governance arrangements were determined by how the LEAs performed. In the case of the weaker performers, a range of alternative approaches to service delivery were introduced that were either private-sector led, public-private partnerships, or public-public partnerships. The key objective for Labour here was to achieve its highest policy goal more effectively. Its strategy allowed it to bypass previously powerful LEAs that were frustrating national policy objectives through political will or administrative incompetence. In this case, the proliferation of new forms of governance was a clear central strategy (Bache 2003) and, more specifically for the focus here, Labour was a keen advocate of partnership arrangements.

Again, pragmatism is generally the key to understanding Labour's approach here, but this understanding must be tempered with some caution, for while it fits well with the discourse and practice of Blair, however dominant the prime minister, the core executive is not homogeneous: the nature of the different departments, the networks that surround them, and the role of key individuals all have an influence on policy development and outcomes. There is no greater illustration in relation to the Blair government than the one already alluded to above, between the approach of the prime minister and that of his deputy. Prescott was more rooted in the political and ideological traditions of the party. Indeed, this was his central value to Blair, who was always one step removed from these traditions. Thus, it is important not simply to refer to government policies as though they are all driven by the same individuals or by the same set of motivations. This point is important here, because it was Prescott who held cabinet responsibility for regional (and urban) policies from 1997 to 2005. He appointed junior ministers who were close to him politically and sought to progress a consistent program of urban and regional development that was not driven simply by pragmatism but was also informed by values. This is illustrated in Labour's approach to domestic urban policy, in which partnerships became more inclusive of socially (and politically) excluded groups and in some areas took on the features of an "embryonic associationalism" (Bache and Catney forthcoming). It was also illustrated in response to the EU's regional policy requirements, which is considered in subsequent chapters.

THE CHANGING NATURE OF BRITISH GOVERNANCE

The discussion above has sketched the contours of change in British governance, albeit briefly. The main characteristic of this change is the moving away from the dominance of the Westminster model toward a multilevel polity. In this emerging multilevel polity, a distinction can be drawn between emerging type I multilevel governance, with clearly and formally defined territorial layers of government proliferated by devolution, and type II multilevel governance, which captures the complex array of quangos, agencies, and partnerships that exist not only at the clearly delineated territorial spaces defined by formal government, but also in the spaces in between and below (intraregional, subregional, sublocal, etc.).

But it is important to speak of *emerging* multilevel governance in Britain, because the transformation is far from complete. Aspects of the Westminster model continue to shape much of the discourse and practice of British politics and many of the tensions inherent in this tradition and those of the emerging multilevel polity remain unresolved. Indeed, the unresolved tensions between these old and new paradigms are a central characteristic of contemporary British politics and how they will be resolved an ongoing puzzle for politicians, policy makers, and academics alike. Table 6.1 characterizes the contrasting features of the Westminster model and the emerging multilevel polity.

While a number of these contrasting features have resonance with debates on multilevel governance, sovereignty stands out as the concept most central to understanding the prospects for multilevel governance through Europeanization (see above). On this, the Labour government has been seen to move away from the concept of indivisible sovereignty, both domestically and internationally, drawing on ideas within its own traditions: "the Party has drawn not just from

Table 6.1.   The contrasting features of the Westminster model and the emerging multilevel polity

Westminster Model Centralized State	Multilevel Polity Disaggregated State
General Principles	
Hierarchy	Heterarchy
Control	Steering
Clear lines of accountability	Multiple lines of accountability
External Dimensions	
Absolute sovereignty	Relative sovereignty
British foreign policy	Multiple foreign policies
Internal Dimensions	
Unitary state	Quasi-federal state
Parliamentary sovereignty	Interinstitutional bargaining
Strong executive	Segmented executive
Direct governance	Delegated governance
Unified civil service	Fragmented civil service

Source: Adapted from Bache and Flinders 2004a, 2004b.

the Westminster model, but also on pluralist and guild socialist conceptions within its own tradition to develop a more nuanced conception of sovereignty" (Richards and Smith 2005, 1–2). Tony Blair (2001) stated:

> I see sovereignty not merely as the ability of a single country to say no, but as the power to maximize our national strength and capacity in business, trade, foreign policy, defence and the fight against crime. Sovereignty has to be employed for national advantage. When we isolated ourselves in the past, we squandered our sovereignty—leaving us sole masters of a shrinking sphere.

This broader view of sovereignty is an important shift in elite perceptions of the EU, even if it is not shared by the public, the mass media, and all elite actors. Geddes (2004, 224) has reported on how studies of television coverage of the EU tend to "reinforce the idea of European integration as a zero-sum game, perhaps reflecting the UK's own 'winner takes all' political system." Yet the position adopted by the Blair government on the EU was more pragmatic than this perception and much closer to viewing Europe in positive-sum terms than its predecessors.

Europeanization Effects

In general terms, a number of EU effects on British central government have been observed. Bulmer and Burch (2006) have spoken of a "quiet revolution" in the way Whitehall manages Britain's dealings with the EU. The changes relate both to formal changes in the machinery of government and less formal changes in organizational values, although the attitude is one of "Europeanization yes, but on our terms." Within Whitehall, the EU's effects on the Foreign and Commonwealth Office (FCO) have included internal restructuring, the creation of new posts, and the diversion of additional human resources to EU matters. More generally, the FCO no longer operates as the gatekeeper of the lines of communication between Whitehall and Brussels, but as one of many interested parties (albeit an important one) within a growing network of actors with an EU role or interest (Allen and Oliver 2006).

The purpose of this book is to understand something of the nature of the EU effect on governance beyond Whitehall and specifically on the emergence of type I and type II multilevel governance in Britain, with a particular focus on the impact of cohesion policy. In relation to the development of type I multilevel governance, the first point of clarification is that the formal devolution of powers to Scotland, Wales, and Northern Ireland has been widely explained as driven by domestic agendas (for example, Bulmer and Burch 2002; Bulmer et al. 2002; Sloat 2002; Smith 2001, 2006); no issue is taken with this argument here. There is some connection between the process of European integration and devolution but it is difficult to assess with any precision. It is generally related to some inestimable contribution of both European integration and globalization (and their interaction) in generating and accelerating a centrifugal force in which the logic of economic competition points to smaller-scale territorial units than nation states and, at the same time, promotes claims to regional and national identity and opportunities to advance them. More estimably, both European integration and globalization were explicit factors in advancing the cause of development agencies in England and for strengthening the devolved institutions elsewhere in the UK. In Scotland, there was an added EU dimension, where the slogan of "Scotland in Europe" was used strategically by nationalists to assuage the concerns of potential supporters insecure about independence from London. Similarly, in relation to devolution for Wales, Griffiths and Lanigan (1999, 13) highlighted the role of the EU in its support for lesser languages, the value of the "Europe of the regions" rhetoric for Welsh nationalists, and the potential of a more European Welsh identity for "weaning Welsh political culture and identity away from a reliance on Britain and British identity to the exclusion of Welsh identity." In both these instances, and in a more general sense, membership of the EU "creates space for the articulation of sub-state national identities within a European framework" (Geddes 2006, 125).

Thus, in a small and indirect way, EU cohesion policy may have put some wind into the sails of devolutionists in Scotland and Wales, but when compared to other effects, this contribution is relatively insignificant. Moreover, it would be more reasonable to expect any EU influence not to be at the level of grand constitutional design, but at the margins and—in line with past practices and British conceptions of sovereignty—at a less visible level. In short, type II multilevel governance is where we are most likely to find Europeanization effects in Britain. However, the relationship between type I and type II multilevel governance may be less clear-cut than it first appears in the potential for the latter to transmute into the former. This suggestion refers to the English regions, which began with governance arrangements that were more type II than type I, with functions limited specifically to economic development. However, there was some anticipation both within government and beyond that at some future point this type II arrangement might lead to type I multilevel governance at the regional level. On this, it is not irrelevant to note that prior to political devolution to Scotland and Wales, each had its own development agency and government office. In short, the addition of the RDAs to the integrated government offices created by the Conservatives in 1994 gave the English regions a similar institutional structure to that in the devolved territories before 1997. How cohesion policy shaped developments up to and after 1997 is considered in the next two chapters.

CONCLUSION

In the postwar period, the nature of British governance has undergone a process of change that promises transformation, but is not yet complete. The dominant Westminster model has been discredited in many ways but continues to prove resilient to change. The first cracks in the edifice of the Westminster model came in the economic crises of the mid-1970s, when the precepts of the postwar social democratic consensus were first challenged.

Yet the process of change was accelerated in the years of Conservative government. Horizontally, a number of policies introduced in these years promoted informal type II multilevel governance. However, this period was also a decisive period in relation to type I multilevel governance, as government policies alienated large chunks of the electorate beyond the south of England and, in particular, fueled the support for greater independence in Scotland. As Gamble (2003, 228) put it, "The Thatcher Government confronted those who opposed it and won some decisive victories, exploiting to the full its constitutional powers. The old Constitution was stretched to breaking point, and it snapped."

After 1997, Labour amended the constitution to strengthen type I multilevel governance and embraced type II multilevel governance, albeit with some differences in emphasis that in some policy areas at least reflected a departure from the values of the previous Conservative governments. Moreover, as the traditional view of sovereignty was reinforced by a particular set of institutional arrangements epitomized by the adversarial style and structure of Westminster politics and the accompanying "winner take all" electoral system, so the changes instigated by New Labour both reinforced and were reinforced by a broader view of sovereignty, with institutional arrangements promoting greater pluralism and, arguably, greater consensualism. There are differences of opinion on this. Peter Mair (2000, 34) has suggested that Labour is "dragging the political system away from an extreme version of majoritarian democracy towards a more institutionally consensual model," while the core argument of Flinders (2005, 63) is that "although New Labour has reformed the British constitution in many important ways this has not led to a far-reaching shift in the nature of democracy." The differences are not hard to understand, given the apparent contradictions that remain in the British system. A key illustration is the juxtaposition of the first-past-the-post electoral system for Westminster elections with the more proportional electoral arrangements for the devolved institutions.

But in some respects, these contradictions may have an underlying pattern and rationale that fit with the argument that Labour is prepared to delegate and experiment where the risks to its priorities are low. Indeed, it is possible to discern in Labour's approach to governance a distinction not only between high politics and low politics, but also between national and subnational levels. Experimentation tends not to take place at the national level: this remains firmly majoritarian both institutionally and politically. However, Labour has promoted consensual institutional arrangements at subnational levels and the more proportional electoral systems for the devolved institutions remains a case in point.[12] But there are other examples. Traditional corporatist-style governing arrangements have not been reinstated at the national level, yet at the subnational level there is an array of institutions, networks, and partnerships in which there are structured relationships between public, private, and voluntary sectors. Moreover, as will be discussed in subsequent chapters, this includes a seat at the table for trade unions.

Further, it is difficult to see how—even under a less sympathetic government—the emerging multilevel governance might be reversed. On this issue, the genie appears to be well out of the bottle. Unintended consequences of devolution, for example, are emerging. The process has already necessitated a culture shift in the formulation of Britain's EU policy, particularly where the devolved institutions have a responsibility for implementation. Bulmer and Burch (2006, 47–48) have argued that "in effect, the basic structure of the state has been changed creating a potentially more varied interpretation of 'national' European interests and objectives." In broader terms, the significance of the reform process has yet to be fully realized and remains disputed. However, the post-1997 reforms have unleashed the prospects for a genuinely differentiated multilevel polity characterized by variation in process and outcome at the subnational level. Moreover, the main features of these reforms are now accepted by all of the major parties: to reject them would be electorally unpalatable.

The changes brought about are, Bulmer and Burch (2002, 133) suggest, "in keeping with European models of multilevel governance." Of course, that developments in British governance are in line with "European models" does not imply causation. The purpose of the remaining chapters is to assess the extent to which EU cohesion policy has had a causal effect.

NOTES

1. H. Wallace, "Contrasting Images of European Governance," in *Linking EU and National Governance*, ed. B. Kohler-Koch (Oxford: Oxford University Press), 1–9.

2. Butler succeeded Gaitskell as chancellor of the exchequer in 1951. Gaitskell went on to be leader of the Labour party between 1955 and 1963.

3. In Scotland there was actually a narrow vote in favor of devolution, but the turnout was less than the 40 percent condition set. In Wales, devolution was rejected by a vote of 4:1.

4. Labour's main constitutional measures and proposals in its first term were: Referendums (Scotland and Wales) Act 1997, Scotland Act 1998, Government of Wales Act 1998, European Communities Amendment Act 1998, Bank of England Act 1998, Human Rights Act 1998, Northern Ireland (Elections) Act 1998, Regional Development Agencies Act 1998, Greater London Authority Act 1998, Registration of Political Parties Act 1998, European Parliament Elections Act 1998, House of Lords Act 1999, Freedom of Information Act 2000, Local Government Act 2000, and the Political Parties, Elections and Referendums Act 2000. The reform process slowed down in its second term (2001–2006), as priorities shifted, but nevertheless continued with the Regional Assemblies (Preparations) Act 2003, Constitutional Reform Bill 2003, and House of Lords Bill 2003 (Flinders 2005, 65).

5. The logic for this choice is straightforward in relation to London, which has never received significant amounts of structural funding. While Northern Ireland has had significant structural funding and the effects on the horizontal dimension have been seen as significant (see Hodgett and Johnson 2001), devolution was aimed primarily at neutralizing sectarian conflict (see Bradbury 2006, 575).

6. The vote in favor was 74.3 percent. In a separate vote, 63.5 percent voted in favor of the Scottish Parliament having tax-varying powers.

7. These included, but were not limited to, education, health, and transport.

8. Inevitably, though, what distinguished foreign and domestic policies would be (increasingly) blurred, not least in relation to the EU. Functionally, the delegation of

"economic development" powers raised the prospect of Scottish actors seeking to act beyond the boundaries of UK territory.

9. The vote in favor was 50.3 percent from a turnout of 50 percent.

10. They were established in eight regions: East of England, East Midlands, North West, North East, South East, South West, West Midlands, and Yorkshire and the Humber. A self-standing development agency for London was also established.

11. The RDAs are public bodies that are directly accountable to government ministers and Parliament. Their aims are to further the economic development of their area, promote business efficiency, promote employment in their area, enhance the development and application of skills relevant to employment in their area, and contribute to the achievement of sustainable development in the United Kingdom, where it is relevant to their area to do so (ODPM 2002, 3).

12. In this case, of course, the potential cost to Labour in limiting its chances of securing majority control in the devolved institutions under proportional representation (PR) is arguably less than the potential benefit of making it unlikely that any of its political opponents can do the same.

7

Cohesion Policy and Governance in Britain: 1989–1997

In the previous chapter, a distinction was made between vertical and horizontal developments in Britain that have led to claims of emerging multilevel governance. In relation to the vertical dimension as it applied to the promotion of type I multilevel governance through devolution to Scotland and Wales, the contribution of the EU generally and cohesion policy specifically has been marginal. Thus, the discussion of the vertical dimension here focuses primarily on developments in England. In relation to the horizontal dimension, the main focus is on the spread of multisectoral partnership as a mode of governance both at and below the regional level. This chapter discusses the effects of cohesion policy from 1989, following the major reform of the structural funds (chapter 4) to the election of the New Labour government in 1997.[1]

Britain has been a major recipient of the regional and structural funds since the introduction of the European Regional Development Fund (ERDF) in 1975.[2] Before 1989, the implementation of the structural funds in the UK (and in most other member states) was a top-down process coordinated by central government and undertaken by local government. The policy priorities generally reflected those of the center (Bache, George, and Rhodes 1996, 301). As discussed in chapter 4, the 1988 reform (effective from January 1989) attempted a step change in the approach to implementation through the guiding principles of additionality, concentration, partnership, and programming. In terms of delivery structures, partnership and programming were the key principles, requiring national, supranational, and subnational actors to come together on a regular basis in each of the assisted regions to make strategic decisions on how best to promote economic development.

To understand the governance effects of the 1988 reform in Britain requires an understanding of the preexisting institutional arrangements in the assisted regions. While political devolution in the late 1990s gave different powers to the component parts of the United Kingdom (chapter 6), these differences reflected asymmetries in the administrative and institutional arrangements that preceded political devolution. A combination of historically ingrained institutional factors and contemporaneous political factors meant that the Scottish Office had greater relative autonomy from Whitehall than did the Welsh Office in the 1990s, although both were departments of state represented in the Cabinet and both had a degree of autonomy not available to the English regions. The English regions had no comparable institutions: there were outposts of individual government departments with a regional dimension, but nothing sufficiently integrated or robust enough to provide any kind of bulwark against Whitehall diktat (see also chapter 8).

Informally, the patterns of territorial networks differed also. The clear territorial delineation of Scotland and Wales and the sense of identity connected with these territories, plus the institutional focal point provided by the territorial ministries, led to the development of defined policy networks in some sectors. Again, as will be discussed below, the degree of cohesiveness in relevant networks in Scotland contrasted favorably with those in Wales. The point here, though, is that in 1989 the English regions were a relative vacuum institutionally, in comparison with both Scotland and Wales: there was no generally accepted territorial delineation of the English regions, little or no sense of identity with "the region," no institutional focal point, and thus no defined policy networks at the regional level. Because of this institutional lacuna, the greatest opportunity for the structural funds to make an institutional impact was in the English regions, and indeed, this is where the impact was greatest.

THE VERTICAL DIMENSION

The English Regions

The underdevelopment of the English regional tier in the late 1980s was illustrated by the absence of an agreed-upon definition of regional boundaries. The most commonly adopted regional classification was that of the "standard region," which originated from the areas covered by the economic planning councils established by the Labour government in 1965. These boundaries (revised to account for changes to local authority boundaries in 1974) remained the basis for most government statistics, and this continued despite the fact that the economic planning councils were abolished in 1979. More important for the discussion here, these boundaries were also adopted by the EU for its regional policies.

Yet while this classification was generally used for statistical purposes by the central government, some government departments adjusted regional boundaries according to their own interpretations and functional requirements. Thus, for its purposes, the Department of the Environment (DoE) treated London as a separate region, while others did not, and the DoE, Department for Trade and Industry (DTI), and Department of Transport (DoT) alone reallocated counties such as Essex and Hertfordshire out of the South East and into the Eastern region (Church 1993, 2). Aside from the central government, the national organizations responsible for the supply of gas, water, and electricity each adopted slightly different definitions of regions.

In this context, English regional identity ranged from weak to nonexistent. To the extent that "regional" identity existed, it was generally connected to historic counties such as Yorkshire (see below) that were not coterminous with the contemporary regional administrative boundaries. Only in the North East region was there any significant "institutional thickening" before the 1988 reform of the structural funds, which was driven by initiatives from within the region (Griffiths and Lanigan 1999, 18). Even here, though, where some comparisons were drawn between the emerging regional governance and that of Wales, it was clear that in terms of culture and identity the North East was very different: "There is nothing remotely comparable to Plaid Cymru, the Welsh Language, St. David's Day, Land of My Fathers or the Welsh Rugby team in North East of England, badges that remind and reinforce a sense of Welshness, even among those who are not strongly 'Welsh'" (Griffiths and Lanigan 1999, 20–21). While Labour was in power (1974–1979), referendums on political devolution to Scotland and Wales had taken place, regional policy remained prominent, and an increased role for the English regions remained possible. Following the election of the Conservative government in 1979, though, the prospects for a strengthened regional tier quickly disappeared. The new government rejected interventionist regional policies on principle and abolished the economic planning councils shortly after taking office.

While the government continued to accept EU regional funds, it did so primarily as a means of securing a rebate for Britain's contribution to the EU budget. As discussed below, the Treasury acted as "financial gatekeeper" over the distribution of these funds, which for the most part stayed in Whitehall (Bache 1999). Moreover, at this stage, there was no EU requirement to develop any regional structures or to involve other actors in decision making over the distribution of this funding. This situation only changed with the 1988 reform of the structural funds, which required the government to establish partnerships of supranational, national, and subnational actors in each of the assisted regions as a condition of funding. This it did, albeit reluctantly,

accepting the boundaries of the "standard regions" that the EU had adopted
for its regional policy purposes. Anderson (1990, 431) noted how the new
structural-funds requirements "coincided with an abrupt shift" in the British
position on national regional aid "which left its regional policy at its weakest
point in 25 years."

The Effects of the 1988 Reform

While partnerships were established in the assisted regions for the structural-
fund program period 1989–1993,[3] their composition was limited primarily to
central government civil servants and local authority officials. Trade unions,
which had been invited to participate in a number of member states, were explicitly excluded from representation in Britain. Central government civil servants based in regional offices and territorial ministries chaired and administered the committees to ensure a firm grip on decisions and Whitehall officials
were often present to oversee proceedings. Local authorities could not be represented by politicians and, in one region, the central government actually appointed the local authority officials to serve on structural-fund committees (see
Bache 2000). The Conservative government's position on this issue was that
structural-fund committees dealt with operational issues and so were more appropriate for officials with a "nonpolitical" background (Bache and George
2000). Officially, the Commission did not take a view on this issue.

Generally, the position of local authorities in relation to the center did not
improve in this early period: in most regions, they participated but had no real
influence over policy decisions. The one region in Britain where partnership
did mean something more than participation was Western Scotland. Here,
there had been a previous history of partnership working for regeneration policy (see chapter 8) and central government (in the form of the Scottish Office)
took a relatively "hands-off" approach to implementation. This was illustrated by the creation of an "independent secretariat" to administer the funds
in 1989, staffed and funded by a range of partners. The European Commission supported this model politically and financially through cofunding. Before 1997, Western Scotland was the only British structural-fund region to operate with this model: this was both a reflection of and reason for relatively
dispersed influence within the partnership. That a cross-sectoral representation of subnational, national, and supranational actors had influence in this region suggested early evidence of multilevel governance.

Despite the controlling influence of central government in most regional
partnerships, their creation and development was not without significance for
the vertical dimension of governance. Indeed, the creation of government offices (GOs) in 1994 was widely seen as an attempt by the central government

to strengthen its capacity to steer the regional networks that the structural funds were instrumental to promoting,[4] a role GOs initially proved capable of playing (Bache 2000). However, the creation of GOs had a number of unintended consequences that actually promoted rather than contained the emergence of the regional tier. In particular, GOs linked the notions of integrated policy and regional delivery in the minds of Whitehall decision makers, encouraged the development of regionally focused interest networks, and gave a push to regional identities by finally establishing what were to become accepted as the standard boundaries for the English regions (Burch and Gomez 2004, 5).

While the central government's control of structural-fund partnerships had exacerbated already difficult relations between central and local government in the regions, in the mid-1990s this began to change and GOs (and territorial ministries) began to soften their attempts at control. This was illustrated by councillors, alongside officers, being allowed to represent local authorities on structural-fund committees in both the North East and North West regions. Even in those regions where no ground was given on this issue, less formal change was starting to take place in the general tone of relations. This change was attributed partly to the experience of day-to-day contact between different partners over structural-fund matters over a number of years. However, the creation of integrated regional offices was also important in giving senior regional civil servants more authority in their dealings with Whitehall and a greater relative autonomy over the conduct of partnership relations. This meant that where the director of a GO felt it was in the region's interests to conduct partnership relations more cooperatively, there was greater scope for this to happen. Thus, while representatives from Whitehall continued to attend regional partnership meetings, the creation of GOs undoubtedly strengthened the autonomy of regional civil servants. One specific initiative that emerged in this period that was reported as particularly helpful in promoting interorganizational understanding was the secondment system that operated within the regions. This system involved officials spending time working inside other organizations within the region as a way of promoting institutional learning, most often through a two-way exchange between local authorities and government regional office (Bache and George 2000).

Thus, the partnership and programming requirements of the 1988 reform provided a focus for activity at the regional level that led to the development of policy networks and contributed to the creation of GOs, which stabilized and strengthened the regional tier as a focus for further activity. However, regional networks remained relatively immature and regional activity limited to a few functional sectors, with economic development predominant. The case study of Yorkshire and Humberside puts these developments into perspective.

Yorkshire and Humberside

As noted above, Yorkshire and Humberside was one of the few regions able
to make some claim to popular identification. Yet it amply illustrated the lack
of coherence in the English regions during this period. Identification with the
historic county of Yorkshire did not correspond with the administrative organization or indeed name of the region. In 1974, the Labour government had
created the county of Humberside, combining parts of East Yorkshire and the
northern parts of the county of Lincolnshire. The new county surrounded the
strategically important Humber estuary. Henceforth, the region became referred to as "Yorkshire and Humberside." This name gained formal status
with the creation of the integrated Government Office for Yorkshire and
Humberside (GOYH) in 1994. Despite the abolition of the county of Humberside in 1996, reference to the Humber remained partly because it highlighted a strategic economic advantage of the region, but also as a concession
to the three formerly Lincolnshire districts who did not wish to see their historic identity submerged by inclusion into an exclusively titled "Yorkshire"
region. Thus, while from the point of view of developing and marketing an
identity there were good reasons for developing "Yorkshire" as a region,
strategically and politically there were more persuasive reasons for keeping
the awkward Humber tag. Thus, from this point the regional government office changed its name to "Yorkshire and Humber" and the regional assembly
of local authorities eventually followed suit.

Research on regional network formation in Yorkshire and Humberside conducted in the months before the 1997 general election revealed that even in
the field of economic development the policy network remained embryonic.
Networks at city and even subregional levels remained more important and
only a few individuals had a high regional profile, with six being identified
by over half the respondents surveyed as "important" at the regional level.
These individuals came from GOYH (1); local government (3); Parliament
(1); and the private sector (1). A further ten individuals were identified by
over a quarter of respondents as "important" at the regional level. These came
from business organizations (2); the private sector (3); Parliament (3); training and enterprise councils (TECs) (1); plus one other.[5]

However, while the economic development network could not yet be described as a policy community, there was evidence that regional-level activity had increased significantly through the 1990s, leading to the creation of a
number of regional partnerships and associations involving a mix of public,
private, and voluntary sector representatives. All interviewees believed that
the regional tier had grown in importance in the 1990s, and a number of explanations were offered for this. Prominent among these explanations was
recognition that regional cooperation was important for competitiveness, par-

ticularly through the development of common strategies. Related to this explanation was the influence of the structural funds, the creation of GOYH, and, latterly, the regional assembly.[6] There was also a perception that the regional tier would be important under a future Labour government, which was an increasingly likely prospect.

Assessing the Effects of the Structural Funds

It is difficult to isolate precisely the role of the structural funds in shaping these developments. However, in the absence of other forms of cooperation at the regional level in 1989, EU regional policy was pivotal in promoting the region as a relevant economic space and provided channels of communication for the various stakeholders concerned. The message that reverberated through these channels was increasingly the same: that cooperation promoted growth and the regional level was an appropriate level at which to cooperate for purposes of economic development. The creation of GOs primarily to control these emerging networks stimulated largely by the structural funds had the unintended consequence of strengthening the regional level further.

These findings are echoed in the work of a number of contributors. John and Whitehead (1997) argued that EU cohesion policy had been a catalyst for the "renaissance" of English regionalism. Martin and Pearce (1999, 47) suggested that while this claim might be overstating the case it was nonetheless true that "in the absence of an elected tier of regional government, the need to respond to EU structural-fund policy has encouraged British local authorities to work more closely with each other through regional forums, regional associations and inter-authority working groups of 'European Officers' as well as with Government Offices," thus leading to the "strengthening of meso-level government." Similarly, Garmise's (1997, 20) study reported that as a result of the EU's policies, actors in the West of England were beginning to "think and act regionally" and that "incentives for funding set by the EU to encourage networking activity have had the spillover effect of spurring regional action in other areas." Moreover, there was evidence of a learning process taking place that was promoting more cooperative behavior through structural programming (Garmise 1997, 20).

Across British regions, the financial incentives provided by the structural funds brought a number of partners together for the first time. However, the partnerships remained relatively narrow in composition in most regions and, despite the government's avowed intention to promote the role of the private sector, were dominated by the public sector. This limited the development of the regional level (Garmise 1997).

In later research, Burch and Gomez (2004, 2006) considered the emergence of a "new English regionalism" in two phases: 1991–1997 and post-1997 (see chapter 8). They suggested that in the first phase, the structural funds both shaped administrative processes at the regional level and also had a regionalizing impact. The funds were said to have had a galvanizing effect in the English regions and were at the very heart of change, although they noted that the degree of change varied significantly across the English regions according to the degree of EU funding and response of key domestic players. Burch and Gomez (2004, 20) pointed to the effects of the ERDF requirements in particular:

> The *programming* concept helped both to develop and consolidate the regional tier by creating a clear focus for activities and opportunities for engagement and activism on the part of regional players. Formal requirements to operate on the basis of *partnership* also exerted a powerful regionalising effect by forcing those actors involved in delivering Structural Funds to devise new ways of working with sub-national interests [italics added].

In terms of domestic factors, they found that there had been increasing dissatisfaction with interregional disparities that had intensified under the period of Conservative governments (see chapter 6), but noted that, with the exception of the North East region, this dissatisfaction was confined to local elites and did not have popular support. Together, this combination of top-down incentives provided by the structural funds and bottom-up dissatisfaction with rising regional inequalities provided the momentum for strengthened English regional governance. The early 1990s was seen as the critical moment when the new English regionalism began to emerge (Burch and Gomez 2006).

In short, there is little doubt that in the period 1989–1997, the structural funds were crucial to the revival of the English regional tier. Despite the steering role of the central government, EU structural policy reinforced the standard regions as the "official" boundaries, gave momentum to the creation of integrated regional government offices, and created embryonic regional networks in England that provided something for the incoming Labour government to build on in its attempts to strengthen the regional tier after 1997 (chapter 8). It is important to note here that the term *revival* is used here to describe developments: the EU may have provided something for Labour to build on in 1997, but the EU did not create the English regional tier. What is clear from this account is that the EU itself drew on boundaries and aspirations that had their origins in domestic postwar initiatives.

Additionality

Alongside the partnership and programming requirements, the strengthened additionality requirement included in the 1988 reform package (chapter 4) had significant implications for Britain. This requirement provided the Commission and subnational governments with new political resources and opportunities that forced a short-term concession on additionality from the British government (Marks 1993). It was a case that was central to the development of the multilevel governance concept, illustrating joint supranational-subnational action against a national authority (chapter 3). However, in the longer term, the dispute did not undermine the British government's ability to continue to use EU regional funds to substitute for domestic spending (see Bache 1999, 34–35) and had no significant vertical effects. Indeed, as Stephen George (2004) observed, the main consequence of this dispute was inadvertent; overall spending on regional development did not increase, but there was a reorientation of policy priorities in favor of the Commission. However, while this consequence may have weakened the position of some government departments in relation to the Commission, it did not strengthen the role of subnational actors within the process and did not, therefore, advance *multilevel* governance.

The case referred to above has been discussed in detail in a number of places (in particular, see Marks 1993; McAleavey 1993; Pollack 1995; and Bache 1999). While it demonstrated the limits to multilevel governance in relation to financial control of EU funds, this was probably the hardest test possible of the 1988 reform in any member state. The British government not only controlled the strongest and most centralized state apparatus in the EU, but was also led by a party whose political values had little sympathy for the supranational and redistributive goals of EU regional policy (chapter 6). Moreover, it was committed to keeping a firm grip on public spending, and EU funds—seen as "our money"—fell into this category. As such, to concede the principle of additionality would, in effect, be to concede formal sovereignty to the EU over the levels of public expenditure. This was not on the Conservative government's agenda. How the Labour government would deal with this issue, particularly in the context of devolution, would be an interesting test of the differences caused by party change (chapter 8).

THE HORIZONTAL DIMENSION

Partnership

In the first phase of structural programming (1989–1993) the partnership requirement was more focused on multilevel government than governance, referring to consultation between "the member states concerned and the competent authorities designated by the latter at national, regional, local or other level" (Regulation [EEC] 2052/88). Before 1993, any involvement of nonstate actors in partnership was at central government discretion and, as discussed above, such discretion was not generally exercised in their favor in Britain. However, the 1993 regulation strengthened the requirement and, problematically for the British government, specified the potential contribution of the social and economic partners in policy making (see chapter 4). The "escape clause" for recalcitrant governments on this issue was the reference to partnership arrangements being "within the framework . . . of current practices," which in Britain very much excluded trade unions. Yet, while there was not a formal requirement for trade unions to be included, the implication was that this was a good practice, which had been adopted in a number of member states before 1993. The EU preference for the involvement of trade unions emerged as an important illustration of the political misfit between cohesion policy norms and the preferences and practices of the Conservative government, which defined itself in large part in opposition to strong trade unionism (chapter 6). That this government would be replaced in 1997 by a Labour government with strong institutional links to the trade union movement made this issue an important test case in understanding the nature of change that took place over the period from 1997 to 2006 (see also chapter 8).

The Trade Unions

Reports produced in 1992, financed by the European Commission, set out the state of "social partner" participation in Scotland and the North West of England. Both reports found that while trade unions were generally well informed on European affairs, they had little knowledge of the structural funds, how they were managed, or what their priorities were (Brunskill 1992; Pillinger 1992, iii). This ignorance was despite Commission arguments that their exclusion was detrimental to effective policy development.

In the fallout from the additionality dispute, the Conservative government announced in February 1992 that it would broaden participation within structural-fund partnerships. However, it made clear that trade unions would not be included and the organizations mentioned by name were generally quasi-governmental bodies led by private sector appointees: British Coal Enterprise, urban development corporations (UDCs), and regional enterprise agencies, who would be put on an "equal footing" with local authorities.[7]

On the continued exclusion of trade unions, the Commission highlighted the increasing isolation of the British government on this issue and argued for a change of policy. However, while the government gave some ground on local councillor involvement (above), before the 1997 general election there was no movement on the principle of trade union representation and no indication that this position would change if the Conservative government were reelected. Trade unions were only invited to take part in structural-fund policy making after the election of Labour in 1997 (see chapter 8).

BEYOND THE REGIONS

As discussed in chapter 1, the literature on the domestic effects of cohesion policy has generally focused on the regional level to the neglect of governance effects at other territorial levels. These effects can be found in the emergence of new subregional structures, which cover a number of local government areas: at the territorial level of the municipal local authority and at levels below the local authority. These type II effects were most evident after 1997 (chapter 8). However, some effects are evident in this earlier period and some of the later effects were the consequence of processes that were in the works then also.

There are two key features of type II governance effects "below the region" that emerged in this period. The first was the contribution of the structural funds to breaking down barriers within local government to the idea of partnership working, which had not been well received initially. The second was the introduction of a bottom-up approach to development (see chapter 4) that was pioneered in the objective 1 program in Merseyside, then incorporated into the EU's Urban program and subsequently brought into all UK structural-fund programs. This approach gave a central role in local development to the voluntary and community sector. We look at each of these effects in turn.

Local Government

Regional partnerships did not exist in the UK in 1989, but many urban areas had partnerships for economic regeneration. However, in this context, partnership was a different beast: it was not aimed at empowering local government, but was employed by the central government to enhance the role of the private sector in local economic development. It is for this reason that the EU's partnership requirement was greeted with some suspicion in British local government circles. There were different political paradigms informing British and EU approaches to partnership at the time: in the language of the "models of capitalism" debate (Hooghe 1998), the British approach was essentially neoliberal and the EU approach informed by regulated capitalism. The emphasis of the former was on rolling back the state to allow market actors a greater role in promoting local development, while the latter promoted a broader range of participants to promote development and secure a more equitable distribution of resources.

The British position on urban policy was informed by U.S. practice, where the business community took a leading role. On the eve of a tour of U.S. cities, Mrs. Thatcher's "inner city supremo," Kenneth Clarke, said he believed "the US is the only country in the world from which Britain has anything to learn about tackling inner city problems" (cited in Carley 1990, 32). However, in the context of the confrontational politics that characterized Britain in the 1980s, public-private partnerships were unlikely to emerge naturally, so central government used its financial levers to ensure that local authorities engaged the private sector in urban partnerships by making it a prerequisite for localities to enter a national competition for urban regeneration funds.

Thus, while the EU model of partnership drew its inspiration from a different set of social democratic ideas and experiences (chapter 4), there was little optimism in British local government that partnership in the context of structural policy would be a transformative process, and, in the first phase of structural policy, this view was accurate. As noted above, the central government established regional partnerships and sought to control them, marginalizing local authority influence in the process. However, over time the operation of structural-fund partnerships in Britain began to evolve to the point that by the mid-1990s, local authorities increasingly saw partnership as an opportunity rather than a constraint and began to adopt practices developed through the structural funds in other areas of their work (chapter 8).

Still, even in this early phase, it was possible to discern a distinct EU impact on partnership, particularly in locations where there had been no similar domestic initiative. Here, rural areas were a case in point, where domestic partnership programs were not prominent, but where EU programs such as Leader provided a stimulus to partnership, particularly in Scotland and Wales. Moreover, these were partnerships that had a distinctive "bottom-up" approach to local development (below). Geddes's (2001, 185) case study of the Western Isles, Skye and Lochalsh in the Highlands and Islands Region of Scotland, found that "the LEADER partnership achieved considerable success in stimulating 'bottom-up' development initiatives and initiating a shift away from a local 'dependency culture'" (Geddes 2001, 185). In this approach, local government was an important partner, but the local voluntary and community sector had a key role also. This leads us to the second important governance effect below the region.

The Voluntary and Community Sector

The "bottom-up" approach to local development that became prominent in British structural-fund programs was termed *community economic development*

(CED). While this approach contrasted with the contemporaneous approach to British urban policy in the early 1990s (below), it is a feature that had its origins in previous British urban policy experiments (Armstrong and Wells 2006, 260). Such experiments can be dated to community-led experiments promoted by the Labour government in the late 1960s and early 1970s.[8]

Promoted by the Commission, CED was introduced as a new theme in the 1994–1999 programs and took an increasing share of allocations.[9] It placed great emphasis on engaging and empowering local community actors in the process of regeneration, not only to contribute to economic regeneration, but also to "build capacity and install social capital in local areas" (European Commission 1996, 18). CED offered a "targeted means to attack social exclusion" and a "direct rather than 'trickle down' contribution to economic and social well-being" (European Commission 1996, 23). The approach acknowledged "the mutually self-reinforcing links between the 'social' and the 'economic' in the endogenous process of community, local and regional conversion" (European Commission 1996, 23): it was explicitly *socioeconomic*. This socioeconomic partnership approach was a central feature of the EU's Urban program, which was adopted in 1994, and initially funded regeneration projects in fifty cities.

CED contrasted with the established British approach to community engagement that was more economistic and, while there had been a move toward greater inclusiveness (Geddes 2001, 177), the emphasis remained on the private sector:

> Given their role in local regeneration and development, local authorities and TECs[10] can be expected to play a central role, but partnerships should include other relevant interests in the private and public sectors, and in local voluntary and community organizations, including faith communities (Government in Partnership 1995, 4).

In the latter view, economic regeneration was prioritized and social regeneration would flow from success in this; in the CED approach, social and economic regeneration were mutually reinforcing. These differences in approach had an impact in terms of voluntary and community sector empowerment. A comparative study of the governance effects of the British Single Regeneration Budget (SRB) and the EU's Urban program in a small area of the city of Sheffield illustrated how these "different seeds in the same plot" produced different outcomes on the ground (Bache 2001). With SRB, the vague requirements on community engagement and empowerment allowed dominant officials from local government and the TECs to determine the policy outcomes. In this case, circumstances motivated these officials to minimize the community role. By contrast, the clearer requirements on community engagement and empowerment within Urban allowed local officials less scope to determine the outcomes. As one key implementer put it, "The Commission model makes you have to stick with it. There's no hiding place" (GOYH civil servant, interview by author, 1997).

Of course, understanding how contrasting political paradigms inform different approaches to urban regeneration governance offers only part of the explanation for the effects on local communities and the outcomes of regeneration policies: the other part of the explanation comes from understanding local circumstances, or the "plot" into which the policy seeds are sown. More specifically, while effective community empowerment requires clear program guidelines, this is a necessary but not sufficient condition. Beyond this clear requirement, there is a need for programs to address the capacity issues of local communities in terms of skills, knowledge, time, and other resources. Less straightforward is the need to address the gatekeeping behavior of local actors who feel their power and authority is being eroded by such initiatives. All these requirements are barriers constraining the development of multilevel governance. However, there were positive experiences of voluntary and community sector involvement in EU structural-fund programs and these successes had an influence on the bottom-up approach adopted by the Labour government in a number of policy fields after 1997 (chapter 8).

CONCLUSION

This chapter has discussed the contribution of EU cohesion policy to the development of two types of multilevel governance in Britain in the period 1989–1997. In doing so, it distinguished between EU effects on vertical and horizontal dimensions. Here, the fit between these two dimensions and type I and type II multilevel governance is not perfect. In particular, the main contribution of EU cohesion policy in relation to the vertical dimension has been to strengthen the English regional tier. This has not led to type I arrangements, but to type II arrangements that may provide the basis for the later development of type I arrangements at this territorial level. The fit between the discussion of the horizontal dimension and type II multilevel governance is better in relation to both effects identified. The first effect has been to encourage elected local governments to work in partnership more, bringing flexibility to local governance arrangements that fit well with type II characteristics. Similarly, the promotion of the voluntary and community sector in local development decision making illustrates a "fit for purpose" design characteristic of type II multilevel governance.

A number of factors explain these developments, but in relation to both vertical and horizontal dimensions, change occurred gradually. In terms of the vertical dimension, the EU's advocacy of an active regional tier was opposed in principle by the central government and it created regional partnerships reluctantly and in exchange for financial resources. Initially, the government sought to control (most of) these partnerships rigidly and succeeded in doing so. However, the creation of GOs to maintain central control in the context of increasingly active and dense policy networks had a number of unintended consequences that gave a momentum for greater regional autonomy. Thus it is reasonable to describe this period as a critical juncture in the revival of the English regional tier. As is generally the case, the significance of a particular juncture is more obvious as time passes and this is certainly the case here. But the key to understanding the impact of the EU on the English regional tier in this period is to understand it as tapping into a prehistory of English regionalization that has its roots in a social democratic political tradition convergent with that which influenced Commission regional policy at the time, and for which there was a domestic political constituency. This constituency, on the left of center in British politics, was one that had suffered a major setback in the 1970s, experienced exclusion from domestic influence in the 1980s, and was in the process of renewal when the vanguard social democratic policy of the Delors Commission was having its greatest impact.

In relation to the horizontal dimension, the process of learning partially explains developments even in this early period. The promotion of partnership was the key change. However, partnership was not new to the UK and its proliferation in public policy making is generally acknowledged to be driven by a range of national and international factors. Specifically, though, the effect of the EU was twofold: to further promote partnership as a mode of governance and to influence the nature and operation of partnerships.

In relation to the first of these points, a further subdivision is useful to distinguish between the direct proliferation of partnerships through EU programs and the indirect effects of breaking down barriers in local government so that partnership became used as a mode of governance more broadly (see also chapter 8). On the second point, there are two main EU influences to highlight. The first was the attempt to promote more inclusive partnerships to incorporate a wider set of social actors than had previously been the case in Britain, notably trade unions; this attempt had little practical impact in this period, but did put the issue back on to the political agenda. The second influence, which is strongly related to the first, was the particular emphasis on local voluntary and community groups promoted through CED. Here the effect was marked, but isolated to a very small number of areas.

However, there are again domestic antecedents that meant the EU was connecting to past domestic practices. Thus, we should keep in mind that while the EU met with strong resistance from the Conservative governments in pushing for trade union inclusion in public decision making, there was a prehistory of trade union participation in public decision making through the corporatist structures that had been a feature of the postwar consensus (chapter 6). So again, the EU was tapping in to a particular tradition for which there was a sympathetic domestic constituency that was being renewed, albeit in a modified form. Moreover, it is probable that this tradition was strongest in Labour's heartlands, where EU regional policy was largely directed, and born of a shared industrial heritage that was cooperative and collectivist in spirit.[11] Similarly, while the EU was crucial in promoting bottom-up approaches to local development through its programs at a time when the inclination of central government (and many local authorities) to local development was often top-down and paternalistic, there were precedents in British urban policy dating back to the 1960s of promoting community-led development. While this approach had been buried in the 1970s, the thinking behind it resonated with the traditions of Labour thought that were becoming popular again in the 1990s and were beginning to inform the Labour party's view on urban and regional policy (Bache and Catney forthcoming).

This discussion is important for understanding Europeanization. It highlights both the importance of the historical dimension in understanding the EU's effects and, in particular, in how the EU's policies, practices, and preferences may consciously or otherwise connect to experiences that can provide a basis for familiarity and fit that may not at first sight be obvious from studying only the recent past. Related to this, it is important to note that the dominant position, practice, narrative, or tradition within the domestic arena is not the only one that matters. Britain may have been a centralized state in this period, with a right-wing and predominantly anti-EU government. However, beyond the executive was a domestic polity characterized by a plurality of perspectives, many of which resonated with the social democratic goals of cohesion policy. This convergence of views was to be found not only in local authorities and trade unions, but also in what was increasingly seen as the government-in-waiting.

NOTES

1. Some of the issues covered in this chapter have been dealt with extensively by the author elsewhere (Bache 1998 and 1999) and so are dealt with summarily here. This material is supplemented by later research by the author and other recent contributions covering the same period.

2. The UK received 28 percent of the ERDF in the first funding period after 1975. Its share of funding was relatively consistent until the Mediterranean enlargements in the 1980s. For the program period 1989–1993, Britain received 7.65 percent of the structural funds and 8.26 percent (€11.04 billion) for the 1994–1999 program period (figures from Bache 1998 and European Commission 2005b, 67). For details of the 2000–2006 period, see chapter 8.

3. In the 1994–1999 programming period the ERDF alone covered almost one-third of the UK population.

4. While the DTI retained overall responsibility for the structural funds in the UK, day-to-day management of the program was devolved to the GOs.

5. From desk research, six "key actors" in the region were identified based on their pivotal positions in the regeneration policy networks. Following the "snowball sampling" technique developed by Goodman (1961), the six initial actors were asked "who else do you think I ought to speak to?" This question was repeated to subsequent interviewees until no new names were put forward by interviewees. This approach was allied with the "reputational" approach (Laumann and Pappi 1973). This approach counts as significant only those individuals nominated as important by at least two key figures in the network. The fieldwork took place between September 1996 and January 1997. See Bache (2000).

6. It is a voluntary local government association known as the Regional Assembly for Yorkshire and Humberside.

7. In local government circles, this announcement was interpreted as an attempt to undermine its role further in the structural policy process, partly as a consequence of its alliance with the Commission over the Rechar program. Further spending constraints on local authorities made it more difficult for them to provide the matching funds and thus allowed other partners to take a greater share of funding. This finding is based on research conducted in 1995 and contained in my unpublished PhD thesis (Bache 1996).

8. The introduction of community development projects (CDPs) by the Wilson government in 1969 was, at the time, a radical departure in the history of British urban policy. Twelve such projects were established between 1969 and 1972, each operating through a local action team that "sought to combine the efforts of national and local government, voluntary groups and universities in finding new ways of supporting (deficient) people in neighbourhoods" (Imrie and Raco 2003, 9–10). They were, as Rhodes (1988, 345) put it, "a political response to a perceived crisis" that "focused on social welfare, that is, on the problems of the individual and not the economic forces transforming cities" (see Bache and Catney forthcoming).

9. Initially CED accounted for around 5 percent of allocations. However, this grew to more than one-quarter of allocations in some regions by 1997–1999 and was continued to be worth around one-quarter of allocations for some regions until 2006 (Armstrong and Wells 2006, 262).

10. The training and enterprise councils (TECs) were private-sector-led agencies set up in England and Wales in the late 1980s and early 1990s. They replaced the Manpower Services Commission (MSC), a corporatist body with representatives from the Confederation of British Interests (CBI) and Trades Union Congress (TUC). The equivalents of TECs in Scotland were local enterprise councils (LECs).

11. On Wales, Osmond (1995, 8) observed that "it remains a paradox, not to say a contradiction, that in the face of a free-market, ideologically aligned Westminster government, Wales' institutions have managed to emulate so much of the more emollient continental patterns of partnership between the public and private sectors." On the North East, Griffiths and Lanigan (1999) identify a history of elite cooperation that led to the creation of the Northern Development Company (NDC) by leading local government, business, and trade union actors in the midst of Thatcherism. They identified a "history of tripartite institutions within the North East of England dating back to the 1930s" (Griffiths and Lanigan 1999, 17). This "cooperative and corporatist" culture was used as a selling point to potential inward investors, indicating a favorable climate of industrial relations in the region.

8

Cohesion Policy and Governance in Britain: 1997–2006

> There has been a sea-change in the UK approach to regional policy: it is now at the top of the agenda.
>
> —Richard Caborn, MP, minister for the regions, 1998

In chapters 6 and 7 it was argued that the explanations for devolution to Scotland and Wales are overwhelmingly domestic and that the vertical effects of EU cohesion policy were found mainly at the level of strengthening the English regions. Here there was potential for the type II arrangements developed for the structural funds to provide the basis for future type I arrangements. Beyond the regions, cohesion policy was promoting type II multilevel governance at both the local and sublocal levels. This chapter continues the discussion from the election of the Labour government in May 1997.

Labour's election victory promised the acceleration of multilevel governance in the UK. The Labour government was committed to political devolution in Scotland, Wales, and Northern Ireland and had proposals for changing governance arrangements for London and the English regions (see chapter 6). In relation to the operation of the structural funds, these changes did not have an immediate impact: the decision was taken to make no administrative changes until the beginning of the new programming period in 2000.[1] However, in other ways, Labour's election did have an immediate impact on structural-fund arrangements in ways that served to embed their main governance effects. This was most obvious in relation to the inclusion of trade unions in structural-fund partnerships, but also in the more general effects of a new government more committed than its predecessor to the EU, to regional policy, and to relevant principles such as partnership. Throughout the period covered here, Britain continued to be a major recipient of the structural funds and, indeed, in the period 2000–2006 had its highest receipts to date.[2]

THE VERTICAL DIMENSION

The English Regions

Governance at the English regional level was strengthened between 1997 and 2006, but while the structural funds remained influential, the most important changes in this period were driven by domestic forces. The creation of regional development agencies (RDAs) and appointed regional chambers (see chapter 6) may not have gone as far as some regionalists would have liked, but were nonetheless very significant developments that strengthened regional governance. In a very direct sense, the new institutions involved a transfer of power to the regional level, particularly in relation to economic development, but also provided a platform for regional actors to engage in a wider range of issues, not least European (Burch and Gomez 2004, 12).

In relation to the development of the new institutions at the regional level, the experience of cohesion policy had lasting effects. In this period, local authorities and other subnational actors who had become used to being involved in the pre-1997 structural-fund arrangements expected to have a role in the new structures. That they did so was taken as "an indication of the extent to which partnership working has penetrated the machinery of government" (Burch and Gomez 2004, 17). The influence of cohesion policy was also evident in the regional economic strategies drawn up by the RDAs and by the government's decision to integrate expenditure on regeneration into a "single pot" for each region (Bachtler and Taylor 2003, 24).

As time passed, though, the effects of EU cohesion policy at the regional level became increasingly indistinguishable from the effects of domestic policies, as the Labour government shared many of its goals and approaches. The embryonic networks that were a feature of the English regions before 1997 (chapter 7) were quickly developing and there was an emerging consensus on regional cooperation: "there is a much wider recognition out there that the region is a unit that makes some sort of sense and there is a sense of the region that perhaps there wasn't before" (Yorkshire and Humberside Regional Assembly official, interview by author 1998). Specifically, though, the principles of partnership and programming that had been promoted longest and clearest by EU cohesion policy became embedded features of regional-level activity (Ecotec 2003, 45; Roberts 2003, 65). While this was partly the result of a learning process that had taken place over almost a decade (see below also), Labour's election had improved the fit between these principles and domestic preferences and the government signaled its approval for these aspects explicitly:

> The Structural Funds programmes have made it possible to plan economic de-velopment on a longer time-frame than most other funding sources allow, and the direct involvement of a wider range of partner organisations in decision-making has delivered distinct benefits in securing consensus on funding priorities that takes an integrated rather than a sectoral approach . . . They have provided a vis-ible pointer to the benefits of EU membership and a catalyst for innovative ways of addressing regional needs. (Treasury/DTI/ODPM 2003, 19)

However, if the "fit" between the goals and requirements of cohesion pol-icy was close in relation to partnership and programming, this could not be assumed for one of the other key principles, additionality. While it had been a Conservative government that had resisted the principle since 1979, and Labour, in opposition, had been critical of the Conservatives' position, Labour had never declared a clear policy position on this issue ahead of the election and an easy acceptance of the principle could not be assumed: it was during the 1974–1979 period of Labour government that Britain's problems with the principle first surfaced. Indeed, the European commissioner who sought to bring the matter to a head in the 1990s (chapter 7) was in part mo-tivated in doing so by his frustrations over the Treasury's approach to addi-tionality when he had been the secretary of state for Scotland in this previous Labour government (McAleavey 1992, 27). Thus, in the post-1997 period, the main question to be answered in relation to vertical governance was whether, in the context of devolution, EU cohesion policy would break the Treasury's stranglehold over the expenditure of EU funds. Here, the critical test case was Wales: the only territory with a newly-devolved political insti-tution that benefited from an increase in structural-fund receipts in the new program period 2000–2006 and thus the only one where demonstrably more spending should have resulted.

Additionality after Devolution[3]

In preparation for assuming formal responsibility for structural-fund program management under the new program period beginning in January 2000, the National Assembly for Wales (NAW) took over some responsibilities from the Welsh Office in July 1999. In doing so, one of its first tasks was to prepare an objective 1 program for the designated areas of West Wales and the Valleys, which had been approved by the Commission in March 1999. The scale of the increase in allocations to Wales under this program made the additionality is-sue crucial: the objective 1 program alone was worth £1.14 billion in EU funding, almost double the previous allocation, and covered 63 percent of the area of Wales and 65 percent of the population.

The principle of additionality is simple enough: EU receipts should be spent in addition to any planned domestic expenditure. However, the reality is more complex and two issues relating to how additionality is implemented in Britain (or not implemented, depending on your view) need some explanation. The first issue is that the Treasury sets overall public expenditure limits for all public authorities. Thus, irrespective of the source of funding, public authorities cannot breach these spending limits without the permission of the Treasury. In other words, public authorities require Treasury consent to spend EU funds in addition to what they already plan to spend. In the jargon, this is known as additional "public expenditure cover" or "PES cover." The second issue is that, under EU rules, structural funding can only contribute a proportion of funding for any project (usually 50 percent). The remaining contribution has to come from domestic sources. This is the "matching funds" requirement and is aimed to ensure that EU and domestic development initiatives are complementary.

After devolution, the Treasury continued to control the public expenditure limit for the NAW, as it had done for the Welsh Office. Within this overall limit, the NAW had scope to switch spending across different budget heads, but required Treasury consent to increase overall expenditure. In the first postdevolution period, public expenditure plans were set by the Treasury's comprehensive spending review (CSR) in July 1998. This included plans for devolved institutions for the three-year period from 1999–2000 to 2001–2002. Thus, the CSR set the budget for the Assembly for the first full year of the implementation of the objective 1 program before eligibility for West Wales and the Valleys had been agreed to. In other words, the Treasury could not have accounted for the extra expenditure required for the program. This situation had echoes of the situation that triggered the Rechar dispute (chapter 7). However, whereas that dispute brought into conflict Labour local authorities and an ex-Labour minister on one side of the argument and a Conservative government on the other, this situation raised tension between a Labour-led devolved institution and a Labour-led central government.

Following negotiations with the central government, the first secretary of the Assembly and leader of the minority Labour administration, Alun Michael, informed the Assembly in June 1999 that the spending consents for Wales would be revised. However, there would be no improvement in the position until April 2001 — some fifteen months into the objective 1 program (National Assembly 1999). This position threatened to place severe budgetary constraints on the Assembly: it implied that any objective 1 funding spent would require a reduction in other areas of NAW spending, such as roads and environmental services. Moreover, it was not clear how much the post–April 2001 change would improve things. The situation affected both the ability of public bodies in Wales to spend EU funds additionally and also their ability to meet the requirement for match funding.

Discontent within the Assembly led to demands for a tougher line to be taken with the UK Treasury. This culminated in the main opposition party, Plaid Cymru, issuing an ultimatum stating that unless an extra £85 million was provided for the first year of the program period, a motion of no confidence in the NAW Executive would be tabled. Opposition parties were also critical over the way in which the Labour leadership of the Assembly had monopolized negotiations with the central government and excluded other parties.

The issue reached up to the highest levels of government, with Prime Minister Blair giving assurances in Parliament that "we do not intend to let the people of Wales down" (House of Commons debates, October 20, 1999, Col. 456), although later stating that "match funding will continue to be the responsibility of the grant applicant and will be largely derived from the existing programmes available to the area . . . I cannot guarantee that more public funding will be available" (reported in House of Commons debates, January 11, 2000, Col. 11 WH).

The response of the central government amounted to no more than a commitment to reviewing the issue in the next CSR in July 2000. This response did not satisfy Labour's opponents in the NAW and the consequence was a vote of no confidence in the leadership of Alun Michael and his concurrent resignation as first secretary on February 9, 2000. Subsequently, the House of Commons Select Committee on Welsh Affairs became involved in the issue. Its report on *The Structural Funds in Wales* (Select Committee on Welsh Affairs 2000) recommended that the UK government make a clear and early commitment to make the provisions necessary to allow Wales to take up its EU funding allocation in full. At this point, the Commission also expressed its concerns following its initial appraisal of the objective 1 single programming document (SPD) for West Wales and the Valleys, published in February 2000: "the Commission needs to be satisfied that future financial resources will be able to provide public funding for the whole programme and cannot be satisfied that this will simply be reviewed in the forthcoming Comprehensive Spending Review. A commitment to this effect needs to be included in the final SPD" (European Commission 2000, 28).

When the July 2000 CSR was announced, it was welcomed by the new (Labour) leadership of the Assembly, but again did not satisfy the opposition parties. The difference in response was partly partisan, but also resulted from the complexities over how much additional provision was needed to meet the requirements for the objective 1 program. In particular, it was difficult to calculate the amount of PES cover required. The amount provided by the CSR 2000, £272 million, was more than the amount considered necessary by the Select Committee on Welsh Affairs and by NAW finance officials, but considerably less than that demanded by the opposition parties. There was also a dispute over the sufficiency of the amount provided by the Treasury for public sector match funding of objective 1. There was a significant increase in the assigned budget to Wales of £1.6 billion between 2000–2001 and 2003–2004, which included extra resources for the purposes of match funding. Again, the Assembly leadership believed this was adequate additional provision, while Plaid Cymru argued that it was not. Again, lack of clarity in the financial details made it impossible to judge which view was more accurate. There was no dispute that, in relation to both PES cover and match funding, the Treasury had improved on the previous position: the dispute was over whether this was sufficient.

Despite the lack of clarity over the adequacy of the financial settlement, the significance of this dispute for the discussion here is that the Treasury retained control over the financial purse strings. Thus, despite political devolution to Wales, EU requirements on additionality did not significantly undermine the position of the Treasury, which demonstrated its continued dominance on the issue within the core executive. Its control of financial resources was important here, but also its control over informational resources, specifically, its ability to frustrate close and effective scrutiny over its calculations. To the extent that extra spending resulted from the objective 1 program, this was primarily a consequence of domestic political factors and processes, although the EU's additionality requirement clearly provided political actors in Wales with resources of political legitimacy to mobilize in their campaigns and give their arguments substance.

In some respects, this case study reflects debates over effective and formal sovereignty, discussed in chapter 6. While the central government retains formal control over public expenditure limits, the combination of EU requirements on additionality and the political exploitation of these requirements by domestic actors whose position was strengthened by devolution may have reduced central government's effective sovereignty over the issue. It remains unclear how much ground the Treasury ultimately gave, but it is clear that devolution placed increased pressure on the center to respond to EU requirements. The creation of the NAW gave Wales greater capacity to highlight the issue and place pressure on the relevant departments of the core executive, than had been the case with the Welsh Office, itself a part of the core executive. In this sense, significant political resources had been transferred away from the core executive to the devolved institution. From the Treasury's perspective, the point in retaining formal sovereignty over the issue is that, in theory at least, what has been given away in one period might be retrieved in another.

THE HORIZONTAL DIMENSION

Partnership

In the previous chapter it was noted that, with a few exceptions, the EU's partnership principle was not initially well received in Britain. However, by the mid-1990s there was evidence of adjustment to the requirement and the beginning of a "thawing" of relations in the English regions between representatives of central and local government, following the creation of government offices (GOs). Post-1997, partnership became "part of the architecture" of governance at the subnational level (Ecotec 2003, 14). As noted above, the change of government was important here, but its influence has to be understood alongside other factors; of particular importance was the process of learning.

In relation to the change of government, Labour had a direct impact on matters by signaling that trade unions should be included in structural-fund partnerships immediately: the effects of this decision are discussed in detail below. Moreover, the new institutions of devolution in Scotland and Wales would take over day-to-day managerial responsibilities for the structural funds from 2000. However, the key period in which partnership became embedded was in the period up to 2000. While this was before the devolved institutions took over responsibility, it is important to note that there were important asymmetries in the institutional arrangements across the UK before political devolution that did affect the development of partnership relations in this period. To account for these asymmetries, the following section discusses developments in two regions covered by different territorial ministries (Western Scotland and South Wales) and two regions covered by different government regional offices (Yorkshire and Humber and the East Midlands).[4]

Western Scotland

"In my experience, the interconnectedness of the polity in Scotland is extremely different from what I've been involved with and seen elsewhere. There is much more discussion between people from different sectors and localities, there is much more joint partnership project working than in England and this was all well before partnership became the vogue buzzword" (local authority official, interview by author 1998).

The relative cohesiveness of the Western Scotland regional partnership was explained by a combination of historical, institutional, and political circumstances particular to the region and nation in which it was embedded.

Partnership working had been a feature of the region since the mid-1970s, when the Strathclyde Regional Council introduced the practice in its efforts to regenerate the city of Glasgow to stimulate regeneration of the broader Strathclyde region. In the view of interviewees, the strategy was born out of desperation with single-agency attempts to address the increasing levels of deprivation in the region. With this background, the EU partnership requirements were relatively easily assimilated into existing practices from 1989. Agreement to create an independent secretariat[5] to administer the funds illustrated the degree of trust developed through prior partnership working between the Scottish Office and other partners. However, this was also an indication of the relative autonomy of the Scottish Office from Whitehall, compared with other institutions of deconcentrated government at this time. This autonomy reflected not only specific historical features of the place of Scotland within the United Kingdom, but increasing central government sensitivity to popular demands within Scotland for greater autonomy. The creation of the independent secretariat further enhanced partnership.

Despite the relaxed role played by the Scottish Office on day-to-day structural-fund matters, it remained the partner with a "golden share." The Scottish Office retained considerable reserve powers, including the right to veto partnership proposals. However, it only used its powers with great reluctance "because it recognizes that it undermines the partnership: it pollutes the atmosphere" (voluntary sector partner, interview by author, 1998).

South Wales

"The simple fact is there is no war in Wales any more" (local government official, interview by author, 1998).

Up to the mid-1990s, South Wales was the British region most characterized by conflict over structural-fund matters. The Welsh Office was viewed by many partners, particularly those in local government, as being very directive and highly bureaucratic. Local authorities felt powerless within partnerships. The conflict over the structural funds became explicitly political: "The local authorities are the political end of the regional partnership and we used our politicians to fight, on occasions, what were administrative issues — that made them political issues. And clearly because it was a Conservative central government that was supporting this line and a Labour group of local authorities that were taking another line, it then became a political issue" (local government official, interview by author, 1998).

Local authorities in particular campaigned long and hard for an independent secretariat, similar to that in Western Scotland. With Commission support, they argued that this would be an important symbol of a move toward a more inclusive partnership and a more effective role for subnational actors. However, for a sustained period after 1988 the Welsh Office resisted this campaign.

From around 1996, the political tensions around the structural funds in South Wales began to ease. A number of developments explain this. The starting point, arguably, was the creation of an independent secretariat, agreed to by the new secretary of state for Wales, William Hague. This signaled a thawing in relations between the Welsh Office and the wider partnership that accorded with Conservative party policies of "open" government in the run-up to the 1997 general election, and also cut central government's administrative costs. In addition, there were personnel changes in the European Affairs Division of the Welsh Office, including the retirement of one senior figure who had a particularly difficult relationship with local authorities (see also WEPE 1998).

By 1998, relations between the Welsh Office and the other partners had improved considerably from their low point in the early 1990s. As one partner put it, "it has influence, but has largely played a reasonably 'hands-off' role" (local authority official, interview by author, 1998). One illustration of improved partnership relations in South Wales was the establishment of a small team to negotiate the 1997–1999 single program document (SPD), cochaired by officials from the Welsh Office and the local government, a development unique in Britain. Despite the creation of the independent secretariat, the Welsh Office retained important reserve powers but the extent and nature of its intervention had changed by 1998.

Yorkshire and Humber[6]

"The whole climate and the environment within which we work in the area of economic development has become much more partnership orientated over the last four or five years . . . people have got used to working together across sectors in a way that simply wasn't the case in the late eighties" (Yorkshire and Humber partner, interview by author, 1998).

As with South Wales, the lack of power felt by local authorities in Yorkshire and Humber resulted in much tension up to the mid-1990s. However, in a relatively short time span, this region moved from being among the most fractured and conflict-ridden British regions to being one of the most cohesive and consensual. A key explanation given for improved partnership relations was the experience of partnership working. From the 1980s onward, partnership became an established prerequisite for funding under both EU and UK regeneration programs. While in many instances these "partnerships" were assembled reluctantly and were in practice largely cosmetic, in others more significant working relationships developed. Thus, partnership "conditionality" undoubtedly made a contribution, however slowly, to improved relations between partners in Yorkshire and Humber.

The development of effective partnerships in this region was accelerated by a change in leadership style demonstrated by regional civil servants. This was helped by changes in personnel within the European Secretariat of the Government Office for Yorkshire and Humberside (GOYH). Several other partners reported positively on changes in style at the government office over the 1994–1999 program period. This was reflected particularly in the way meetings were chaired and the responsiveness to partners' requests of the European Secretariat. By mid-1998, GOYH was generally seen to be facilitating rather than dominating partnerships, which was not a perception of partners during the early part of the program period. No one was under any illusion about the underlying authority of the government office—it retained the key political and administrative functions within the partnerships and did not create an independent secretariat. However, GOYH had chosen to exercise its authority differently, allowing local authorities and other partners more influence. While this change was essentially voluntary, it was also partly a response to dysfunctional partnership relations that hindered policy performance and threatened the region's access to additional structural funding allocated at the Commission's discretion. Regional civil servants reported that, on their visits, "the word in Brussels" was that the region was underperforming in terms of economic development outputs of the structural funds. While this affected all partners, it reflected most damagingly on GOYH as the lead partner. Moreover, as the lead partner, it was essential that GOYH take the initiative to resolve this.

Thus, the Commission undoubtedly played a role in developing partnership relations in Yorkshire and Humber. In addition to its role in allocating discretionary funds, it also generated awareness within the region of how others viewed it negatively. Moreover, the Commission continued to be approachable and constructive in its relations with the wider partnership. Certainly, in the early part of the program period, the Commission was viewed by most partners as having a more "even-handed" approach to partnership than the government office. Not surprisingly, therefore, where there was tension with the Commission, it was in its relationship with GOYH rather than with the wider partnership.

East Midlands

"The main problem for the East Midlands is that it doesn't have a common identity . . . I think it is one of the peculiar areas that really hasn't got anything that links it all together" (East Midlands partner, interview by author, 1998).

The findings on the operation of structural-fund partnerships confirmed the widely held view of this region as relatively fragmented. Here, the Government Office for the East Midlands (GOEM) was closer to Whitehall in its implementation of policy than were government departments in the other regions. Civil servants interpreted their role strictly along the lines of directives from Whitehall and in accordance with EU regulations. One regional civil servant (interview by author, 1998) commented that "the (Conservative) government took a clear view that all decisions were to be made by government officials and that the role of the committees was to pass an opinion and monitor the implementation of the program." In the view of GOEM, the change of government in 1997 made no difference to this policy, because all of the programs had been agreed to or were about to be agreed to by the time the government was elected (GOEM official, interview by author, 1998).

In this region, too, local authorities felt they had little influence over structural policy making up to the mid-1990s and the partnership was characterized by tension, not least between the Commission and GOEM officials, who saw the Commission as having a "political agenda with a small 'p.' . . . It wants to see more regionalization of programs. It doesn't like national programs. . . . It wants to see independent secretariats free from central government control" (regional civil servant, interview by author, 1998). In policy terms, little changed immediately after Labour's election in 1997: regional program priorities had been set by then and would not be altered. Moreover, while partners reported an improved change in the tone of exchanges with GOEM officials from around this time, GOEM officials remained less approachable and less innovative in their approach in this period than their counterparts in Yorkshire and Humber. This may have been partly to do with different personnel, but also that the East Midlands region received considerably smaller amounts in structural funding than Yorkshire and Humber. As such, there was less experience of partnership working and less of an onus on making partnerships work in terms of the net impact on economic performance and external perception of the region.

Analyzing Developments

As suggested above, the general acceptance of partnership began before Labour's election. However, the change of government contributed to the enhancement of partnership in a number of ways. Generally, Labour was more pro-EU and more pro–regional policy than the Conservative government had been. Moreover, in party political terms, Labour's election victory, coupled with Labour dominance of local government in this period, meant that for the first time there was an absence of significant ideological and party political conflict underpinning the institutional conflict between center and locality in relation to structural-fund partnerships. As one Labour council leader in York-shire and Humber (interview by author, 1998) put it, "I think that subordina-tion is now starting to disappear. Certainly, from our perspective, it's because we've got a Labour government. It's somewhere else to go if we're not happy. Previously there was nowhere else to go." The same council leader suggested that without the change of government, "partnership would have developed but it would have struggled."

Yet Labour's contribution to enhancing partnership relations should be un-derstood in the context of a more general process of learning taking place in relation to partnership working at the subnational level. This took place at dif-ferent times and to different degrees in different locations, and the different institutional arrangements that predated political devolution partly explained this, but there was evidence of a general trend toward more effective partner-ship working across the regions studied. In Western Scotland, where partner-ship was initially most successful, there had been the longest experience of partnership working facilitated partly by the cooperative political culture but also by the relative autonomy of the Scottish Office from Whitehall, which allowed that culture to flourish. In other parts of Britain, where the institu-tional arrangements were different, Whitehall was much more influential and partnership much more constrained. However, as institutional constraints were eased by the creation of GOs and changes in the Welsh Office, partner-ship began to flourish. On the surface, this may have been surprising, but most of the regions assisted by EU structural funds were very similar to West-ern Scotland historically, with strong industrial traditions that often generated cooperative cultures and also a general interest in securing effective eco-nomic development to regenerate their communities that were suffering hard-ship. In other words, the principle of cooperation that informed partnership had a legacy to draw on in all of the assisted regions once political and/or in-stitutional circumstances allowed.

The timing and extent of the changes depended partly on the financial fac-tors specific to each region. The Commission could make use of the financial resource to promote change, but the extent of its leverage was related to the importance of the structural funds within each region. Of the regions studied, the East Midlands received the smallest amount of assistance from the struc-tural funds, and consequently the funds had the least impact on governance in this region: there was less experience of partnership here and less of an in-centive to work through conflicts between organizations to improve development policies. By contrast, in Yorkshire and Humberside the importance of structural funding generally and the Commission's use of its control over discretionary funding were important factors in promoting more cooperative working.

Yorkshire and Humber also illustrated, though, that other factors were important. Beyond the initial external push from the Commission using the financial resource, partners within the region began to embrace multiagency cooperation as an effective way to promote development. Here, there was clear evidence of changing actor preferences over time. This meant that rather than being a laggard, the region became a leader in partnership relations and one the Commission held up as a model for others to follow:

> Taking South Yorkshire as an example. It is a very participative process. The South Yorkshire Forum was set up with a very wide representation from NGOs/ civil society, also business and social partners in general, with political representation at the local level and even MPs and MEPs being involved in the process. So it is a good example of a region pulling together all of its forces to develop a vision for the programming. (DG Regio official 2, interview by author, 2006)

That the structural funds had been key to understanding the transformation of partnership relations in South Yorkshire was felt both within Brussels and the region itself. Moreover, this was seen as one of the major contributions of the structural funds to the region. An official of the Yorkshire and Humberside Regional Assembly (interview by author, 2006) commented: "In South Yorkshire, partnership has been one of the biggest successes. Before [the structural funds] the partners often wouldn't speak to each other. Now they're all involved."

However, change had not just taken place subnationally, but also within the central government. This was partly through the change of party in government, but change was also identified within the Whitehall department directly responsible for the structural funds, the Department of Trade and Industry (DTI). Here again, the process of learning was deemed important: "There is a wide difference between the DTI now and say fifteen years ago, where it had the idea that the same program could suit all regions. DTI has evolved. It is now much more sensitive to effective partnership, considering partnership as a way by which regions take their responsibilities" (DG Regio official 3, interview by author, 2006). Here the emphasis was on institutional evolution, rather than political direction by the incoming government. The explanation offered for this evolution was that "I think the ministry of industry has learned that partnership may be a success factor: it may be improving the efficiency of measures" (DG Regio official 3, interview by author, 2006).

While partnership governance became part of the architecture across Britain, there were variations in how partnerships were organized in different regions, even in relation to the same program. For example, some British objective 1 regions became more proactive than others in embracing the EU's objective of promoting equal opportunities in structural policy, with different regions setting different targets for female participation (Select Committee on Welsh Affairs 2002). Moreover, while West Wales and the Valleys sought to operate a "three-thirds" principle, through which public, private, and voluntary sectors would be represented in equal numbers on all of the local and regional partnerships, other program areas did not aspire to this split. Indeed, as the program progressed, South Yorkshire moved away from an emphasis on sectoral representation to finding "the right person at the right time doing the right job" (Yates 2002, 16). In Cornwall, a distinction was made between the higher-level decision-making bodies, where a sectoral balance was sought, and more task-specific lower-level bodies where the principle was related more to being fit for purpose: "for example, we have a taskforce on the SME agenda which is entirely private sector. They wanted that and we were very keen to see private sector engagement" (Bayly 2002). The arrangements in Cornwall in particular closely resembled the characteristics of type II multilevel governance.

The Trade Unions

As discussed in the previous chapter, despite pressure from the Commission, the Conservative government refused to allow trade unions a role in structural policy making. However, following the May 1997 general election, the Labour government was quick to signal to civil servants in England and Wales that trade unions should be included on program-monitoring committees (PMCs). This move was generally welcomed by other structural-fund partners who accepted that the trade unions had a potentially important contribution to make in the planning, implementation, and evaluation of structural-fund activities. Interviews for this research[7] covered partners from all sectors and revealed no opposition to trade union involvement with the structural funds and many positive responses. Views ranged from acceptance of the inclusion of trade unions as legitimate partners to the belief that their involvement had made partnerships more complete.

For many, the debates that had previously taken place in monitoring committees around social partners' participation had been an unhelpful distraction to the main business of structural policy. As one regional civil servant (interview by author, 1998) put it, "A whole load of wasted time has been saved. Not just wasted time, but time that was creating a whole adversarial approach when we wanted to build up a more cooperative partnership. Obviously, if you've just spent half an hour arguing about why the social partners aren't there it's quite difficult to say 'let's go to the next part of the agenda' and have a cooperative discussion about that."

Despite this view, the speed with which the government's policy change was operationalized varied across regions. Central to this was the established civil service habit of not inviting unions, which appeared difficult for some to break. Some Trades Union Congress (TUC) regional officials considered this a genuine oversight. As one put it, "they've forgotten to send us things because they haven't sent it us for so long" (TUC regional secretary, interview by author, 1998). Despite delays in some regions, ultimately regional TUC officials in all regions received letters from GOs in England and the Welsh Office in Wales inviting participation on the PMCs. Ironically perhaps, given its tradition of inclusive partnerships, Scotland was an exception on this issue. The Scottish Office, in consultation with other partners, took the view that to introduce new partners midway through the 1994–1999 programming period was inappropriate, although the unions would be involved in preparing the next round of programs and would be included on PMCs from 2000.

While the English regional TUCs and the Wales TUC welcomed the opportunity to be involved with the structural funds in the mid-program period, in reality their initial participation was without real influence. That the inclusion of trade unions on structural-fund committees for the first time coincided with increased opportunities in other domains through devolution placed an even greater strain on the limited resources of the TUCs in these regions than before 1997. Yet even when the TUC representatives managed to attend structural-fund meetings and had briefed themselves, their influence was still limited. One TUC regional secretary (interview by author, 1998) noted, "We've spent ages trying to get on the monitoring committees, now we find there are all these subcommittees where the real action takes place. Then you find that even at those meetings there are three to four people [who] have carved it up before the meeting, so you never quite get to the center of power."

Having been excluded for so long, trade unions found the culture and process of structural policy making a further barrier to influence. As another regional secretary (interview by author, 1998) put it, "There's far too much paperwork, far too much jargon. They are trying to do something about it, but instinctively they're not good at making things accessible because they're working in an environment where they develop a language of their own and it's exclusive. A lot of it's to make themselves more comfortable—because if you have your own language, it's much harder for people to ask searching questions that you've got to answer."

The lack of trade union resources at the regional level was partly a problem that was internal to the organization of the TUC. Having developed in a centralized polity, the TUC was itself heavily centralized and there was a feeling in the regions that the center was underestimating the effects and opportunities coming from EU regional policies and domestic devolution. Beyond the problem of resource constraints, though, the trade union movement faced an obstacle to effective participation in terms of the mind-set of many trade unionists, who "in the past eighteen years have developed a different agenda altogether, which is about firefighting, fighting redundancies, defending members' jobs and going out there increasingly and recruiting members" (TUC regional secretary, interview by author, 1998). To become influential players in structural funding required additional resources in the regions and also a cultural shift in relation to participation in the public policy-making process.

Over time, there was some improvement on both counts. However, the improvements were uneven across regions. On resources, some regional TUCs were given assistance by their RDAs to improve their capacity to engage, while others were not and staffing remained at pre-1997 levels. Typically, this meant a very small number of policy officials. Thus, in the Yorkshire and Humber region there was one such official (the regional secretary), and there were only two officials covering the Midlands (the size of two standard planning regions). This meant that while there had been a generally positive response across the TUC regions to the new postdevolution opportunities, the ability to participate effectively remained constrained by resource limitations (regional TUC official, interview by author, 2006).

BEYOND THE REGIONS

Local Government

While cohesion policy had begun to have an effect on local government in the period up to 1997, this effect became clearer and more pronounced as time passed, with learning over time being a more significant dynamic than the change of government. British local authorities had long been prominent in making representations to Brussels (John 2001), but the download effects of Europeanization took longer to embed. Marshall (2005) identified changes in both the attitudes of elite actors within local government and the delivery structures adopted for regeneration and other domestic programs that reflected "European" modes of partnership working and project design.

A study of Birmingham and Glasgow (see Bache and Marshall 2004; Marshall 2005, 2006) found that while the initial response to structural-fund requirements was instrumental, there was a gradual move away from parochial attitudes toward holistic, longer-term, and regionally focused approaches toward regeneration. There was a drive in both cases to construct a regional consciousness around the "engine" of the central city and local encouragement for the development of regional bodies. One local politician in Birmingham suggested that the implementation of the structural funds had forced a sort of paradigm shift, stating that "Birmingham now operates not as a city, but as a city-region. In an economic sense, we have moved from a city to a regional perspective" (interview cited in Bache and Marshall 2004, 19). Here, the development of regional programs for structural funding was the key. More generally, the research found that there was "a commitment to joint working, capacity-building and holistic thinking that is less evident in non-beneficiary cites across Britain" (Marshall 2004, 15).

In the post-1997 period, the domestic agenda affecting local authorities was shaped by a Labour government for the first time since the 1988 reform of the structural funds. While Labour policies were in many ways more devolutionary and inclusive than the Conservative government's had been, at times there were tensions between these policies and the center's desire to retain control. Labour maintained a strict regime of audits and inspections in relation to local government that reflected this desire. However, in a number of policy initiatives, Labour's approach to local delivery was highly convergent with the principles of EU cohesion policy, such as partnership and programming. As such, Labour's approach to partnership was generally seen by local government as less threatening than that of the Conservatives, and as these domestic and EU policy principles began to converge, identifying the distinct EU effect became more difficult. The extent to which Labour's approach was informed by its engagement with the EU is also difficult to discern, although elsewhere it has been observed that many of the key figures in the Labour government were individuals who in the 1980s had turned to Brussels as local government leaders and trade unionists, when British government doors were closed (Bache and Jordan 2006c, 275). This was a period when some important trade unions became attracted to the "European social model" (Van der Maas 2006) and the activities of a wider array of public and voluntary interests became Europeanized (Bache and Jordan 2006d). There are further reflections on these arguments in the concluding chapter.

The Voluntary and Community Sector

In opposition, the Labour party had been heavily critical of the limited role the Conservative government had allowed for the voluntary and community sector in both structural policy and domestic initiatives. On this issue, the

Labour government's requirements were clearer and stronger: "mere existence of community representatives in partnerships is not enough to ensure a
significant say in decisions. They need to play a full and effective role in the
partnership and be supported by local structures that allow the community
viewpoint to be heard and partnership decisions to be fed back to the community" (DETR 1999, 1.4.4).

In its own policies, Labour's guidance documents placed a greater emphasis on building the capacity of community actors to allow them to lead partnerships. More practically, the government earmarked up to 10 percent of its
Single Regeneration Budget (SRB) funding specifically for capacity-building
measures, either as part of a wider regeneration project or as a stand-alone attempt to provide local people with participatory skills (Bache and Catney
forthcoming). That the government was prepared to use SRB funding for capacity-building measures not linked to specific economic regeneration projects illustrated the new government's emphasis on the intrinsic value of engaging and empowering local community actors.

Labour's approach to voluntary and community sector engagement was
close to that promoted by the Commission in its community initiatives such as
Urban and Leader and through the CED component of mainstream structural
funding. The extent to which Labour policy was informed by the experience
of EU approaches is unclear, although there is evidence of some learning. CED
has been seen as influential over domestic policies for community-based regeneration, such as New Deal for Communities and the SRB (Bachtler and
Taylor 2003, vi). As with partnership more generally, the influence of the EU's
bottom-up approach was beginning to wane by Labour's second term, but
there was continuing evidence that "lessons are still being learnt about bottom-
up approaches to community development and are being applied through domestic programmes" (Ecotec 2003, 20).

At the same time as noting the EU's effects on domestic policies and practices, it is important to note that key experiments informing the EU's approach on these issues took place in Britain. Particularly influential was the
"Pathways to Employment" experiment within the Merseyside 1994–1999
objective 1 program, which was identified by the national government as a
model of best practice and informed domestic programs aimed at addressing
social exclusion (Ecotec 2003, 19). At the neighborhood level, there was also
evidence that lessons had been drawn from practices developed in EU programs and incorporated into domestic practices locally (Catney 2005, 198).

In the program period 2000–2006, the EU continued to pursue voluntary
and community sector participation through structural policy. This had continuing effects on the ground in Britain. Chapman (2004, 2006) highlighted
an "increasing emphasis" on involving community actors through her study

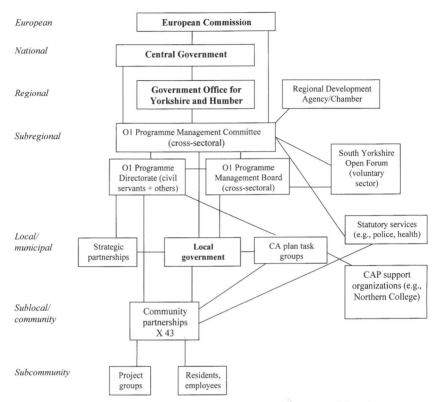

Figure 8.1.   **Mapping type II multilevel governance onto type I multilevel governance: Community action planning in the South Yorkshire objective 1 structural fund program (type I institutions in bold)**
Source: Developed from Chapman 2005; Yates 2005.

of the implementation of EU structural-fund programs in South Yorkshire. The Chapman study illustrated how this emphasis increased the complexity of multilevel governance (see figure 8.1).

Tofarides (2003) reported similar effects in relation to London. In relation to Merseyside, Evans (2002, 506) argued that the "Pathways" approach had "generally fostered 'community' empowerment in the sense that they have improved residents' and local groups' representation on key decision-making structures, knowledge of the program and ability to procure resources." Each of the studies emphasized the need to understand the relative influence of European guidelines in the context of specific local factors, including the strength of preexisting community networks and the responsiveness of local elites to bottom-up governance approaches. However, each also highlighted a process of learning in relation to making community engagement more effective.

In relation to Birmingham and Glasgow, Marshall (2005) showed how the areas demarcated for priority investment on domestic maps were adjusted to match European target zones and, simultaneously, the organization of local partnership groups was altered to include more stakeholders in the decision-making process. This process of geographic and organizational adjustment enabled local partnership groups to meet EU criteria for multiannual funding support. Whereas Birmingham historically favored highly visible public-private "flagship" projects (Loftman and Nevin 1998) and Glasgow quietly developed area-based initiatives aimed at employment issues or social exclusion (Pacione 1995), both cities altered their local development strategies to ensure consistency with the vision promoted by the European Commission.

What is particularly interesting, given the focus here, is that Britain appears to have gone furthest in relation to embracing this feature of EU governance. Kelleher, Batterbury, and Stern (1999, 10) described voluntary and community sector involvement in Britain as "atypical of the general trend." One Commission official commented on the creation of up to forty community partnerships by one strand of the South Yorkshire objective 1 program: "this shows you how far the UK is now going: they are getting close to the field. The UK is at the forefront of this" (DG Regio official 4, interview by author, 2006). Another official with long-standing responsibility for a number of programs in the UK emphasized how this change had taken time: "I had a lot of problems with the UK because it [creating community partnerships] was not seen as the right thing to do. But after a number of years I think the practice was proven and the practice was demonstrated to be a nonaggressive practice toward the institutions. It convinced a lot of people that, after all, this was not a bad thing" (DG Regio official 5, interview by author, 2006).

Again, this is ostensibly a case of Europeanization (as defined in chapter 1) but resonates with past British practices and with an enduring tradition in social democratic thought that had its advocates within the Labour government. These practices have resurfaced under Labour's own urban policy initiatives, with the development of governance structures that reflected associationalist ideas with a long history in the tradition of the British Labour movement (Bache and Catney forthcoming). The change of government has thus been important here, but is not the only explanatory factor. Alongside this has been a process of learning and accepting the principle of partnership in general terms and, in some contexts, the centrality of the voluntary and community sector to the process of development. Understanding the detail of how the learning process has taken place is difficult. Many of the actors involved in the domestic implementation networks for EU urban and regional policies were also involved in the networks for British urban and regional policies. The scope for learning is obvious, but this was a process of mutual learning. As the discussion above has suggested, this is true both in relation to the exchange of ideas over the principles of local development governance and also how this was implemented in practice. The result was an ongoing process of action, learning, and feedback into policy design and implementation.

CONCLUSION

In the period discussed above, Britain went from being a hesitant implementer of EU cohesion policy requirements to being a leading light in relation to some key principles. Interviews with Commission officials revealed a consensus that, in relation to partnership in particular, Britain had become a model for other member states to follow.[8] The period saw the further development of type II structures, particularly at the local and sublocal level, both for EU cohesion policy purposes and for domestic initiatives also. The potential for the type II arrangements being transformed into type I structures through the creation of directly elected regional assemblies was not realized following the "no vote" for this in the North East in November 2004.[9] However, type II arrangements moved closer to type I governance as an increasing number of competences were bundled together at the regional level.[10]

Ironically, though, while the Labour government embraced some key principles of EU cohesion policy that strengthened horizontal governance in particular, it also demonstrated discomfort with other principles that might have strengthened further the vertical dimension of multilevel governance. Reluctance to devolve responsibility over the implementation of additionality remained the most obvious case in point.

Given the Treasury's historic hostility on the additionality issue, it is perhaps not surprising that it was this government department that led the British call for a partial renationalization of EU cohesion policy in the negotiations leading up to the 2006 reform of the structural funds. Although the document outlining the arguments for renationalization was published jointly with the DTI and the ODPM,[11] it was the chancellor of the exchequer, Gordon Brown, who took the lead publicly in promoting the arguments it contained. The document acknowledged the need for EU cohesion policy to continue assisting the poorer member states after 2006, but argued that financial transfers should end between the wealthiest member states (i.e., those with an average GNP per capita at greater than 90 percent of the EU average). This would reduce the contributions of the wealthier states who could then redirect the savings toward domestic regional policy measures. The argument put forward was that the English RDAs and the devolved institutions of Scotland and Wales would be given "greater power and flexibility to decide their own priorities ... the best regional policy is now the most decentralised" (Brown 2003, 20). The government's proposals would retain an overarching EU framework that would retain a supranational dimension to local projects, but "Commission regional policy resources would in future be focused on supporting capacity building of institutions and infrastructure in those member states which need it" (Treasury/DTI/ODPM 2003, 28). Moreover, the government was clear that should it be successful in renationalizing its share of structural funding, it would retain the "strengths" of long-term funding and partnership working (Treasury/DTI/ODPM 2003, 29): further evidence of deep learning.

While there was a development rationale for the approach of the British government, it was one that also had echoes of previous Conservative governments' calls for "getting our money back from Brussels." Institutionally, this view has long characterized the position of the Treasury in relation to the EU budget generally and the structural funds specifically. Politically, however, it could be argued that Gordon Brown and other Labour ministers had different purposes for any reimbursed funds than their Conservative predecessors, who did not value interventionist regional development measures in principle. Either way, the British position was ultimately rejected. We return to the most recent developments in cohesion policy in the concluding chapter.

NOTES

1. Although the new institutions of Scotland and Wales took over the day-to-day management of the structural funds in 2000, the Department of Trade and Industry (DTI) retained overall responsibility for the funds in the UK. Government offices (GOs) retained day-to-day management responsibility in the English regions.

2. In the period of 2000–2006, the UK received €16.4 billion, the sixth largest amount in the EU. This compared to €11.04 billion in 1994–1999. Six subregions received objective 1 funding, two of which were in a phasing-out period: Cornwall, Merseyside, South Yorkshire, West Wales and the Valleys, Northern Ireland (transitional), and Highlands and Islands (transitional). In addition, objective 2 funding went to East Midlands, East of England, London, North East, North West, South East, South West, West Midlands, Yorkshire and the Humber, Eastern Scotland, South of Scotland, Western Scotland, East Wales, and Gibraltar (Shutt and Koutsoukos 2004, 2). In addition to these were a number of Community initiative programs.

3. This section draws on research published jointly with Gillian Bristow (Bache and Bristow 2003). I am very grateful to Gillian for allowing me to produce this summary version here.

4. This section draws on interview material from the ESRC-funded research project Implementing EC Regional Policy in the UK: Multi-Level Governance in Action? (grant no. R000222447). This research was conducted jointly with Stephen George. I am grateful to Stephen for allowing me to use some of our material here. For a fuller discussion, see Bache and Jones (2000) and Bache (2004).

5. This would be staffed by individuals from a range of partner organizations and beyond to replace the previous arrangement of administration by the Scottish Office.

6. As noted in the previous chapter, this region was generally referred to as Yorkshire and Humberside until the abolition of the county of Humberside in 1996. From around this time the term Yorkshire and Humber was more widely used.

7. See note 4.

8. One commented, "I have been quite amazed by the strength of the partnership in the UK. It is a highly democratic situation in that all partners are consulted before a decision is made" (DG Regio official 4, interview by author, 2006). Another stated, "My finding is that the UK is a best-practice example in partnership involvement in the developing of preparing a strategy, and in the delivery of the program, plus evaluation of the programs. . . . In my experience, the partnership model really worked" (DG Regio official 2, interview by author, 2006).

9. Labour had planned to hold referendums in each of the three northern regions—the North East, the North West, and Yorkshire and Humberside. However, after the decisive vote to reject elected regional government in the North East—the region deemed most likely to vote "yes"—the planned referendums in the other two regions were canceled.

10. As one interviewee (Regional Assembly official, interview 2006) put it, "We haven't got regional democracy, but regional administration is alive and well. In spite of the North East vote, the regional level is accumulating competences: for example, on rural policy. There's also a regional housing board, transport board, regional planning competences."

11. Treasury/DTI/ODPM 2003.

9

Conclusion

This book has explored the relationship between two concepts—Europeanization and multilevel governance—that are concerned with explaining the transformation of governance in Europe. The main purpose has been to establish whether EU cohesion policy (independent variable) has promoted multilevel governance in Britain and other member states (dependent variable) and, therefore, to assess whether any governance change identified can be characterized as a process of Europeanization. In doing this, a distinction was made between the effects of cohesion policy on the vertical and horizontal dimensions of multilevel governance and these were related to the development of type I multilevel governance (general purpose bodies) and type II multilevel governance (functionally specific bodies). Beyond this, the book sought to identify the important intervening variables facilitating or constraining change. As a general intervening variable, Schmidt's categories of simple and compound polities were employed in the comparative study. This chapter reflects on these questions and also considers two related issues set out in chapter 1: the implications of any changes in governance for the role, power, and authority of the state and the utility of the analytical tools employed.

The structure of the chapter is as follows: the first section considers whether EU cohesion policy has promoted multilevel governance within member states and whether this should be understood as a process of Europeanization. In doing so, it considers developments across both simple and compound polities and discusses the important intervening variables. This section closes with reflection on the significance of developments in Britain, in particular for the role, power, and authority of the central state. Section two of the chapter reflects on the analytical tools of Europeanization and multilevel governance, and the third and concluding section recaps the main findings of the book and raises issues for further investigation.

COHESION POLICY AND MULTILEVEL GOVERNANCE

Has EU cohesion policy promoted multilevel governance within Britain and other member states and should this be understood as a process of Europeanization? The simple answer to this question is yes. But this answer comes with a number of important qualifications about the process and nature of change.

The first thing to state is that while various aspects of EU cohesion policy may have been "uploaded" from different member states at different times, the overall policy framework set in 1989 was heavily influenced by the Commission and was distinctly European. Moreover, those aspects of this framework most relevant to the development of multilevel governance—the prominence of regional objectives, the partnership principle, and the programming requirement—remained in place throughout the period investigated here (1989–2006).[1] Thus, any domestic effects arising from this policy should be understood as a process of Europeanization in the widely accepted sense of the term as domestic change through EU membership and in specific relation to the definition adopted here of Europeanization as "the reorientation or reshaping of politics in the domestic arena in ways that reflect policies, practices, or preferences advanced through the EU system of governance" (chapter 2).

Second, in understanding multilevel governance as a process of Europeanization, much needs to be unpacked, as will be done below. At this stage, though, there is one important observation to make: that we can now speak about the promotion of multilevel *governance* through Europeanization rather than multilevel *government*. It was a reasonable criticism of the first wave of studies in this field that the concept of multilevel governance was developed at a time when there was little evidence of changes in horizontal relations within states and, indeed, this was not the main focus of the relevant research. Thus, the Hooghe (1996a) study addressed specifically the impact of cohesion policy on territorial relations, and in comparing member states distinguished between federal and unitary states as the main intervening variable. While some effects were found, the conclusion to the study cautioned against expecting to find dramatic institutional change resulting so soon after the introduction of cohesion policy (Marks 1996, 413–14). Over a decade later, we can come to firmer conclusions, particularly in relation to those states that were members when cohesion policy was introduced in 1989. Moreover, we can now speak of horizontal as well as vertical effects. In adopting this dual focus, the multidimensional simple or compound polity distinction provides a more relevant broad intervening variable for the comparative analysis than the federal-unitary state categorization used in this earlier study. Complementary to this conceptual refinement, the distinction between type I and type II multilevel governance provides greater clarity for categorizing change arising from greater vertical and/or horizontal interaction and interdependence (below).

Comparing Simple and Compound Polities

In relation to the simple or compound polity distinction, the evidence from cohesion policy is broadly in line with Schmidt's (2006, 63) argument that while the EU generally enhances interest-based, consensus politics across its member states, it has "tended to put more of a damper on the more highly polarized, politically charged politics of the majoritarian representation systems of simple polities than on the more consensus-oriented (albeit partisan) politics typical of the proportional systems of more compound polities." The greater misfit with simple polities has meant that, generally speaking, the EU's impact on these states has been greatest. However, there have been effects on both vertical and horizontal relations across Europe.

While cohesion policy has mobilized actors and influenced processes below the regional level, the most prominent vertical effect across the EU is the strengthening of the regional tier through the requirement for regional administrative processes. Yet while regional structures have been developed as a condition of funding in even the most centralized states, it is important to recognize the limits to what the EU can achieve in producing transformative domestic change. The EU can create statistical regions and restructure opportunities within the domestic arena, but real shifts toward greater regional autonomy must also have a powerful domestic imperative. Moreover, in smaller member states, promotion of the regional tier has not been a consistent feature of the Commission's approach to cohesion policy (chapter 5). In terms of horizontal effects, EU cohesion policy has generally advanced cross-sectoral engagement and interdependence through the requirements of partnership and programming.

In all cases of change, across both vertical and horizontal dimensions, understanding specific domestic factors beyond the broad simple/compound distinction is the key to understanding the timing, tempo, and nature of change. As Schmidt (2006, 232) acknowledged, the typologies of simple and compound polities are broad and exceptions to the general rules of this distinction should be expected and were found here. Thus, Germany experienced greater problems accepting the EU's approach to partnership than the broad distinction might suggest, and there was evidence of some horizontal change even in the statist polities such as Greece, Portugal, and Spain. Moreover, there were important variations not only across states, but also within them, depending on different regional circumstances (e.g., the level of formal institutional development, the cohesiveness of policy networks, or the prominence of political entrepreneurship). However, a common thread was that the longer the period of engagement with cohesion policy, the greater the likelihood of thick learning taking place.

Learning

It is clear that EU policies provided pressures (and incentives) for changes in domestic governance, but there is also plenty of evidence in relation to the EU15 in the period up to the mid-1990s that most of the changes introduced were superficial and that established power relations survived the surface changes. If there was learning in this period, it was of the "thin" type—that is, a readjustment of the strategies of actors to allow them to achieve the same objectives in a new context. However, from around the mid-1990s—after several years of a relatively stable structural policy framework—there was greater evidence of "thick" learning in the EU15, in which key actors involved changed their goals and preferences. This was evident in the transference of lessons drawn from EU policies into domestic policies (chapters 7 and 8).

The relationship between time and learning is not straightforward and is shaped by a number of other factors. These include the political will of domestic actors to embrace the EU policies, the institutional capacity to implement the policies, and the amount of funding available as an incentive for domestic actors to respond to the EU's requirements. Based on the evidence presented in chapters 5 to 8, it is reasonable to claim that the process of learning is initially strategic and only becomes deeper over time and according to other variables.

An important variable in this regard was scale of funding. This was illustrated in the comparative study of two English regions (chapter 8), which held as constant the broader political and institutional context. The evidence suggested that the greater the financial stakes for the region, the higher the number of actors involved, the denser the networks, and the greater the incentive for cooperation.

Yet large-scale funding alone does not promote thick learning. Evidence of thick learning in even the neediest regions in the first structural-fund programming period after 1989 was scarce, as was evidence of thick learning

within the 2004 entrants. Thick learning occurred when and where key domestic actors were persuaded that the benefits of adopting the principles that
underlay cohesion policy outweighed the costs.[2] In particular, the principle
of partnership is one that state leaders have learned to trust and mobilize for
their own purposes.[3] If this means that control is lost at the margins, the
overall gains are seen as greater. That a rationalist logic still comes into play
is evident not only in explaining why some EU principles have been accepted over time, but also why some are obstructed. Thus, the British Treasury remains yet to be persuaded of the benefits of the additionality principle (see chapter 7).

A final aspect to understanding the learning process may be specific to the
nature of the policy area. EU cohesion policy has placed a great emphasis on
monitoring and evaluation as an important part of the policy process and this
has been seen as an important cause of innovation. The monitoring and evaluation requirements have promoted analysis and reflection in relation to
agreed objectives and targets. As Bachtler and Taylor (2003, 40) have argued,
"monitoring provides management information on an ongoing basis, while
regular evaluation feeds in more substantive reflection on impact and strategic direction. Both activities generate a flow of feedback which helps to inform the steering of the programmes. In this way, a culture of learning becomes integral to the Structural Funds."

Analyzing Developments in Britain

The importance of going beyond the broad structural categorizations of simple and compound polities was amply illustrated by the study of Britain. In
the period under observation (1989–2006), the British polity experienced profound change to the extent that it was increasingly described as a system of
multilevel governance (chapter 6). Some of these changes were formal and
high profile, such as political devolution to Scotland and Wales, while others
were more informal and lower profile, such as the proliferation of agencies,
networks, and partnerships. While these changes have been widely documented there has been no attempt before now to distinguish between two
types of multilevel governance emerging in Britain and to relate these developments to the process of European integration generally or to EU cohesion
policy specifically. In short, Europeanization through cohesion policy is evident in both vertical and horizontal changes that promoted type II multilevel
governance at the level of the region and below.

The main effect of cohesion policy on vertical relations in Britain was its
role in the revival of the English regional tier in the period 1989–1997. As

discussed in chapter 7, the structural funds reinforced the "standard regions" as the official boundaries for the English regional tier, created regional networks, and gave momentum to the creation of the integrated government offices (GOs) that subsequently served to strengthen the regional dimension further. This effect meant that when Labour came to power in 1997 it had much more to build on in developing the English regions than it would have had otherwise. It did not need to have arguments about the definitions of regional boundaries, or create regional networks, or generate from nothing the support of regional elite actors for its plans.

In relation to the horizontal dimension, change occurred gradually. Partnership was not new to Britain in 1989 and its development has been driven by a range of factors (below). However, the EU partnership requirement (alongside programming) had a number of effects. Very directly, it promoted partnership as a mode of governance in Britain through providing financial incentives for domestic actors to collaborate across sectors (and levels). Of particular note, cohesion policy helped to break down barriers within local government to partnership working. The effect of this was that local governments were more inclined to work in partnership in other (domestic) policy areas, promoting more flexible type II arrangements across local governance. This occurred at the level of the individual local authority, but also increased interlocal cooperation at the subregional level (e.g., South Yorkshire, Merseyside, and Cornwall; see chapter 8). In the longer term, the partnership principle helped to generate a norm of inclusion of a wide range of organizations in public decision making. A feature of this inclusiveness of the EU partnership approach was the promotion of the role of the voluntary and community sector in local decision making. This again spilled over into domestic policies, further enhancing type II multilevel governance (chapters 7 and 8).

The Diversity of Traditions and Ideas in British Politics

On the surface, there is a high degree of misfit between the compound polity requirements of EU cohesion policy and the simple British polity. However, the detailed study revealed a high level of resonance between aspects of the EU's approach to cohesion policy with past practices and periodically marginalized but nevertheless constantly present ideas within British politics. This relates to both vertical and horizontal dimensions.

In relation to the vertical dimension, it is important to emphasize the influence of the EU on the *revival* of the English regional tier, rather than on its creation. The EU's policies had built on the boundaries (standard regions), ideas (regional planning), and aspirations (interregional redistribution) that had precedents in domestic policies in the earlier postwar period (chapter 6). In the language of historical institutionalism, the 1989 reform of the structural funds should properly be understood as a critical juncture in this revival.

In relation to the horizontal dimension, while the Conservative governments had a clear approach to partnership that did not include trade unions, trade union participation in public decision making had been the norm in the postwar period up to the election of the Conservatives in 1979. Moreover, much of what cohesion policy aimed to do reflected and connected to a social democratic tradition that was strongest in those British regions that it was trying to assist: traditional industrial areas (chapter 7). Thus, despite apparently strong dissimilarities at first blush, the inclusive, cooperative, and redistributive aspirations of EU cohesion policy were actually a good fit with the values of many of the constituencies in Britain that it sought to serve.

Similarly, the EU's approach to bottom-up decision making had precedents in Labour government policies of the 1960s and in traditions of Labour thought (chapter 8). Indeed, even in the encouragement of cooperation at the subregional level, the EU was far from starting from scratch. In the cases of Merseyside and South Yorkshire, discussed above, metropolitan authorities had covered these territories until being abolished by the Thatcher governments in the 1980s, and even in this decade there were some residual structures (e.g., for emergency services). In relation to Cornwall, the EU's coverage mapped onto a historic county with which there is a strong sense of identity.

In short, EU cohesion policy contributed to a revival of both the regional tier and of a loose neocorporatism, exactly the types of developments the Thatcher governments feared would be brought back into Britain through the "back door" of Brussels. Yet ironically, without the Thatcher governments' exclusion of a broad range of interests from public policy making, its reductions in domestic regional policy expenditure, and its tendency toward political centralization, this revival would have been far less likely. It was the very marginalization of important social democratic constituencies in this period—in local government, the trade unions, and the voluntary and community sector—that intensified domestic receptiveness for what EU cohesion policy sought to achieve. As one former Labour council leader of the 1980s and 1990s later put it, "in the 1980s we turned to Europe because there was nowhere left to turn" (interview by author, 2003).

Moreover, under the leadership of Tony Blair, Labour's shift away from class-based politics (incorporated in the idea of *New* Labour) signaled an attempt to move away from the traditional adversarial style and majoritarian system of British politics, and provided greater consonance with EU norms of pluralism and consensualism. In relation to this shift, too, the years of Conservative government played an important role. As Gamble (2003, 228) argued, "One of Thatcher's most enduring achievements was to transform the Labour Party, forcing the party to end the pretence that it was seriously committed to extending socialism through centralized state control."

Thus, part of the understanding of change in this case rests on an appreciation of the diversity of traditions and ideas within British politics and how EU policies connect or "fit" with these differently. It is equally important to recognize that the influence of these traditions and ideas is not static but informs the position of key actors within institutions differently over time. This is most obvious when the governing party changes.

The Significance of Emerging Multilevel Governance in Britain

While EU cohesion policy has made a distinct contribution to emerging multilevel governance in Britain, the overall effects on the British polity to date should not be overstated. The English regions have undoubtedly been strengthened in the past two decades and there is evidence that the structural funds have played an important role in this. However, English regional governance remains relatively weak within the UK's constitutional arrangements, not least in comparison to the devolved institutions of Scotland and Wales. As such, despite shifts toward multilevel governance, the UK state remains "highly unitary," with 85 percent of the population remaining centrally governed (Schmidt 2006, 86). Thus, while Britain may be understood as a *regionalizing* state—that is, one in which the regions have increasing autonomy, but where the central state remains formally unitary and still expects to exercise power over the periphery—it still has some way to go before it can genuinely be described as *regionalized* in the same sense as Spain (chapter 1). The idea of elected general-purpose bodies for the English regions is an idea whose time has not yet come (chapter 6). On this type I issue, there is an interesting point of contrast with the proliferation of type II multilevel governance and task-specific partnership governance in particular, an idea whose time *has* clearly arrived and which is now an established part of the landscape of British politics at the regional level and below. Here, the EU's cohesion policy has played a key role in promoting the role of nonstate actors.

In summary, Britain is increasingly characterized by multilevel governance: vertical interdependence has increased significantly, since the mid-1990s in particular, and horizontal interdependence has similarly increased, particularly at the subnational level. Moreover, there is evidence that the EU cohesion policy has played a role in promoting these developments. Its effects on type I multilevel governance are less pronounced than on type II, but are nonetheless discernible in both cases. While these Europeanization effects are distinct, they should not be exaggerated either in comparison with domestic explanations, or in terms of their impact on the redistribution of power. Most commentators would argue that while the nature of British governance is changing, the state remains more than first among equals in the context of multilevel governance. This paradox demands clarity in our understanding of the notion of multilevel governance.

THE ANALYTICAL TOOLS

Europeanization

The starting point for the Europeanization framework that was developed in chapter 2 was the three-step approach developed by Risse, Cowles, and Caporaso (2001). This framework was subsequently adapted to highlight the nature, precision, and status of EU requirements and their goodness of fit with member states; the potential importance of Europeanization as a dynamic or circular process involving repeated interactions between the EU and individual states (as well as a top-down process of change); the potential importance of non-EU factors in explaining change; and the inclusion of a test variable to find if in-depth change has occurred in behavior.

The Force and Fit of EU Requirements

While the requirements of cohesion policy were contained within the governing regulations for a sustained period of time and were legally binding, their wording generally left much room for interpretation. Notable domestic examples of this were the role of member states in shaping the role and influence of different partners within partnership arrangements and in the interpretation of the additionality principle. Equally important was how the Commission appeared to view the requirements differently in different contexts, particularly in the run-up to the 2004 enlargement (chapter 6). In this sense, the "force" of the EU's requirements was inherently situational.

The notion of "goodness of fit" provided a useful point of departure in relation to understanding the varying degrees of adaptational pressure on member states from cohesion policy. However, as a conceptual tool, the "goodness of fit" notion is relatively static: over time a state can move from a position of relative misfit to relative fit (or vice versa) in relation to the EU. This fluidity of "fit" is well illustrated by the contrast between Britain and Germany.

Whereas the fit between British governance and politics and those of the EU has moved closer in the recent past, Germany has been seen to move in the opposite direction, with a "breakdown" in the goodness of fit caused by "new adaptational pressures rooted in wider dynamics of change in both domestic and EU politics" (Jeffery 2003, 98). Moreover, there is also a need to be cautious in treating fit or misfit as something that can be easily measured. Even a cursory examination of debates in British politics would reveal differences in the way in which the idea of "fit/misfit" with the EU is politically constructed in the domestic arena (see Geddes 2004). Finally, there is greater scope for learning than the goodness of fit idea suggests. The notion of "adaptational pressure" arising from misfit implies a degree of coercion that understates the importance of learning in the process of Europeanization, particularly in the later phase of the period considered here (above).

Top-down and Circular Dynamics

Modeling for top-down processes in this study was valuable in that, while there was evidence of uploading from member states, the policy framework remained broadly stable from 1989 and the requirements from this point on were effectively "coming down" from the EU level. However, keeping the analytical framework open to consideration of two-way or circular dynamics was important in identifying the role of member states in uploading specific ideas and practices to the EU level that had a subsequent effect on their reception within the domestic context. This was true not only of specific ideas uploaded to the framework agreed in 1989, such as programming (France), but also about refinements to the conception of partnership that were subsequently developed, such as the emphasis on the voluntary and community sector, which came out of experiments in Britain. As one Commission official put it, "These things feed on each other. It is not as if the Commission invented these principles from nowhere: they came from member states' experiences and the UK's experience has obviously fed into the regulations for the structural funds and then the application of the regulations has obviously reinforced these ideas within the UK. So there are feedback loops that work in both directions" (DG Enlargement official 1, interview by author, 2006).

Non-Europeanization

In chapter 2 it was acknowledged that a reasonable criticism of research on Europeanization was that those looking for it tend to find it.[4] Consequently, the conceptual framework that was developed modeled explicitly for consideration of non-EU effects in explaining the emerging pattern of multilevel governance in Britain and elsewhere. It has been argued here that the EU has shifted its member (and accession) states closer to its own image, but it is also clear that Europeanization is not the only explanation for trends toward multilevel governance across Europe.

Increasingly, there is no easy separation to be made between domestic, EU, and international drivers of change, with governance change generally taking place in the "shadow of the market" (Kohler-Koch 1999, 31). In this context there are global trends of neoliberal decentralization and destatization. Thus, while there has been a public reform program in Britain since the early 1980s that has proliferated multilevel governance (chapter 6), these domestic policies cannot be understood without reference to global economic changes. Further, the process of European integration itself has a complex relationship with economic globalization. A result of these complex interrelated processes has been a challenge to traditional forms of the state, which are seen as too small to deal adequately with the challenges of a globalizing economy and too big and inflexible to deal with the differing needs of diverse local communities (Benington 2001, 209). Thus, the first explanation for the emergence of partnership and other forms of type II multilevel governance relates to their relatively greater flexibility, compared to either markets or hierarchies, to respond to broad changes in international political economy.

Yet while it is important to understand that partnership as a mode of governance is driven by the logic of contemporary political economy, this does not explain the particular approach to partnership promoted by the EU. This is explained by a combination of social democratic ideas and the prevailing wisdom on the most effective way to deliver social and economic development. Moreover, a separate set of analytical tools is needed to understand how this supranational approach is then mediated in different states and their regions, tools drawn from the new institutionalisms and the policy networks approach. It is not the purpose of this study to focus on the links between these tools and macro theories of political economy, but simply to highlight here some important non-EU sources of change that promote multilevel governance and, in doing so, to place Europeanization effects in the context of other international and domestic drivers for change.

The Test Variable

As discussed in chapter 2, the purpose of including a test variable in the analytical framework was to isolate evidence of in-depth change. In this case, the test variable for indicating deep Europeanization was evidence of EU policies, practices, and preferences being voluntarily applied by domestic actors to domestic policies and practices as a result of their preferences changing through engagement with the EU. Moreover, given that the dependent variable here is multilevel governance, deep Europeanization of this type would display related characteristics.

The incorporation of a test variable was useful in distinguishing between the type of multilevel governance through Europeanization that is strategic and procedural—for example, the creation of regional-level partnerships to ensure continued EU funding—and multilevel governance through Europeanization that has been embraced and becomes embedded—for example, the creation of partnerships for domestic policy programs. The other examples of deeper change where there is a distinct EU influence relate primarily to ongoing regionalization and continued experiments with bottom-up approaches to policy making, notwithstanding the arguments above about the domestic antecedents of some of these policies and the other drivers of change.

Multilevel Governance

As a concept multilevel governance has been criticized for its failure to distinguish between governance and participation (or dialogue). In chapter 3 it was suggested that missing from the debate so far has been the identification of empirical indicators that tell us whether what we are witnessing is governance or participation: to paraphrase Radaelli (2003, 38), the need to locate the "fence" that separates the two. It was argued that the essential difference between the two concepts is that participation refers to engagement in decision-making processes, while governance implies engagement that involves influence over the outcomes of these processes. Thus, the empirical fence is whether or not participants influence decision making. In terms of linking Europeanization to multilevel governance, the key indicator is whether EU policies, practices, and preferences increase the influence of subnational and nonstate actors, either by redistributing resources in their favor (rationalist explanation) or by reshaping the preferences of domestic actors (reflectivist explanation); the effect in both cases is that influence over decision making and its outcomes becomes more diffuse.

To assist in this empirical investigation, the tools of the policy networks approach were included as a conceptual bridge between Europeanization and multilevel governance. In its early manifestations the Rhodes model adopted a predominantly rationalist approach, but the reflectivist arguments relating to the model were subsequently strengthened. In rationalist terms, cohesion policy has strengthened the resources of subnational and nonstate actors within the domestic arena—informational, through bringing them into decision-making arenas and giving them access to knowledge; constitutional-legal, through their status as recognized policy actors in EU regulations; political, by acknowledgment of their legitimate role in development policies as actors close to the ground (local authorities and community actors) or through their sectoral expertise and representation (trade unions and nongovernmental organizations); and financial, by giving them access to EU funding. It is, as a result, widely recognized across the British regions and within the EU institutions that control over decision making within regional partnerships has gradually become more dispersed (chapters 7 and 8). However, while this has involved some redistribution of power resources, it has also involved a process of learning, within which the process of decision making and actors' conceptions of power have changed as the networks have taken on characteristics of policy communities.

In short, neither the rationalist nor the reflectivist perspective alone explains the process of Europeanization. The process is most pronounced where there is a convergence over time of domestic and EU actors' preferences, partly through the interaction of these actors in territorial overarching policy networks. This is true in relation to changes in both the vertical and horizontal dimensions of multilevel governance.

Multilevel Governance and the Role of the State

Understanding the changes taking place within domestic politics as emerging multilevel governance, with its emphasis on how informal and disorderly governance relates to and overlays orderly and formal governance, brings into focus a different set of questions about the mechanisms, strategies, and tactics through which decisions are made in contemporary politics, not least those employed by the central state. This presents a paradox when multilevel governance is seen to be emerging in a unitary state such as Britain, but it is important to acknowledge that multilevel governance should not be equated with the argument that the state is in the process of irreversible decline or even that state power is necessarily undermined. Rather, it should be understood as a challenge to the role, authority, and perhaps nature of the state, but a challenge that in some circumstances at least might be met.

That this point is often misunderstood may point to a weakness in the literature on governance generally, the lack of specification in the concept, and, in particular, how it relates to power. There is no easy solution to this problem, although a starting point may be at least to classify governance not only in relation to types, but also in relation to the degree of interdependence between actors. Referring to the discussion above, the question of governance

Figure 9.1.   Governance and interdependence

or participation is one of substance, a question of whether actors are interdependent or simply interconnected. Drawing on the tools of the policy networks approach, one way of understanding this is to place governance and participation on a continuum of power dependence. For the sake of simplicity, participation is here equated with weak governance (see figure 9.1).

From a rationalist perspective, degrees of interdependence explain the extent and nature of interaction between state and nonstate actors at different territorial levels. To relate this argument to multilevel governance, it is necessary to distinguish between horizontal and vertical dimensions. Strong multilevel governance has both high vertical and high horizontal interdependence, while weak multilevel governance may be high on one dimension, but should have at least some interdependence along both dimensions (see table 9.1).

In empirical terms, the way to measure whether interdependence is strong or weak is to identify the influence of different actors on policy outcomes, and in doing so to focus both on routine decision making and on the critical cases where there is much at stake and where the underlying distribution of power is often most clearly revealed. The history of additionality in Britain is one such critical case that highlighted the successful resistance to change by the government (chapters 7 and 8). Strong multilevel governance will be characterized by a high degree of dispersal of influence over outcomes.

This characterization does not of course account for learning. While learning does not depend on the preexistence of high levels of vertical and/or horizontal interdependence, it clearly accelerates through interaction. Thus, for this reason, the emergence of weak multilevel governance can be important

Table 9.1.   Strong and weak multilevel governance

	Vertical Interdependence		*Horizontal Interdependence*
Strong multilevel governance	High	and	High
Weak multilevel governance	Medium-high	and	Low-medium
		OR	
	Low-medium	and	Medium-high

in generating change in policy outcomes through learning, which does not necessarily result from nor lead to a redistribution of power resources, but may result from a reconceptualization of how power is understood and therefore used. Here the case of regional partnerships in Britain is most instructive, with the case of the changing role played by civil servants in Yorkshire and Humberside particularly so (chapters 7 and 8).

In this book, there is evidence of Europeanization both through the redistribution of power resources and through the process of learning. In the case of Britain, there is evidence both that the state has managed to retain control over key power resources in the context of emerging multilevel governance and of a change in some state preferences that suggests validity in the argument that state actors have sought to address "a strategic alternative to zero-sum power struggles, directed towards building new frames for intergovernmental consensus" (Gualini 2003, 619). It is important not to overstate this case: much tension remains between the central state and substate and nonstate actors. Over time though, there is evidence in relation to EU cohesion policy of a shift away from a bargaining mentality to one of problem-solving and positive-sum outcomes. This is not to claim problem solving as the dominant characteristic of partnership in Britain even in relation to cohesion policy. However, there has been a perceptible change in this direction since 1989, when partnership across the board (with the possible exception of Western Scotland) was characterized by distrust, hard bargaining, and zero-sum conceptions of power. In relation to this, as Paraskevopoulos (2001, 260) suggested, the norm of generalized reciprocity is important, based on "a continuing relationship of exchange involving mutual expectations that a benefit granted now should be repaid in future." Here, the principle of programming is important in locking in actors over a substantial time period, usually six years, to create a linked range of issues that can transform zero-sum relations into positive-sum relations.

In short, structural-fund networks in Britain have demonstrated the capacity to generate social capital that facilitates collective action and learning. However, on different issues and across different parts of the core executive there are different responses to EU cohesion policy. Partnership is increasingly accepted as positive-sum, while control over public expenditure is considered zero-sum. The Treasury's determination to keep a firm hold of the financial purse strings in the emerging multilevel polity provides evidence of this.

In other words, there is a need to place the view that multilevel governance equals decline of state power alongside the understanding that multilevel governance can lead not only to new state strategies based on rational calculations, but may also reflect the reshaping of state preferences. Viewed in this way, multilevel governance draws attention not only to the distribution of various types of power resources, but also to how power is both conceived and exercised differently by the same actors in different circumstances and by different actors within the same institutions. This understanding offers part of the explanation for why states behave differently in different contexts. On this point, it may be helpful to incorporate Sabatier's (1987) ideas about the structure of beliefs—deep core, near core, and secondary—to provide a more nuanced understanding of when learning is likely to take place. In this view,

> policy-oriented learning is . . . the process of seeking to realize core beliefs until one confronts constraints or opportunities, at which time one attempts to respond to this new situation in a manner that is consistent with the core. Although exogenous events or opponents' activities may eventually force the re-examination of core beliefs, the pain of doing so means that learning occurs most in secondary aspects of a belief system or governmental action programme. (Sabatier 1987, 675)

Economic geographers have long argued that regions that collaborate gain a competitive advantage: the idea of the "learning" region (Morgan 1997). The findings of this book suggest that alongside the notion of the learning region, we should place the notion of the "learning state" to emphasize the interaction between interests and ideas in the process of change at the heart of emerging multilevel governance.

BEYOND THE TRIADIC DYNAMIC

The approach developed in the opening chapters of this book combined institutions, interests, and ideas in a framework that used policy networks to link Europeanization and multilevel governance. This framework identified the importance of both institutional interests and the private preferences of actors within institutions in advancing the shift toward multilevel governance across Europe.

The pattern of change is inevitably uneven across and within states, and domestic factors are central to understanding how EU requirements are refracted differently in different contexts. The argument developed is not that the emerging patterns of multilevel governance in Britain and elsewhere are due primarily to engagement with the EU, but that it is not possible to understand fully the nature and pace of change in domestic governance without reference to the EU, and EU cohesion policy specifically has had distinct contributory effects in Britain and elsewhere, providing momentum for change and shaping its direction.

Both in Britain and elsewhere, though, the effects on type II multilevel governance are more pronounced than on type I, with EU cohesion policy proliferating ad hoc and functionally specific governance arrangements at various territorial levels involving a diverse mix of actors. However, there has been a reinforcement of type I governance at the regional level through cohesion policy in some cases and the development of type II arrangements at the regional level and below in a number of states where little or nothing previously existed. Moreover, while the governance structures that were promoted were often established instrumentally in the first phase of cohesion policy, there is evidence in a number of cases that what began as a strategic response led to a deeper transformation in actor preferences over time. The most obvious example here is the acceptance of multilevel and cross-sectoral partnerships as part of the institutional architecture in states where this was a novel or underdeveloped mode of governance before the emergence of cohesion policy.

Moreover, the study of Britain revealed that these shifts not only involved the strengthening of the regional tier, as has been observed in previous research, but also suggest that the predominant focus of previous research on the regional tier has obscured other important governance effects of cohesion policy, both vertical and horizontal. This is important in taking the debate on cohesion policy and multilevel governance beyond the typical focus on the "triadic dynamic" between regions, nations, and the EU institutions, to highlight a less orderly and more complex reality both across and within European states. Further, the distinction between type I and type II multilevel governance highlights how informal and disorderly governance relates to orderly and formal governance. Understanding this relationship is important, but in future research it will be important to link these insights more closely to debates on the distribution of power to strengthen the theoretical dimension of the multilevel governance concept, so that it asks not only who participates, but also who decides and who benefits. This would connect the debate on Europeanization and multilevel governance more directly to wider debates on the nature and exercise of power beyond the state and through increasingly complex sets of social relations.

NOTES

1. These requirements remained in place for the programming period 2007–2013 also.

2. Bachtler and Taylor (2003, 22) spoke of how the cohesion policy provided a "powerful demonstration effect and played an influential role in the change of 'paradigm' among national regional policies in many parts of the EU."

3. Of course, this is not to claim that partnership does not also create problems. There are many examples of where partnership working is not efficient, duplicates activity, and wastes resources. Moreover, policy makers have been known to complain of "partnership fatigue" (see Kelleher, Batterbury, and Stern 1999, 145).

4. Although similar criticisms might also be made about much research starting from either a "domestic" or an "international" politics perspective.

References

Aalberts, T. 2004. The Future of Sovereignty in a Multilevel Governance Europe—A Constructivist Reading. *Journal of Common Market Studies* 42 (1): 23–46.

Adshead, M. 2002. *Developing European Regions? Comparative Governance, Policy Networks and European Integration.* Aldershot, England: Ashgate.

Adshead, M., and I. Bache. 2000. Developing European Regions? Unity and Diversity in the New Europe. Paper presented to the Annual Conference of the Political Studies Association of Ireland, Cork, October 13–15.

Albers, D., ed. 1992. European Trade Unions' Regional Policy—A Comparative Summary. Final report, phase 1, for the EC Commission, DG XVI. Bremen: University of Bremen, May.

Allen, D. 2000. Cohesion and the Structural Funds: Transfers and Trade-offs. In *Policy-making in the European Union,* 4th ed., ed. H. Wallace and W. Wallace, 243–66. Oxford: Oxford University Press.

Allen, D., and T. Oliver. 2006. The Foreign and Commonwealth Office. In *The Europeanization of British Politics,* ed. I. Bache and A. Jordan, 52–66. Basingstoke: Palgrave Macmillan.

Anderson, J. 1990. Skeptical Reflections on a Europe of Regions: Britain, Germany, and the ERDF. *Journal of Public Policy* 10:417–47.

Anderson, J. 1996. Germany and the Structural Funds: Unification Leads to Bifurcation. In *Cohesion Policy and European Integration: Building Multi-level Governance*, ed. L. Hooghe, 163–94. Oxford: Oxford University Press.

Andreou, G. 2006. EU Cohesion Policy in Greece: Patterns of Governance and Europeanization. *South European Society and Politics* 11 (2): 241–60.

Armstrong, H., and P. Wells. 2006. Structural Funds and the Evaluation of Community Economic Development Initiatives in the UK: A Critical Perspective. *Regional Studies* 40 (2): 259–72.

Bache, I. 1996. EU Regional Policy: Has the UK Government Succeeded in Playing the Gatekeeper Role over the Domestic Impact of the European Regional

Development Fund? Unpublished PhD thesis, Department of Politics, University of Sheffield.

Bache, I. 1998. *The Politics of European Union Regional Policy: Multi-level Governance or Flexible Gatekeeping?* Contemporary European Studies Series. Sheffield: UACES/Sheffield Academic Press.

Bache, I. 1999. The Extended Gatekeeper: Central Government and the Implementation of EC Regional Policy in the UK. *Journal of European Public Policy* 6 (1): 28–45.

Bache, I. 2000. Government within Governance: Steering Economic Regeneration Policy Networks in Yorkshire and Humberside. *Public Administration* 78 (3): 575–92.

Bache, I. 2001. Different Seeds in the Same Plot? Competing Models of Capitalism and the Incomplete Contracts of Partnership Design. *Public Administration* 79 (2): 337–59.

Bache, I. 2003. Governing through Governance: Education Policy Control under New Labour. *Political Studies* 51 (2): 300–14.

Bache, I. 2004. Multi-level Governance and European Union Regional Policy. In *Multi-level Governance*, ed. I. Bache and M. Flinders, 165–78. Oxford: Oxford University Press.

Bache, I. 2006. The Politics of Redistribution. In *Handbook of European Union Politics*, ed. K. Jorgensen, M. Pollack, and B. Rosamond, 395–412. London: Sage.

Bache, I. 2007. Cohesion Policy. In *Europeanization: New Research Agendas*, ed. P. Graziano and M. Vink, 239–52. Basingstoke: Palgrave Macmillan.

Bache, I., and G. Bristow. 2003. Devolution and the Core Executive: The Struggle for European Funds. *British Journal of Politics and International Relations* 5 (3): 405–27.

Bache, I., and P. Catney. Forthcoming. Embryonic Associationalism: New Labour and Urban Governance. *Public Administration.*

Bache, I., and M. Flinders. 2004a. Multi-level Governance and the Study of British Politics and Government. *Public Policy and Administration* 19 (1): 31–52.

Bache, I., and M. Flinders. 2004b. Multi-level Governance and British Politics. In *Multi-level Governance*, ed. I. Bache and M. Flinders, 93–106. Oxford: Oxford University Press.

Bache, I., and M. Flinders. 2004c. Conclusions and Implications. In *Multi-level Governance*, ed. I. Bache and M. Flinders, 195–206. Oxford: Oxford University Press.

Bache, I., and S. George. 2000. *Administering the Structural Funds: Multi-level Governance in Action?* Sheffield: University of Sheffield.

Bache, I., and S. George. 2006. *Politics in the European Union.* 2nd ed. Oxford: Oxford University Press.

Bache, I., S. George, and R. A. W. Rhodes. 1996. Cohesion Policy and Subnational Authorities in the UK. In *Cohesion Policy and European Integration*, ed. L. Hooghe, 294–319. Oxford: Oxford University Press.

Bache, I., and R. Jones. 2000. Has EU Regional Policy Empowered the Regions? A Study of Spain and the United Kingdom. *Regional and Federal Studies* 10:1–20.

Bache, I., and A. Jordan, eds. 2006a. *The Europeanization of British Politics?* Basingstoke: Palgrave Macmillan.

Bache, I., and A. Jordan. 2006b. Introduction. In *The Europeanization of British Politics*, ed. I. Bache and A. Jordan, 3–16. Basingstoke: Palgrave Macmillan.

Bache, I., and A. Jordan. 2006c. Europeanization and Domestic Change. In *The Europeanization of British Politics*, ed. I. Bache and A. Jordan, 17–36. Basingstoke: Palgrave Macmillan.

Bache, I., and A. Jordan. 2006d. The Europeanization of British Politics? Comparative Conclusions. In *The Europeanization of British Politics*, ed. I. Bache and A. Jordan, 265–179. Basingstoke: Palgrave Macmillan.

Bache, I., and A. Marshall. 2004. Europeanisation and Domestic Change: A Governance Approach to Institutional Adaptation in Britain. Europeanisation Online Papers No. 5/2004, Queen's University, Belfast. www.qub.ac.uk/schools/SchoolofPolitics InternationalStudies/Research/PaperSeries/EuropeanisationPapers/PublishedPapers.

Bache, I., and J. Mitchell. 1999. Globalisation and UK Regions: The Prospects for Constituent Democracy. Paper presented to the ECPR Annual Conference, Workshop 23 (Regionalism Revisited), Mannheim, Germany, March 26–31.

Bache, I., and J. Olsson. 2001. Legitimacy through Partnership? EU Policy Diffusion in Britain and Sweden. *Scandinavian Political Studies* 24:215–37.

Bachtler, J., and S. Taylor. 2003. *The Added Value of the Structural Funds: A Regional Perspective: IQ-Net Report on the Reform of the Structural Funds*. Glasgow: European Policies Research Centre, University of Strathclyde.

Bailey, D., and L. De Propris. 2002. EU Structural Funds, Regional Capabilities and Enlargement: Towards Multi-level Governance? *Journal of European Integration* 24:303–24.

Balme, R., and B. Jouve. 1996. Building the Regional State: Europe and Territorial Organization in France. In *Cohesion Policy and European Integration*, ed. L. Hooghe, 219–55. Oxford: Oxford University Press.

Baun, M. 2002. EU Regional Policy and the Candidate States: Poland and the Czech Republic. *Journal of European Integration* 24 (3): 261–80.

Bayly, R. 2002. Evidence to the House of Commons Select Committee on Welsh Affairs by the Director of Devon and Cornwall in the Government Office for the South West, January 15, Cm. 200102. www.publications.parliament.uk/pa/cm200102/cmselect/cmwelaf/520/2011502.htm (accessed July 17, 2006).

Benington, J. 2001. Partnerships as Networked Governance? Legitimation, Innovation, Problem-solving and Co-ordination. In *Local Partnerships and Social Exclusion in the European Union*, ed. M. Geddes and J. Benington, 198–219. London: Routledge.

Benz, A., and T. Eberlein. 1999. The Europeanization of Regional Policies: Patterns of Multi-level Governance. *Journal of European Public Policy* 6 (2): 329–48.

Bevir, M., and R. Rhodes. 2003. *Interpreting British Governance*. London and New York: Routledge.

Blair, T. 2001. Speech to the European Research Institute, University of Birmingham, November 23. http://politics.guardian.co.uk/euro/story/0,,604413,00.html (accessed January 1, 2007).

Bogdanor, V. 2005. Footfalls Echoing in the Memory: Britain and Europe, the Historical Perspective. *International Affairs* 81 (4): 689–701.

Bomberg, E., and J. Peterson. 1998. European Union Decision Making: The Role of Sub-national Authorities. *Political Studies* 46 (2): 219–35.

Börzel, T. 1999. Towards Convergence in Europe? *Journal of Common Market Studies* 39 (4): 573–96.

Börzel, T. 2002. Pace-Setting, Foot-Dragging, and Fence-Sitting: Member State Responses to Europeanization. *Journal of Common Market Studies* 40:193–214.

Börzel, T., and T. Risse. 2003. Conceptualising the domestic impact of Europe. In *The Politics of Europeanization*, ed. K. Featherstone and C. Radaelli, 57–82. Oxford: Oxford University Press .

Bradbury, J. 2006. Territory and Power Revisited: Theorising Territorial Politics in the United Kingdom after Devolution. *Political Studies* 54 (3): 559–82.

Brown, G. 2003. As the EU Expands, We Must Repatriate Some of the Power from Brussels. *The Times*, March 6.

Brunskill, I. 1992. *Social Partner Participation in the Operation of the European Structural Funds in the United Kingdom: A Study of Scotland*. Report to the European Commission. Glasgow: University of Strathclyde.

Brusis, M. 2002. Between EU Requirements, Competitive Politics, and National Traditions: Re-creating Regions in the Accession Countries of Central and Eastern Europe. *Governance* 15 (4): 531–59.

Buãkek, J. 2002. Regionalization in the Slovak Republic—From Administrative to Political Regions. In *Regionalization for Development and Accession to the European Union: A Comparative Perspective*, ed. G. Marcou, 143–77. Budapest: Open Society Institute.

Buller, J. 2006. Monetary Policy. In *The Europeanization of British Politics*, ed. I. Bache and A. Jordan, 201–15. Basingstoke: Palgrave Macmillan.

Bulmer, S. 1992. Britain and European Integration: Of Sovereignty, Slow Adaptation, and Semi-detachment. In *Britain and the European Community: The Politics of Semi-detachment*, ed. S. George, 1–29. Oxford: Clarendon.

Bulmer, S. 1997. Shaping the Rules? The Constitutive Politics of the European Union and German Power. In *Tamed Power: Germany in Europe*, ed. P. J. Katzenstein, 47–79. Ithaca and London: Cornell University Press.

Bulmer, S. 2007. Theorizing Europeanization. In *Europeanization: New Research Agendas*, ed. P. Graziano and M. Vink, 46–58. Basingstoke: Palgrave Macmillan.

Bulmer, S., and M. Burch. 1998. Organising for Europe—Whitehall, the British State and the European Union. *Public Administration* 76 (4): 601–28.

Bulmer, S., and M. Burch. 2002. British Devolution and European Policy Making: A Step Change towards Multi-level Governance. *Politique Européenne* 6:114–36.

Bulmer, S., and M. Burch. 2005. The Europeanisation of UK Government: From Quiet Revolution to Explicit Step-Change. *Public Administration* 83 (4): 861–90.

Bulmer, S., and M. Burch. 2006. Central Government. In *The Europeanization of British Politics*, ed. I. Bache and A. Jordan, 37–51. Basingstoke: Palgrave Macmillan.

Bulmer, S., M. Burch, C. Carter, P. Hogwood, and A. Scott. 2002. *British Devolution and European Policy-making: Transforming Britain into Multi-level Governance*. London: Palgrave.

Bulmer, S., C. Jeffery, and W. Paterson. 2000. *Germany's European Diplomacy: Shaping the Regional Milieu*. Manchester: Manchester University Press.

Bulmer, S., and C. Lequesne. 2005. The EU and Its Member States: An Overview. In *The Member States of the European Union*, ed. S. Bulmer and C. Lequesne, 1–24. Oxford: Oxford University Press.

Bulmer, S., and C. Radaelli. 2004. The Europeanisation of National Policy? Europeanisation Online Papers, Queen's University Belfast, No. 1/2004, www.qub.ac.uk/schools/SchoolofPoliticsInternationalStudies/Research/PaperSeries/EuropeanisationPapers/PublishedPapers/.

Bulmer, S., and C. Radaelli. 2005. The Europeanisation of National Policy. In *The Member States of the European Union*, ed. S. Bulmer and C. Lesquesne, 338–59. Oxford: Oxford University Press.

Burch, M., and R. Gomez. 2004. Europeanisation and the English Regions. Paper presented to the ESRC/UACES Conference on Britain in Europe and Europe in Britain: The Europeanisation of British Politics, Sheffield Town Hall, July 16.

Burch, M., and R. Gomez. 2006. The English Regions. In *The Europeanization of British Politics*, ed. I. Bache and A. Jordan, 82–97. Basingstoke: Palgrave Macmillan.

Carley, M. 1990. *Housing and Neighbourhood Renewal—Britain's New Urban Challenge*. Policy Studies Institute. London: Pinter Publishers.

Catney, P. 2005. Urban Partnerships under New Labour: Associative Governance in Action? PhD diss., University of Sheffield.

Chapman, R. 2004. Europeanization and the Third Sector. Paper presented at the ESRC/UACES conference on Britain in Europe and Europe in Britain: The Europeanization of British Politics, Sheffield Town Hall, July 16.

Chapman, R. 2005. Third Sector Empowerment and Legitimacy in a Multi-Level Polity: The Politics of Implementing Community Economic Development in the 2000–2006 South Yorkshire Objective 1 Structural Fund Programme. PhD diss., University of Sheffield.

Chapman, R. 2006. The Third Sector. In *The Europeanization of British Politics*, ed. I. Bache and A. Jordan, 168–86. Basingstoke: Palgrave Macmillan.

Checkel, J. 2005. *It's the Process, Stupid! Process Tracing in the Study of European and International Politics: Working Paper No. 26*. Oslo: Arena.

Chroszcz, D. 2005. The EU New Cohesion Policy and Its Decentralized Implementation System in Poland beyond 2006. Master's thesis, Aarhus School of Business, MSc in EU Business and Law.

Church, J. 1993. The Provision of Regional and Local Statistics: UK Overview. Paper given to the Statistics' Users Council Annual Conference, November 16. Esher: IMAC Research.

Conejos i Sancho, J. 1993. Los fondos estructurales de las Comunidades Europeas: aplicación en España y participación regional. In *Informe Comunidades Autónomas 1992*, 327–42. Barcelona: Instituto de Derecho Público.

Cowles, M., J. Caporaso, and T. Risse, eds. 2001. *Transforming Europe: Europeanization and Domestic Change*. Ithaca and London: Cornell University Press.

Czernielewska, M., C. Paraskevopoulos, and J. Szlachta. 2004. The Regionalization Process in Poland: An Example of "Shallow" Europeanization? *Regional and Federal Studies* 14 (3): 461–95.

Daugbjerg, C. 1999. Reforming the CAP: Policy Networks and Broader Institutional Structures. *Journal of Common Market Studies* 37 (3): 407–28.

DETR. 1999. *Single Regeneration Budget Round 6 Bidding Guidance*. London: Department for the Environment, Transport and the Regions.

DETR. 1997. *Building Partnerships for Prosperity: Sustainable Growth, Competitiveness and Employment in the English Regions*, CM3814. London: HMSD.

Dieringer, J., and N. Lindstrom, with J. Bajaczek and I-S. Moisa. 2002. The Europeanization of Regions in EU-Applicant Countries: A Comparative Analysis of Hungary, Poland, Romania and Slovenia. Paper for the 7th EACES Conference in Forli, June.

Dyson, K., and K. Goetz, eds. 2003. *Germany, Europe and the Politics of Constraint.* Oxford: Oxford University Press.

Ecotec. 2003. Evaluation of the Added Value and Costs of the European Structural Funds in the UK. *Final Report to the Department of Trade and Industry (DTI) and the Office of the Deputy Prime Minister (ODPM)*. London: ECOTEC Research and Consulting Limited.

European Commission. 1975. *Report on the Regional Problems in the Enlarged Community (presented to the Council on May 4): Bulletin of the European Communities* 6 (8/73). Brussels: European Communities.

European Commission. 1989. *Guide to the Reform of the Community's Structural Funds.* Brussels and Luxembourg: European Communities.

European Commission. 1993. *Community Structural Funds 1994–1999, Revised Regulations and Comments.* Brussels and Luxembourg: European Communities.

European Commission. 1996. *Social and Economic Inclusion through Regional Development: The Community Economic Development Priority in European Structural Funds in Great Britain.* Brussels: European Commission.

European Commission. 1997. *Eighth Annual Report on the Structural Funds, COM (97) final, 30 October.* Luxembourg: Office for Official Publications of the European Communities.

European Commission. 1999. *Agenda 2000: For a Stronger and Wider Europe.* Brussels and Luxembourg: European Commission.

European Commission. 2000. *Response to the Single Programming Document for the Objective 1 Programme in West Wales and the Valleys 2000–2006, Report of the Commission Services.* Brussels: European Commission.

European Commission. 2004. *A New Partnership for Cohesion: Convergence—Competitiveness—Cooperation: Third Cohesion Report, COM(2004)107.* Brussels: European Commission.

European Commission. 2005a. Inforegio Website on the European Regional Development Fund. http://europa.eu.int/comm/regional_policy/funds/prord/prord_en .htm (as of July 27, 2005).

European Commission. 2005b. The Impact and Added Value of Cohesion Policy, Evaluation Unit, Directorate General for Regional Policy, http://ec.europa.eu/regional_policy/sources/docgener/evaluation/pdf/impact_en.pdf (accessed September 9, 2006).

Evans, R. 2002. The Merseyside Objective One Programme: Exemplar of Coherent City-regional Planning and Governance or Cautionary Tale? *European Planning Studies* 10 (4): 495–517.

Faro, J. 2004. Europeanization as Regionalisation: Forecasting the Impact of EU Regional-policy Export upon the Governance Structure of Slovenia. www.ksg.harvard .edu/kokkalis/GSW7/GSW%206/Jeremy%20Faro%20Paper.pdf (accessed September 4, 2006).

Featherstone, K., and C. Radaelli, eds. 2003. *The Politics of Europeanization*. Oxford: Oxford University Press.

Ferry, M. 2003. The EU and Recent Regional Reform in Poland. *Europe-Asia Studies* 55 (7): 1097–1116.

Flinders, M. 2005. Majoritarian Democracy in Britain. *West European Politics* 28 (1): 61–93.

Gamble, A. 1981. *Britain in Decline*. London: Macmillan.

Gamble, A. 1988. *The Free Economy and the Strong State: The Politics of Thatcherism*. Durham: Duke University Press.

Gamble, A. 2000. Policy Agendas in a Multi-Level Polity. In *Developments in British Politics* 6, ed. A. Gamble et al., 290–307. London: Macmillan.

Gamble, A. 2003. *Between Europe and America: The Future of British Politics*. Basingstoke: Palgrave Macmillan.

Garmise, S. 1997. The Impact of European Regional Policy on the Development of the Regional Tier in the UK. *Regional and Federal Studies* 7 (3): 1–21.

Geddes, A. 2004. *The European Union and British Politics*. London: Palgrave Macmillan.

Geddes, A. 2006. Political Parties and Party Politics. In *The Europeanization of British Politics*, ed. I. Bache and A. Jordan, 119–34. Basingstoke: Palgrave Macmillan.

Geddes, M. 2001. Local Partnership and Social Exclusion in the United Kingdom: A Stake in the Market. In *Local Partnerships and Social Exclusion in the European Union*, ed. M. Geddes and J. Benington, 170–97. London: Routledge.

George, S. 2001. The Europeanisation of UK Politics and Policy-making: The Effect of European Integration on the UK. Queen's Papers on Europeanisation No. 8/2001. Belfast: Institute of European Studies, Queen's University of Belfast.

George, S. 2004. Multi-level Governance and the European Union. In *Multi-level Governance*, ed. I. Bache and M. Flinders, 107–26. Oxford: Oxford University Press.

Getemis, P., and L. Demetropoulou. 2004. Towards New Forms of Regional Governance in Greece: The South Aegean Islands. *Regional and Federal Studies* 14 (3): 355–78.

Glowacki, W. 2002. Regionalization in Poland. In *Regionalization for Development and Accession to the European Union: A Comparative Perspective*, ed. G. Marcou, 105–40. Budapest: Open Society Institute.

Goodman, L. 1961. Snowball Sampling. *Annals of Mathematical Statistics* 32:148–70.

Government in Partnership. 1995. *Partners in Regeneration: The Challenge Fund, a Guide to Bidding for Resources from the Government's Single Regeneration Budget Challenge Fund*. April.

Greenleaf, W. 1983. *The British Political Tradition, Vol. 1: The Rise of Collectivism.* London: Methuen.

Griffiths, D., and C. Lanigan. 1999. The Strategic Uses of Regionalism: Regionalist Rhetoric in the North East of England and Wales. Paper presented to the ECPR Workshop: Regionalism Revisited—Territorial Politics in the Age of Globalisation, ECPR Joint Sessions, Mannheim, Germany, March 26–31.

Gualini, E. 2003. Challenges to Multi-level Governance: Contradictions and Conflicts in the Europeanization of Italian Regional Policy. *Journal of European Public Policy* 10:616–36.

Haas, E. 1958. *The Uniting of Europe: Political, Social and Economic Forces 1950–1957.* London: Library of World Affairs.

Hall, P., and R. Taylor. 1996. Political Science and the Three New Institutionalisms. *Political Studies* 44:936–57.

Hay, C. 2002. *Political Analysis: A Critical Introduction.* Basingstoke: Palgrave Macmillan.

Hill, D. 2000. *Urban Policy and Politics in Britain.* Basingstoke: Macmillan.

Hix, S. 1994. The Study of the European Community: The Challenge to Comparative Politics. *West European Politics* 17 (1): 1–30.

Hix, S., and K. Goetz. 2000. Introduction: European Integration and National Political Systems. *West European Politics* 23 (4): 1–26.

Hodgett, S., and D. Johnson. 2001. Troubles, Partnerships and Possibilities: A Study of the Making Belfast Work Development Initiative in Northern Ireland. *Public Administration and Development* 21 (4): 321–32.

Hoffmann, S. 1964. The European Process at Atlantic Crosspurposes. *Journal of Common Market Studies* 3:85–101.

Hoffmann, S. 1966. Obstinate or Obsolete? The Fate of the Nation State and the Case of Western Europe. *Daedalus* 95:862–915.

Hooghe, L., ed. 1996a. *Cohesion Policy and European Integration: Building Multilevel Governance.* Oxford: Oxford University Press.

Hooghe, L. 1996b. Building a Europe with the Regions: The Changing Role of the European Commission. In *Cohesion Policy and European Integration*, ed. L. Hooghe, 89–128. Oxford: Oxford University Press.

Hooghe, L. 1998. EU Cohesion Policy and Competing Models of Capitalism. *Journal of Common Market Studies* 36:457–77.

Hooghe, L., and M. Keating. 1994. The Politics of EC Regional Policy. *Journal of European Public Policy* 3 (3): 367–93.

Hooghe, L., and G. Marks. 2001. *Multi-level Governance and European Integration.* London: Rowman & Littlefield.

Hooghe, L., and G. Marks. 2003. Unravelling the Central State, But How? Types of Multi-level Governance. *American Political Science Review* 97 (2): 233–43.

Hübner, D. 2004. Lisbon and Cohesion Policy: Complementary Objectives. Speech by the member of the European Commission responsible for regional policy, UNICE Competitiveness Day, Brussels, December 9. http://europa.eu/rapid/pressReleases Action.do?reference=SPEECH/04/535 (accessed June 1, 2006).

Hughes, J., G. Sasse, and C. Gordon. 2004. Conditionality and Compliance in the EU's Eastward Enlargement. *Journal of Common Market Studies* 42 (3): 523–51.

Hughes, J., G. Sasse, and C. Gordon. 2005. *Europeanization and Regionalization in the EU's Enlargement to Central and Eastern Europe: The Myth of Conditionality*. Basingstoke: Palgrave Macmillan.

Imrie, R., and M. Raco, eds. 2003. *Urban Renaissance? New Labour, Community and Urban Policy*. Bristol: The Policy Press.

Jachtenfuchs, M. 2001. The Governance Approach to European Integration. *Journal of Common Market Studies* 39 (2): 245–64.

Jachtenfuchs, M., and B. Kohler-Koch. 2004. Governance and Institutional Development. In *European Integration Theory*, ed. A. Wiener and T. Diez, 97–115. Oxford: Oxford University Press.

Jacoby, W. 2005. External Incentives and Lesson-Drawing in Regional Policy and Health Care. In *The Europeanization of Central and Eastern Europe*, ed. F. Schimmelfennig and U. Sedelmeier, 91–111. Ithaca and London: Cornell University Press.

Jeffery, C. 2000. Sub-national Mobilization and European Integration: Does It Make Any Difference? *Journal of Common Market Studies* 38 (1): 1–23.

Jeffery, C. 2003. The German Lander: From Milieu-Shaping to Territorial Politics. In *Germany, Europe and the Politics of Constraint*, ed. K. Dyson and K. Goetz, 97–108. Oxford: Oxford University Press.

Jessop, B. 2004. Multi-level Governance and Multi-level Metagovernance. In *Multilevel Governance*, ed. I. Bache and M. Flinders, 49–74. Oxford: Oxford University Press.

Jewtuchowicz, A., and M. Czernielewska-Rutkowska. 2006. Between Institutional Legacies and the Challenges of Europeanisation: Governance and Learning in Regional and Environmental Policies in Poland. In *Adapting to Multi-level Governance: Regional and Environmental Policies in Cohesion and CEE Countries*, ed. C. Paraskevopoulos, P. Getemis, and N. Rees, 137–76. Aldershot: Ashgate.

John, P. 2001. *Local Governance in Western Europe*. London: Sage.

John, P., and A. Whitehead. 1997. The Renaissance of English Regionalism in the 1990s. *Policy and Politics* 25 (1): 7–18.

Jones, R. 1998. Beyond the Spanish State? Relations between the European Union, Central Government and Domestic Actors in Spain. PhD diss., Loughborough University.

Jones, R., and R. Scully. 2003. The Legitimacy of Devolution: The Case of Wales. Paper presented to the Annual Conference of the Political Studies Association, Leicester, UK, April.

Jordan, A. 2001. The European Union: An Evolving System of Multi-level Governance . . . or Government? *Policy and Politics*, special issue, 29 (2): 193–208.

Jordan, A., and D. Liefferink, eds. 2004. *Environmental Policy in Europe: The Europeanization of National Environmental Policy*. London: Routledge.

Kelleher, J., S. Batterbury, and E. Stern. 1999. *The Thematic Evaluation of the Partnership Principle: Final Synthesis Report*. London: The Tavistock Institute Evaluation Development and Review Unit.

Kettunen, P., and T. Kungla. 2005. Europeanization of Sub-national Governance in Unitary States: Estonia and Finland. *Regional and Federal Studies* 15 (3): 353–78.

Kjaer, A. 2004. *Governance*. Cambridge: Polity Press.

Knill, C. 2001. *The Europeanization of National Administrations: Patterns of Institutional Change and Persistence.* Cambridge: Cambridge University Press.

Knill, C., and D. Lehmkuhl. 1999. How Europe Matters: Different Mechanisms of Europeanization. *European Integration Online Papers* 3 (7): June 15, 1999.

Knill, C., and D. Lehmkuhl. 2002. The National Impact of EU Regulatory Policy: Three Mechanisms. *European Journal of Political Research* 41 (2): 255–80.

Kohler-Koch, B. 1996. Catching Up with Change: The Transformation of Governance in the European Union. *Journal of European Public Policy* 3 (3): 359–80.

Kohler-Koch, B. 1999. The Evolution and Transformation of European Governance. In *The Transformation of Governance in the European Union*, ed. B. Kohler-Koch and R. Eising, 14–35. London: Routledge.

Ladrech, R. 1994. Europeanization of Domestic Politics and Institutions: The Case of France. *Journal of Common Market Studies* 32 (1): 69–88.

Laumann, E., and F. Pappi. 1973. New Directions in the Study of Elites. *American Sociological Review* 38:212–30.

Leonardi, R. 2005. *Cohesion Policy in the European Union: The Building of Europe*. Basingstoke: Palgrave Macmillan.

Leontitsis, V. 2006. Territorial Restructuring in Greece: A Case of Europeanisation? Paper presented at the UACES Annual Conference at Limerick, Ireland, August 31–September 2, 2006.

Lijphart, A. 1984. *Democracies*. London: Yale University Press.

Lijphart, A. 1999. *Patterns of Democracy*. London: Yale University Press.

Lindberg, L. 1963. *The Political Dynamics of European Economic Integration.* Stanford: Stanford University Press; London: Oxford University Press.

Loftman, P., and B. Nevin. 1998. Pro-Growth Local Economic Development Strategies: Civic Promotion and Local Needs in Britain's Second City, 1981–1996. In *The Entrepreneurial City*, ed. T. Hall and P. Hubbard, 129–48. Chichester: John Wiley.

Lowi, T. 1964. American Business, Public Policy, Case Studies and Political Theory. *World Politics* 16 (4): 677–715.

Mair, P. 2000. The Limited Impact of Europe on National Party Systems. *West European Politics* 23 (4): 27–51.

Mair, P. 2004. The Europeanization Dimension. *Journal of European Public Policy* 11 (2): 337–48.

Maniokas, K. 2005. Presentation to the Thematic Stocktaking Conference on Multi-level Governance in Europe: Structural Funds, Regional and Environmental Policy, organized by the Connex Network of Excellence, Athens, Greece, May 5–7.

March, J., and J. Olsen. 1998. *Rediscovering Institutions: The Organizational Basis of Politics.* New York and London: Free Press.

Marcou, G., ed. 2002. *Regionalization for Development and Accession to the European Union: A Comparative Perspective, Local Government and Public Service Reform Initiative.* Budapest: Open Society Institute.

Marek, D., and M. Baun. 2002. The EU as Regional Actor: The Case of the Czech Republic. *Journal of Common Market Studies* 40 (5): 895–919.

Marinetto, M. 2003. Governing beyond the Centre: A Critique of the Anglo-Governance School. *Political Studies* 51:592–608.

Marks, G. 1992. Structural Policy in the European Community. In *Euro-Politics: Institutions and Policymaking in the "New" European Community*, ed. A. Sbragia, 191–224. Washington, D.C.: Brookings Institution.

Marks, G. 1993. Structural Policy and Multilevel Governance in the EC. In *The State of the European Community, Vol. 2: The Maastricht Debates and Beyond*, ed. A. Cafruny and G. Rosenthal, 391–410. Boulder: Lynne Rienner; Harlow: Longman.

Marks, G. 1996. Exploring and Explaining Variation in EU Cohesion Policy. In *Cohesion Policy and European Integration*, ed. L. Hooghe, 388–422. Oxford: Oxford University Press.

Marks, G., and L. Hooghe. 2004. Contrasting Visions of Multi-level Governance. In *Multi-level Governance*, ed. I. Bache and M. Flinders, 15–30. Oxford: Oxford University Press.

Marks, G., L. Hooghe, and K. Blank. 1996. European Integration from the 1980s: State-Centric v. Multi-level Governance. *Journal of Common Market Studies* 34 (3): 341–78.

Marsh, D., and R. Rhodes, eds. 1992. *Policy Networks in British Government*. Oxford: Oxford University Press.

Marsh, D., D. Richards, and M. J. Smith. 2003. Towards a Model of Asymmetrical Power. *Government and Opposition* 38:306–32.

Marsh, D., and M. Smith. 2000. Understanding Policy Networks: Towards a Dialectic Approach. *Political Studies* 48:4–21.

Marshall, A. 2004. Europeanisation at the Urban Level: Evaluating the Impact of the EU on Local Governance in Britain. Paper presented to the UACES/ESRC one-day conference on Britain in Europe and Europe in Britain: The Europeanisation of British Politics, Sheffield, UK, July 16, 2004.

Marshall, A. 2005. Europeanization at the Urban Level: Local Actors, Institutions and the Dynamics of Multi-level Interaction. *Journal of European Public Policy* 12: 668–86.

Marshall, A. 2006. Local Governance. In *The Europeanization of British Politics*, ed. I. Bache and A. Jordan, 98–118. Basingstoke: Palgrave Macmillan.

Martin, S., and G. Pearce. 1999. Differentiated Multi-level Governance? The Response of British Sub-national Governments to European Integration. *Regional and Federal Studies* 9 (2): 32–52.

McAleavey, P. 1992. *The Politics of European Regional Development Policy: The European Commission's RECHAR Initiative and the Concept of Additionality.* Strathclyde Papers on Government and Politics 88. Glasgow: University of Strathclyde.

McAleavey, P. 1993. The Politics of the European Regional Development Policy: Additionality in the Scottish Coalfields. *Regional Politics and Policy* 3 (2): 88–107.

Ministerio de Economía y Hacienda. 1995. *La Planificación Regional y Sus Instrumentos, Informe Anual 1994*. Madrid: Dirección General de Planificación.

Morata, F., and X. Muñoz. 1996. Vying for European Funds: Territorial Restructuring in Spain. In *Cohesion Policy and European Integration*, ed. L. Hooghe, 195–218. Oxford: Oxford University Press.

Moravcsik, A. 1991. Negotiating the Single European Act. *International Organization* 45:19–56.

Moravcsik, A. 1993. Preferences and Power in the European Community: A Liberal Intergovernmentalist Approach. *Journal of Common Market Studies* 31:473–519.

Moravcsik, A. 1994. *Why the European Community Strengthens the State: Domestic Politics and International Cooperation.* Center for European Studies, Harvard University, Working Paper Series 52.

Moravcsik, A. 1998. *The Choice for Europe: Social Purpose and State Power from Messina to Maastricht.* London: UCL Press.

Morgan, K. 1997. The Learning Region: Institutions, Innovation and Regional Renewal. *Regional Studies* 31:491–503.

Nanetti, R., H. Rato, and M. Rodrigues. 2004. Institutional Capacity and Reluctant Decentralization in Portugal: The Lisbon and Tagus Valley Region. *Regional and Federal Studies* 14 (3): 405–29.

National Assembly. 1999. Minutes of the Economic Development Committee Meeting, June 30, 1999 (EDC-02–99 min). National Assembly for Wales, www.wales.gov.uk.

Novotny, V. 2000. The European Union and the Emergence of Regional Institutions in Czechia. Paper presented to the University Association for Contemporary European Studies (UACES) 30th Anniversary Conference and 5th Research Conference, Central European University, Budapest, April 6–8.

ODPM. 2002. *Your Region, Your Choice: Revitalising the English Regions, Cm 5511.* London: Office of the Deputy Prime Minister.

Olsen, J. 2002. The Many Faces of Europeanization. *Journal of Common Market Studies* 40:921–52.

Olsson, J., and J. Astrom. 1999. Europeanization and Regionalism in Sweden. Paper presented at the 27th ECPR Joint Session of Workshops, University of Mannheim, Germany.

Osmond, J. 1995. *Welsh Europeans.* Bridgend: Seren Press.

Pacione, M. 1995. *Glasgow: The Socio-spatial Development of the City.* Chichester: John Wiley.

Pálné Kovács, I., C. Paraskevopoulos, and G. Horvárth. 2004. Institutional "Legacies" and the Shaping of Regional Governance in Hungary. *Regional and Federal Studies* 14 (3): 430–60.

Paraskevopoulos, C. 2001. Social Capital, Learning and EU Regional Policy Networks: Evidence from Greece. *Government and Opposition* 36 (2): 251–77.

Paraskevopoulos, C., P. Getemis, and N. Rees. 2006. *Adapting to Multi-level Governance: Regional and Environmental Policies in Cohesion and CEE Countries.* Aldershot: Ashgate.

Peterson, J. 2004. Policy Networks. In *European Integration Theory*, ed. A. Wiener and T. Diez, 117–36. Oxford: Oxford University Press.

Peterson, J., and E. Bomberg. 1993. *Decision Making in the European Union: A Policy Networks Approach*. Paper prepared for presentation to the Annual Conference of the UK Political Studies Association, Leicester, April 20–24.

Peterson, J., and M. Sharp. 1998. *Technology Policy in the European Union*. Basingstoke: Macmillan.

Pierre, J. 2000. *Debating Governance: Authority, Steering and Democracy.* Oxford: Oxford University Press.

Pierre, J., and G. Stoker. 2000. Towards Multi-level Governance. In *Developments in British Politics*, 6th edition, ed. P. Dunleavy, A. Gamble, I. Holliday, and G. Peele. London: Macmillan.

Pierson, P. 1996. The Path to European Integration: A Historical Institutionalist Analysis. *Comparative Political Studies* 29:123–62.

Pierson, P. 2000. Increasing Returns, Path Dependence, and the Study of Politics. *American Political Science Review* 94 (2): 251–67.

Pillinger, J. 1992. *Social Partner Participation in the Operation of the European Structural Funds in the United Kingdom: The North West of England*. Report to the European Commission. Barnsley: Northern College.

Pollack, M. 1995. Regional Actors in an Intergovernmental Play: The Making and Implementation of EC Structural Policy. In *The State of the European Union, Vol. 3: Building a European Polity?*, ed. S. Mazey and C. Rhodes. Boulder: Lynne Rienner.

Pollack, M. 2005. Theorizing the European Union: International Organization, Domestic Polity, or Experiment in New Governance? *Annual Review of Political Science* 8:357–98.

Radaelli, C. 2000. Whither Europeanization? Concept Stretching and Substantive Change. *European Integration Online Papers* 4 (8).

Radaelli, C. 2003. The Europeanization of Public Policy. In *The Politics of Europeanization*, ed. K. Featherstone and C. Radaelli, 27–56. Oxford: Oxford University Press.

Rees, N., B. Quinn, and B. Connaughton. 2004. Ireland's Pragmatic Adaptation to Regionalization: The Mid-West Region. *Regional and Federal Studies* 14 (3): 379–404.

Rhodes, R. 1986. *The National World of Local Government*. London: Allen and Unwin.

Rhodes, R. 1988. *Beyond Westminster and Whitehall*. London: Unwin and Hyman.

Rhodes, R. 1997. *Understanding Governance: Policy Networks, Reflexivity and Accountability*. Buckingham: Open University Press.

Rhodes, R., I. Bache, and S. George. 1996. Policy Networks and Policy-Making in the European Union: A Critical Appraisal. In *Cohesion Policy and European Integration*, ed. L. Hooghe, 367–87. Oxford: Oxford University Press.

Richards, D., and M. Smith. 2002. *Governance and Public Policy in the United Kingdom.* Oxford: Oxford University Press.

Richards, D., and M. Smith. 2005. Analysing the Competing Interpretations of Sovereignty within the Labour Party. Paper presented to the 55th PSA Annual Conference, University of Leeds, UK, April 5–7.

Richardson, J. 1998. Series Editor's Preface. In *Regions in Europe*, ed. P. Le Galès and C. Lequesne, vii–ix. London and New York: Routledge.

Risse, T., M. Cowles, and J. Caporaso. 2001. Europeanization and Domestic Change: Introduction. In *Transforming Europe: Europeanization and Domestic Change*, ed. M. Cowles et al., 1–20. Ithaca: Cornell University Press.

Roberts, P. 2003. Partnerships, Programmes and the Promotion of Regional Development: An Evaluation of the Operation of the Structural Funds Regional Programmes. *Progress in Planning* 59:1–69.

Rodgers, W. 2004. House of Lords debates. December 1: Regional Agencies and Bodies, http://theyworkforyou.com/lords/?id=2004–12–01a.512.2 (accessed September 29, 2006).

Rosamond, B. 2000. *Theories of European Integration.* Basingstoke and London: Macmillan.

Rosenau, J. 2004. Strong Demand, Huge Supply: Governance in an Emerging Epoch. In *Multi-level Governance*, ed. I. Bache and M. Flinders, 31–48. Oxford: Oxford University Press.

Sabatier, P. 1987. Knowledge, Policy-Oriented Learning, and Policy Change. *Knowledge* 8 (June): 649–92.

Saurugger, S. 2005. Europeanization as a Methodological Challenge: The Case of Interest Groups. *Journal of Comparative Policy Analysis* 7 (4): 291–312.

Scharpf, F. 1988. The Joint Decision Trap: Lessons from German Federalism and European Integration. *Public Administration* 66:239–78.

Scharpf, F. 1994. Games Real Actors Could Play: Positive and Negative Coordination in Embedded Negotiations. *Journal of Theoretical Politics* 6 (1): 27–53.

Schimmelfennig, F., and U. Sedelmeier, eds. 2005. *The Europeanization of Central and Eastern Europe.* Ithaca: Cornell University Press.

Schmidt, V. 2003. The Europeanization of Governance in Larger European Democracies. Paper prepared for presentation at the biannual conference of the European Studies Association, Nashville, Tenn., March 26–29.

Schmidt, V. 2006. *Democracy in Europe.* Oxford: Oxford University Press.

Scott, J. 1995. *Development Dilemmas in the European Community: Rethinking Regional Development Policy.* Buckingham and Philadelphia: Open University Press.

Select Committee on Welsh Affairs. 2000. European Structural Funds, First Report. HC 46, 1999/2000 Session, February 17, 2000.

Select Committee on Welsh Affairs. 2002. Minutes of Evidence, Cm. 200102. www.publications.parliament.uk/pa/cm200102/cmselect/cmwelaf/520/2011502.htm (accessed July 17, 2006).

Shutt, J., and S. Koutsoukos. 2004. *Emerging Lessons from the Mid-term Evaluation in 2003 of EU Structural Funds.* Special Policy Briefing 019/04. London: LGIU.

Sloat, A. 2002. *Scotland in Europe: A Study of Multi-level Governance.* Oxford: Peter Lang.

Smith, J. 2001. Cultural Aspects of Europeanization—The Case of the Scottish Office. *Public Administration* 79 (1): 147–65.

Smith, J. 2006. Government in Scotland. In *The Europeanization of British Politics*, ed. I. Bache and A. Jordan, 67–81. Basingstoke: Palgrave Macmillan.

Smith, M. J. 1990. *The Politics of Agricultural Support in Britain.* Aldershot and Brookfield, Vt.: Dartmouth.

Smith, M. J. 1999. *The Core Executive*. Basingstoke: Macmillan.

Smyrl, M. 1997. Does European Community Regional Policy Empower the Regions? *Governance* 10 (3): 287–309.

Steclebout, E. 2002. Europeanization of Regional Policies and Conflicts over Power and Information: The Case of the French Region of Nord-Pas de Calais. Paper presented at the third workshop of the European Young Researchers Network on EU Spatial Policies, Venice, Italy, October 21–23.

Stoker, G. 1998. Governance as Theory: Five Propositions. *International Social Science Journal* 155:17–28.

Thielemann, E. 1999. Institutional Change and European Governance: An Analysis of Partnership. *Current Politics and Economics of Europe* 9 (2): 181–97.

Thielemann, E. 2000. Europeanisation and Institutional Compatibility: Implementing European Regional Policy in Germany. *Queen's Papers on Europeanization* No. 4/2000.

Tofarides, M. 2003. *Urban Policy in the European Union: A Multi-level Gatekeeper System.* Aldershot: Ashgate.

Tomaney, J. 1999. New Labour and the English Question. *Political Quarterly* (January–March): 83–90.

Tommel, I. 1998. Transformation of Governance: The European Commission's Strategy for Creating a "Europe of the Regions." *Regional and Federal Studies* 8 (2): 52–80.

Treasury/DTI/ODPM. 2003. *A Modern Regional Policy for the United Kingdom, HM Treasury, Department of Trade and Industry and the Office of the Deputy Prime Minister.* Norwich: HMSO.

Van der Maas, E. 2006. Trade Unions. In *The Europeanization of British Politics*, ed. I. Bache and A. Jordan, 152–67. Basingstoke: Palgrave Macmillan.

Verney, S., and F. Papageorgiou. 1993. Regional Planning and the Integrated Mediterranean Programmes. In *The Regions and the European Union*, ed. R. Leonardi, 109–38. London: Frank Cass.

Vink, M. 2003. What Is Europeanisation? *European Political Science* 3 (1): 63–74.

Wallace, H. 1977. The Establishment of the Regional Development Fund: Common Policy or Pork Barrel? In *Policy-Making in the European Communities*, ed. H. Wallace, W. Wallace, and C. Webb, 137–63. London: John Wiley and Sons.

Wallace, H. 2000. Europeanisation and Globalisation: Complementary or Contradictory Trends? *New Political Economy* 5:369–82.

Wallace, H. 2003. Contrasting Images of European Governance. In *Linking EU and National Governance*, ed. B. Kohler-Koch, 1–9. Oxford: Oxford University Press.

Wallace, W. 1986. What Price Independence? Sovereignty and Interdependence in British Politics. *International Affairs* 62 (3): 367–89.

Warleigh, A. 2006. Conceptual Combinations: Multi-level Governance and Policy Networks. In *Palgrave Advances in European Union Studies*, ed. M. Cini and A. Bourne, 77–95. Basingstoke: Palgrave Macmillan.

Welsh, S., and C. Kennedy-Pipe. 2004. Multi-level Governance and International Relations. In *Multi-level Governance*, ed. I. Bache and M. Flinders, 127–46. Oxford: Oxford University Press.

WEPE. 1998. *Welsh European Programme Executive: Business Plan 1998–1999.* Mountain Ash/Machynlleth: Welsh European Programme Executive.

Wilson, D. 2003. Unravelling Control Freakery: Redefining Central-local Government Relations. *British Journal of Politics and International Relations* 5 (3): 317–46.

Wintour, P. 2006. Ministers Split on Regional Government. *The Guardian*, July 21.

Wright, V., and J. Hayward. 2000. Governing from the Centre: Policy Co-ordination in Six European Core Executives. In *Transforming British Government, Vol. 2, Changing Roles and Relationships*, ed. R. Rhodes, 27–46. London: Macmillan.

Yates, S. 2002. Evidence to the House of Commons Select Committee on Welsh Affairs by the Director of the South Yorkshire Objective 1 Programme. January 15, Cm. 200102, www.publications.parliament.uk/pa/cm200102/cmselect/cmwelaf/520/2011502.htm (accessed July 17, 2006).

Yates, S. 2005. Presentation by the Director of the South Yorkshire Objective 1 at the Conference on Participative Strategic Development, hosted by the Pendik Municipality, Istanbul, Turkey, November.

Index

About the Author

Ian Bache is a reader in politics at the University of Sheffield. He took his first degree in politics and parliamentary studies at the University of Leeds and worked as a researcher in the House of Commons, the U.S. Congress, and for a UK/EU public-sector interest group before completing an MA in international studies, PhD and MEd at the University of Sheffield. He has published widely on the European Union and related issues, including: *The Politics of European Union Regional Policy* (1998); *Politics in the European Union*, with Stephen George (2001; 2nd edition 2006); *Multilevel Governance*, with Matthew Flinders (2004; pbk 2005); and *The Europeanization of British Politics*, with Andrew Jordan (2006; pbk 2008). Between 2003 and 2005, Dr. Bache convened the ESRC Seminar Series and UACES Study Group on the Europeanization of British Politics and Policy-Making.